Before the Lights Go Out

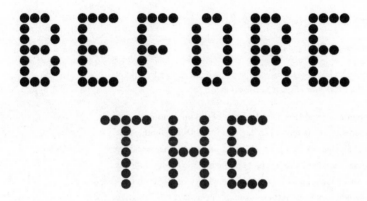

BEFORE THE

A SEASON INSIDE A GAME WORTH SAVING

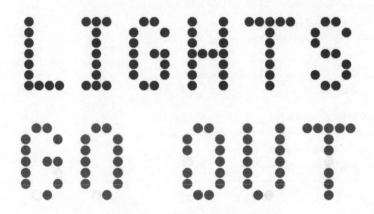

LIGHTS GO OUT

SEAN FITZ-GERALD

McCLELLAND & STEWART

Hardcover edition published 2019

McClelland & Stewart and colophon are registered trademarks of
Penguin Random House Canada Limited.

Library and Archives Canada Cataloguing in Publication data
is available upon request

ISBN: 978-0-7710-2419-1
ebook ISBN: 978-0-7710-2420-7

Typeset in Adobe Garamond by M&S, Toronto
Printed and bound in Canada

McClelland & Stewart,
a division of Penguin Random House Canada Limited,
a Penguin Random House Company
www.penguinrandomhouse.ca

1 2 3 4 5   23 22 21 20 19

Penguin
Random House
McCLELLAND & STEWART

For Caroline, Brendan, and Molly

CONTENTS

PREFACE

On the first morning of our first season in minor hockey, maybe two dozen parents were bent shoulder to shoulder over their children in the dressing room. The children were five and six years old, all nattering happily over the soundtrack of tearing Velcro and gentle parental requests to please-stop-kicking-while-I'm-tying-your-skates. It was a bright Saturday in September, and everyone was getting dressed for a pre-season tyke practice—the entry point of the entry point into organized hockey.

A few sets of shoulders away, two fathers were comparing notes on their summers. One family went to a lakefront retreat, the other went somewhere else—Everest or Jupiter, for all that it mattered. The vacations were friendly small talk, inconsequential appetizers for the main course: the continued professional development of their children.

One child went to one summer hockey school, the other to another. As they tightened laces and snapped tiny chinstraps into place, the fathers marvelled at a special kind of treadmill available for use at one of the local universities. It was designed for skating, not running. Coaches could evaluate every stride a skater made, and could identify and correct almost imperceptible imperfections.

The oldest child in the room that morning was a few days into grade one.

Ours was in kindergarten, and it had never dawned on us to register him for summer hockey school before he was enrolled in actual school. Like the delinquent parents we were, we allowed him to play soccer, to grow out of his old skates while they lay dormant in the basement. We had never, not even once, strapped him into a fancy child-sized treadmill. What would happen if Hockey Canada's executive board caught wind of our transgressions?

In that moment, and in many more to follow, minor hockey seemed as if it existed within a walled city. It had its own politics, rituals, and dialect. The easily accessible version of the sport Roch Carrier described in his beloved short story "The Hockey Sweater" was hidden from view, if it existed at all anymore.

The idea that grew into this book was rooted in that shift. Hockey became an official Canadian sport by Act of Parliament in part to highlight national unity in the face of a looming referendum in Quebec. The great on-ice triumphs are known by colloquial shorthand: the Summit Series, the Golden Goal. Historically, it is not so much a sport as it is an instrument with which Canadians scratch the surface of what it means to live in the frozen half of North America. The game has become foundational to this country's identity.

So what happens if the foundation starts to crack? What if the strain of known pressures combines with newer forces to diminish the game and weaken its hold on the Canadian imagination? What would that look like, and what might it mean not just for the future of how Canadians relate to each other, but to the understanding of what it means to be here?

The road to exploring these ideas led 90 minutes northeast of Toronto, up a windswept highway to the city of Peterborough. It has elements of cities and towns across Canada: an urban downtown core, an outer ring of suburban tract housing, and a short drive to farmland and, finally, to open wilderness. It is a Canadian test market for consumer goods and political policy. More than that, it is a hockey town.

For years, the Peterborough Memorial Centre has been one of the most efficient places in all of Ontario to get your teeth knocked out. It's home to the Petes, a junior hockey team that incubated innovation and developed a specific line of National Hockey League stars through the 1970s and 1980s. If they came from Peterborough, it meant that they knew how to play the game hard and fast. The proof has been hung from the rafters, with banners of players and coaches who also maintain an eternal second residence in the Hockey Hall of Fame.

Scotty Bowman and Roger Neilson coached the Petes. Steve Yzerman scored 42 goals in 56 games for Peterborough the year the Detroit Red Wings picked him fourth overall in the NHL draft. Chris Pronger honed the sharp edges of his game in the arena's famously square corner boards. So numerous are the Petes alumni around the NHL, they are sometimes referred to as members of the "Peterborough Mafia."

The Petes won the Memorial Cup in 1979, and the maroon and white on their jerseys seemed like it might become a symbol of perpetual success. As the business of the game began to evolve— not to mention the world around it—the wheels turned slowly in Peterborough. The oldest continuously operating franchise in the Ontario Hockey League began to show its age.

When rival cities built modern arenas with contemporary amenities, the political class in Peterborough held firm. Players still had a tiny dressing room, and front office managers had to squeeze new hires into desks crammed inside the copy room. The roof sprung a leak. The floor needed repairs. The team sank from the crest of the wave to the bottom of the sea.

There were reports of young players refusing to report to Peterborough. Others wanted out after they arrived. The players were changing and so were the parents, having often invested tens of thousands of dollars—or more—into their child's career long before the OHL draft. Some of the same forces shifting the landscape in minor hockey could be seen pushing and pulling at the Petes.

Peterborough would be the perfect place to explore Canada's evolving relationship with hockey.

I followed the team for more than a year, beginning with their unexpectedly deep run in the 2017 OHL playoffs. They returned months later in September, loaded with the expectation of even more, and of finally driving the franchise back into the national conversation. I watched practices and attended games, riding the team bus on a road trip through Windsor, Ontario, and across the border to Michigan, into Flint and Saginaw. I sat in on banking and sports psychology seminars with players. I listened to them carol at the team Christmas party.

There was a dramatic night in Oshawa, a night of heartbreak in Owen Sound, and countless journeys up and down Highway 115, which turns into a four-lane bobsled track depending on its wintry whims. There were trips to Saskatoon, Chicago, Montreal, Ottawa, and Buffalo. There were meetings with executives and politicians and artists who helped shape the way we look at the game in Canada. I spoke with hundreds of people in Peterborough and around the country.

"The consequence of the high cost is that the sport is being cut to a great deal of possible stars, possible champions," Carrier, the author, said in his living room one rainy afternoon in Montreal. "The sport has cut itself from the people who could bring something to the sport."

The version of hockey in his famous short story—played outdoors, and requiring only skates, gloves, sticks, and an abiding love of the game—has been replaced with an industry catering to minor hockey families. There are power-skating courses, goaltending specialists, and professional coaches. Those expenses are only one brick in the wall that has risen around the game.

Minor hockey can devour whole weekends with a single tournament. It can demand weeknight practices, summer training camps, and skating on PA days. Even at the lower end of the competitive spectrum, a family that enjoys skiing or ice fishing or winter vacations can struggle to become a family in hockey.

Minor hockey executives acknowledge shortcomings in attracting new Canadians to the rink. Women and girls are playing in greater numbers, but overall registration has been flatlining or falling across a number of markets, including Peterborough. There are growing concerns around the long-term risk of concussions. Children and parents have more choice in winter sports, if they want to play them at all. Rising global interest in competitive video games. Climate change threatening backyard rinks.

Tom Renney, the chief executive at Hockey Canada, the sport's national governing body, knew about the challenges. So did James Bradburn, the president of the Peterborough Hockey Association. Their challenge: how to fix it. How do you break down the walls and make a sport more accessible? How can you sell a sport that, until recently, had never needed selling north of the 49th parallel?

Our son was already sold. He started playing mini-sticks in the basement almost as soon as he could walk, and then he moved to playing ball hockey on the back deck. He requested No. 9 for his jersey, because that was the number all the children wanted in "The Hockey Sweater," which we read more nights than either of us could remember.

He was one of the only children in his class to be registered in hockey. It would not be long before we were living deep within the walled city, signing up for hockey camps over March break and Christmas and any other days off from school. He became friends with teammates, and we became close friends with their parents. We became a winter caravan, criss-crossing the city for games and practices, tournaments and skills camps. Birthday parties were also sometimes held inside arenas.

We lived the winter of warm-hearted television commercials and established national narratives, the stuff of Tim Hortons and Canadian Tire commercials. The arena lights still burned bright inside the wall, even as they flickered outside.

PROLOGUE

They started trickling onto the bus after practice, the veterans piling supplies on the choice seats at the back, leaving the rookies to fight for space near the front, closer to the adults. Some of the older players made a leisurely candy run to the convenience store across the street before settling in for a five-hour ride that would trace half the northern shore of one Great Lake and most of another.

"I forgot my fucking headphones," one of the younger players moaned. "I forgot my fucking pillow."

He had, however, remembered to pack his video game system.

It was the first real road trip of the season. The Petes would be gone for four nights, stopping in Windsor before crossing the border into Michigan for games in Flint and Saginaw. Protocol mapped out the seating chart: the coach got the first two seats by the front door, with one of his assistants in the row behind him, and the other two across the aisle. Each coach got two seats.

The trainer, his two assistants, and the radio announcer were next, forming the human breakwall between coaches and players.

There was no sign to indicate who sat where, but everyone found their place with the seamless intuition of migrating birds.

"This might be the comfiest five-hour ride I've ever had in my life," one of the older defencemen grumbled as he squeezed into his seat.

Their bus could be temperamental. On an earlier trip to Hamilton, the heating controls got jammed on full-blast and players stripped off layers of clothing in the aisle as they sweated every passing kilometre. The previous spring, right in the middle of the playoffs, it stopped working altogether.

This time was different. As the charter finally pulled away from the Peterborough Memorial Centre and onto Roger Neilson Way, if felt like nothing was going to slow them down.

The Petes had won their last four games, and six of their previous seven. Their starting goaltender was earmarked for stardom, drafted by the Edmonton Oilers and signed to an NHL contract. Four forwards had also been drafted. They were thin on defence, but there was an assumption management would find a way to patch the hole with an eventual trade. They were leaving Peterborough with the air of teenaged conquerors, on a mission to reclaim glory for their forgotten outpost.

Suddenly, there was a popping sound near the front of the bus. It sounded like hail, but the mid-October sky was clear and warm. There was another, moments later. *Crack.* Then another. *Crack.* The frequency was increasing. *Crack . . . crack . . . pop.*

"Ow," one of the rookies cried.

The veteran players were throwing their recently purchased candy from the back. They had started slowly but were now abandoning any hint of mercy. The arsenal of soft, forgiving Gummi Bears had yielded to more painful sweets. Hard candy fell from the sky like cluster bombs.

"I'm getting lit up," the helpless rookie yelped.

The barrage intensified.

"It's like *Saving Private Ryan*," the rookie said, anguished. "And I'm dead in the first 10 minutes."

Some of the adults took notice. Brian Miller, the head trainer and all-around handyman whose duties included skate-sharpening, stood up and glared wordlessly at the back of the bus.

The barrage ebbed.

They were past the mall now, turning toward the Costco and the building site of a 30,000-square-foot casino near the ramp to Highway 115, leading out of town. Two minutes after the silent warning, two more stray rounds of candy came from the back of the bus.

Miller stood up again, moving into the aisle this time.

"Hey, boys," he shouted. "We get hit with anything more up here, I'm not sharpening your skates all weekend."

With that, the storm passed and the bus grew quiet. A moment later, an email pinged. It was from the Canadian Hockey League, the national governing body for junior hockey. It was the weekly ranking report. The Petes were being rewarded on the national stage. After opening the season with a 7–2–0–1 record, they were named as one of the 10 best teams in the country.

There were 60 teams in the league. The Petes were now listed as number 10.

A cheer rose up from the rows of seats.

Jody Hull, the head coach, glanced back from his seat at the front. He had salt-and-pepper hair and weary eyes that sometimes conveyed a sense they had maybe seen too many things over a lifetime in the game. Teenagers can be unpredictable at the best of times, but overconfident teenagers can be unbearable. As the celebration continued, Hull turned and looked ahead through the windshield, speaking just loudly enough for his three assistants to hear: "Oh, I don't like that."

The bus eased onto the southbound 115, rolling into the rest of the season.

•••

Breakfast was scheduled for 9:30 a.m., but Hull was downstairs early, reading the newspaper at a table in the bright kitchenette next to the front desk in Windsor. He had booked the Stonecroft Inn, on Dougall Avenue. It was a clean roadside motel, sandwiched between a funeral home and a pharmacy on a commercial strip six kilometres from the downtown core. That seemed like a reasonable distance from the bars and strip clubs for which the city had become known.

Hull greeted two of his assistants when they walked in a few minutes later: "Good afternoon."

Hull appreciated punctuality and order in equal measure. Back at his office in Peterborough, he kept his desk showroom-clean; sometimes, in conversation, he would spot a piece of lint visible only to his eyes, trap it with the point of his index finger, and drag it from the surface. On the bus, he noticed who boarded early and which players were pushing deadline. Being five minutes early meant you were five minutes late.

He was 48 years old, and had spent more than 800 games in the NHL as a forward who was both respected and unremarkable. Hull was raised in Southwestern Ontario but spent his junior career in Peterborough. He raised his own family nearby, and had been coaching the team for more than 275 games. It was easy to know when he was at work, because his black Hummer was visible from a block away down Lansdowne Street. He always pulled it snug to the west wall of the arena, next to the white sign with bright red lettering: "Reserved parking at all times, Jody Hull, Petes head coach."

Hull had begun both of his hockey careers in Peterborough, first as a player, then as a coach. He moved to the city from Cambridge, Ontario, as a teenager. He averaged more than a point per game over three seasons with the Petes, but never led the team in scoring; his value was as a utility player, a forward who could fill more than one role on the ice. The year he became eligible for the NHL draft—the year prospects try to put their best foot forward—the team needed him to play defence. So he moved back.

The Hartford Whalers admired those qualities enough to take him in the first round of the 1987 draft, ahead of forwards such as John LeClair and Theoren Fleury. The latter two would become stars, but Hull still scratched out a career that lasted more than a decade. He played for six teams, and more than once he landed on the roster of a team coached by a charter member of the Peterborough Mafia.

Roger Neilson, whose name now adorns the road in front of the Memorial Centre, coached Hull on four different teams: New York, Florida, Philadelphia, and Ottawa. Neilson was an assistant with the Senators in 2002 when, with two games to go in the regular season, coach Jacques Martin stepped aside. It was a noble gesture: Neilson had been head coach in the NHL for 998 games, and with those two final games, he would be able to reach 1,000 for his career. He had been battling cancer for years, and the milestone would also be a farewell to the game.

The Senators were hosting the Toronto Maple Leafs in the season finale. Both teams were on their way to the playoffs, so the result did not matter in the standings. But it still mattered for Hull. Toronto led 2–0 after the first period, and 3–1 after the second. It was early in the third period—4 minutes and 19 seconds after intermission, to be precise—when Hull scored for the Senators.

It was only his second goal of the season, and the Leafs still won the game, 5–2. No matter the score, the game carried special meaning for Hull. His goal was the last anyone would score with Neilson behind the bench as an NHL head coach. His long-time coach and mentor died 14 months later.

Hull softened whenever he spoke of Neilson, the gruff comportment of a weary authority figure melting into wistful reminiscence. Neilson was a devout Christian, and while Hull did not consider himself deeply observant, he kept a symbol of faith in the top drawer of his desk: a pocket Bible he suspected Neilson gave him as a gift somewhere on the road they travelled together. He still flipped through it. It helped him to deal with stress. He turned to it whenever he felt he needed "a little pick-me-up."

"At the beginning," he said, flipping through the first few pages, "it tells you when you're anxious or you're afraid or discouraged . . . it shows you readings."

He flipped through every time, because he would never, not even for a favourite passage, think about dog-earing a page.

Neilson was a role model and a mentor, but his lessons could only extend only so far. He never played in the NHL, and even as the most innovative coach of his era, he was never a constituent in dressing room politics. Hull still felt an attachment to some of the echoes of his former life—his eye would twinkle when players teased each other or shared an inside joke within earshot. There was recognition, maybe even a desire to take part. He would smile as the players walked past, but he usually resisted the urge to join in. There was a wall between a head coach and his roster, and he seemed to worry that getting too close would erode the divide.

The players and coaches ate breakfast at separate tables. The restaurant was connected to the motel, and the coaches could see which players arrived alert and who had just rolled out of bed. They watched everyone. Who arrived alone? Who arrived with their roommate? Who was grumpy? Who was sleepy? Who was late? Who was eating, and who should be eating more?

It was game day, and the Petes would not have to be on the ice for another nine hours. Hull planned to take his players to the rink in the morning to set up their visiting dressing room and sort their equipment, but not to skate. It was not critical work—more a way to get them out of their motel rooms with a sense of purpose for a few hours.

They filed onto the bus just after 10 a.m.—veterans at the back, rookies at the front—just as they had the day before in Peterborough. But something was different. Players noticed before they made it four steps past the front door.

"This bus stinks."

"This bus smells like fucking fish."

"It smells like rotten dink in here."

"It smells like shit."

"Wow. Good smell."

"Holy fuck."

"Why does it smell in here? It smells like piss."

The correct answer was it smelled like all of those things, and the source was never identified.

If there was good news, it was that the players would not have to suffer for very long. It was only a 14-minute drive from the motel to the WFCU Centre, the nine-year-old cathedral to junior hockey built in a quiet part of town. It seated 6,400 fans for hockey—about 2,000 more than the Peterborough Memorial Centre.

The Windsor Spitfires had been housed in an ancient arena downtown, but emerged as a national power after moving into their new home. They won their first national championship—the Memorial

Cup—the year after the arena opened. They won it again the following year, in 2010, and then for the third time in franchise history in 2017, catching and passing the Petes in less than a decade.

Windsor was defending champion in name only, though: the nature of junior hockey meant that many of their biggest talents had graduated and moved on. The Petes, meanwhile, were only getting stronger, with two key players coming back from injury. Defenceman Matthew Timms was set to return, as was Cole Fraser, the most physically imposing blueliner on the roster.

Peterborough scored 38 seconds into the first period. Christopher Paquette, a 19-year-old forward and a Tampa Bay Lightning draft pick, scored the game's next three goals, a natural hat trick. The Petes were up 4–0, and everything was unfolding in line with preseason expectations. The offence was running the other team out of the building, while the goaltender, Dylan Wells, stopped everything thrown at him.

It was an extension of the hope from the previous spring, when the Petes tore through two rounds of the OHL playoffs without a single loss. Their run ended abruptly in the conference final, when Mississauga overpowered their defence and the Steelheads launched an unholy torrent of shots on Wells. The Petes were swept without mercy, but many of those players were returning, hardened and hungry. What the Spitfires were hearing—what the entire OHL would hear this season—was the redemption song of the Peterborough Petes.

Except, aside from the score, the Petes were playing terribly. Rookie forward John Parker-Jones sent a clumsy backhand clearing attempt over the glass and had gone to the penalty box with a two-minute minor for delay of game in the first period. Moments later, defenceman Declan Chisholm had tried to whip the puck around his own net but ended up shooting it toward the bottom corner. Wells made the save.

He had already made several saves. Chisholm and Timms allowed the Spitfires a breakaway later in that period, but they escaped without consequence when the shot missed the net. By the end, the Petes had blown Windsor out, 5–1, but none of the coaches were celebrating.

The Petes had been outshot 41–17. As a rule, teams conceding 24 more shots than they take on net do not usually leave the arena in a good mood at the end of the night. Peterborough got lucky.

"Well," assistant coach Derrick Walser said, back on the bus, "we did our best for 60 minutes to try to piss that one away."

"In the first three shifts," Hull added, "we had four shots on our own net."

The players had dinner at the motel restaurant. Shortly after they dispersed, Hull bought two rounds of beer for the adults at his table, including his assistant coaches and the radio play-by-play announcer. He gently refused any offer of repayment and settled in to decompress.

The previous May, following the hopeful playoff run, the team's executive rewarded general manager Mike Oke with a two-year contract extension. Oke did not extend the favour to Hull. Hull had been on the coaching staff since 2010 and had been the head coach since 2012. Without a new contract, his fate was tethered more tightly to the team's than anyone else's in the organization, his job security largely in the hands of teenagers who had not yet finished high school.

The server delivered the beer.

Around the table, the adults wondered how the victory would play out back home. The team's media relations department had a difficult job: the post-game press release always sought the most upbeat tone, regardless of whether the Petes had won or lost. Andrew Verner, the senior assistant coach who had once played goal in Peterborough, smiled mischievously. With close to four dozen shots allowed against, he workshopped a possible headline: "Petes make Spits' arms tired."

•••

Mike Duco, the ginger-haired junior assistant on Hull's staff, grew up in the Beach, an upscale east-end Toronto neighbourhood overlooking the shore of Lake Ontario. He played in the OHL, scratched his way into 18 NHL games, and spent most of his career bouncing from league to league and team to team. He was not an imposing physical force on the ice, but he would happily punch you in the face.

He and Walser had joined the Petes a few months earlier, over the summer, after Hull's former assistants left for jobs with other OHL teams. Duco was 30 years old, only about 10 years older than the veterans on the roster. Even though he grew up in Toronto, his vowels seemed to roll out with a gentle Prairie drawl. He also had a superpower that made him stand out on road trips: he could fall asleep anywhere, with almost no warning. On the bus, he could fall asleep in the time it's taken you to read this sentence. Or this one. Or this.

"It's unbelievable," his older brother, Johnny marvelled.

Johnny Duco was the head coach of the men's hockey team at Ryerson University in Toronto. When they were teenagers, Johnny was responsible for driving them both to practice. It did not matter if the practice was in the morning or the afternoon—if they were in the car, it was the same story.

"I'd look over, he'd be asleep. We'd get there and he was, 'Oh, we're here.' Practice would end, we'd get in the car, he'd fall asleep. We'd pull into the driveway: 'Oh, we're home.'

"I was like, 'Yeah, you're good company.'"

The Petes had a day off after their win over the Spitfires. They held a light workout in Windsor before loading everything back onto the bus. Unlike in the NHL, where teams employ workers to load and unload equipment, the Petes did their own heavy lifting. The skate sharpener had to be packed. So did the sticks and the bags. Once the metal doors snapped shut, the bus pulled out of the parking lot, bound for Michigan, with weekend games against the lowly Flint Firebirds and the middling Saginaw Spirit.

Duco flexed his muscle quickly. He settled into his seat with his sunglasses on his face and his burnt-orange neck pillow securely fastened.

"Fuck, Dukes," one of the players yelled forward, "does that thing float, too?"

Duco was sound asleep as the team zoomed north along the I-75 on a cloudless Friday afternoon. It was quiet, and Verner, the ranking assistant coach, felt it was maybe too quiet. He turned around in his seat to snap a photo of his slumbering colleague. He smiled to himself as he looked at his phone.

Unsatisfied, a few miles farther down the road, Verner crossed the aisle to Duco's. With the stealth of a cat burglar, he snatched the green apple Duco had left by his hip before surrendering consciousness, and placed it near his crotch, near the edge of the seat. With any sudden movement, the apple would roll off and land on the floor with a thud. Duco did not move. He was a breathing corpse.

Verner waited for 20 minutes. When nothing happened, he returned to the apple. This time, rather than relocating it, Verner took two large bites and placed it back between his colleague's legs.

Duco finally stirred when the bus slowed for traffic just outside Flint. He looked down at the apple through his dark sunglasses and grimaced. He shook his head and lobbed it back to the only logical suspect. Verner was giggling to himself.

Hull turned around at the commotion.

"He took two bites out of my apple!" Verner complained loudly.

The bus eased off the highway. Every trace of sound seemed to whoosh out of the cabin as the driver made his first turn onto a city street. There was no music playing, no conversation, no echoes wafting forward from the euchre game in the back. They were in Flint.

If they watched the news, they might have known about the drinking-water crisis. If they were fans of old documentaries, they might have seen *Roger & Me*, and followed director Michael Moore through the thorough destruction of the local economy. Even then, even if they had seen all of that, very few of them had first-hand experience of the stark poverty that was now passing outside their windows.

The Petes were from Oakville and Mississauga, Markham and Bowmanville. They were from many of the same places that have become Canadian hockey factories. In 2016, the *Hamilton Spectator* printed the results of a year-long investigation into the changing face of minor hockey. Journalist Teri Pecoskie had requested the postal codes of players from all 20 OHL franchises in order to map the sport's supply chain, which had been shifting for a generation.

She heard back from 13 teams, giving her data points for 218 OHL players. What she found, comparing the postal codes to information from Statistics Canada, was that 80 per cent of OHL players were raised in parts of Ontario where residents earned higher than the provincial median. Some earned much, much more than the average Ontarian.

Three years earlier, Jim Parcels and Ken Campbell had published a seminal exploration into the cost of modern minor hockey. In *Selling the Dream*, they highlighted a handful of eye-catching examples of the spiralling expenses. Matt Duchene, then an NHL-bound forward who had grown up in cottage country a few hours north of Toronto, was one of those case studies. His parents estimated it cost $300,000 to get him through minor hockey.

Many of the Petes came from similar circumstances: the sons of civil servants on Ontario's so-called Sunshine List of public employees earning more than $100,000; the sons of money managers who'd handled the fortunes of Old Hollywood; the sons of families who, one way or another, had found their way inside the safety of the walled city.

They stared through the bus windows.

"Holy fuck," a veteran boomed through the silence. "This place is nice."

A KFC and a gas station stood at the foot of the off-ramp; across the intersection was an abandoned office, with its white vinyl awning torn and lapping the ground in the breeze. They kept rolling, past cracked sidewalks overgrown with weeds, homes with boarded windows, and a cluster of three-storey apartment buildings that appeared to have been abandoned.

On the left was a squat one-storey liquor store with a half dozen cars in the parking lot. Farther ahead was Walter E. Scott School, which had been closed for two years, after the Flint Board of Education voted to shutter three elementary schools to make up for a $22-million (U.S.) deficit in 2015. It stood eerily vacant in the middle of a school day.

"When we get to the hotel, we're not leaving," a rookie whispered to his seatmate. "Even if there's a fire."

The bus pulled up to the Dort Federal Credit Union Event Center, a 50-year-old building that somehow felt a bit older. Folding chairs comprised the first several rows of seating in the arena bowl. There were cobwebs on some of the ones closest to the glass. An arena worker greeted the Petes cheerfully as they filed off the bus: "Welcome to Flint—the people are nicer than the water."

He followed up quickly: "Don't drink the water."

The crisis began in 2014, when the city, as a cost-cutting measure, switched its water supply from Lake Huron to the less-than-potable Flint River, but really it began well before that: the city's economy cratered when General Motors scaled back operations more than two decades earlier; a company that had once offered 80,000 good-paying jobs in the area was now reportedly only employing about 2,000. A month before the Petes pulled into town, data from the U.S. Census Bureau showed Flint was the poorest city in the country. Half of all residents lived below the poverty line. Childhood poverty rates skyrocketed against the national average. Meanwhile, the state was still providing bottled water to the area amid lingering fear of dangerously high levels of lead in the supply.

The Petes did not stay at a hotel near the arena. Hull had booked them into a comfortable chain hotel by the airport. There was an Arby's next door, a McDonald's across the parking lot, near a Tim Hortons, and a vast suburban shopping mall across the intersection. Hull had a treat planned for that first night in Flint, too—the Petes were going to have a steak dinner at a roadhouse near the hotel.

It was the most expensive meal of the five-day trip. They ordered 34 New York strip sirloins, with 12 orders of pretzel logs as an appetizer for the group. There were six glasses of Coke, six iced teas, four Sprites, and nine ginger ales. Hull spent $1,036.62 (U.S.), including tip. (The team had two dinners in Windsor, and the total was about $1,200.)

Food became a running theme in Flint, not because the menus were unfamiliar, but because the portion sizes seemed so foreign. On the afternoon of their game against the Firebirds, the team went to a clean and friendly Italian restaurant for lunch, where they ordered 33 plates of chicken Parmesan with pasta, along with salad and bread. When the food arrived, each piece of chicken was half the size of an American football, the pasta formed 33 tomato-covered foothills, and the bread was bottomless.

Players were going to have to skate, hit, and forecheck when they got on the ice; they would have to be nimble and lean when the puck dropped. Midway through the meal, some of the adults had begun to wonder just how nimble and how lean the players would be with five pounds of pasta sitting in their bellies. The puck was supposed to drop five hours after the bill arrived at the table.

Hull had not joined the team for lunch. Walser, one of the new assistant coaches, wondered if the team would have to tell Hull they needed to adjust the game plan because of the heavy meal.

He was joking. But only a little bit.

Every now and again, in a special alcove the restaurant had reserved for the Petes, a player would tap a fork on their plate. It was like a wedding reception, except instead of requesting a kiss, they wanted to signal that there was a new victim. The prank had no name—"Shoe Check" was one suggestion—and it did not discriminate. The goal was to sneak up on an unsuspecting victim and smear butter on their shoe while evading detection.

By tapping a fork on the plate, they sounded the alarm.

The alarm sounded several times over the hour the team spent at the table.

They were back at the hotel by 2:50 p.m., which did not leave much time to digest before the pre-game nap. Players and coaches were back on the bus by 4:40, en route to the rink for a game that had the potential to soothe any nerves jangled in Windsor. The Flint Firebirds—who were the Plymouth Whalers until the franchise was sold and relocated in 2015 — were not a strong team.

The Petes, meanwhile, were a power. They had won 8 of their first 11 games, and were sitting atop the OHL's Eastern Conference standings. Less than a month into the season, they were a full 13 points clear of the Mississauga Steelheads, who languished at the bottom of the conference.

They were on the road to somewhere, and Flint was just a toll booth.

Flint was whistled for a penalty 47 seconds into the game. Peterborough had all of its important forwards healthy and active. The defence was approaching full strength. Wells, the 19-year-old goaltender and Oilers draft pick, was almost certainly going to be invited to selection camp for the world junior team, where Hockey Canada convened the very best junior-age players in the country.

As the Petes went onto the power-play, on that Saturday night in late October, they were getting ready to speed away from the Firebirds. All they had to do was hit the gas.

The Firebirds got a partial breakaway on the penalty kill. They took another penalty five minutes later and got another short-handed breakaway. This time they scored, taking a 1–0 lead. Over the first 10 minutes of the game, the Petes allowed three break-aways on Wells.

Flint scored twice in the first four minutes of the second period, both off Peterborough giveaways. The Firebirds scored four more times in the third period. As the crowd filtered out into the autumn darkness, the Petes filed onto the idling bus in stunned silence, having absorbed a 7–3 loss.

Hull stared through the front window. Walser and Duco sat thumbing their mobile phones, not saying a word. Players avoided eye contact with all four coaches as they slipped past toward their seats in the back.

It was quiet when the bus pulled away from the arena, and it was still quiet 15 minutes later when they arrived back at the roadhouse where they had dined on steak the previous night. It was after 10 p.m., and Hull had arranged for them all to have burgers.

Slowly, life returned to the group. At the adult table, Hull passed a pen and a piece of paper a few seats down to where Larry Smith was sitting. Smith, a kindly man with short-cropped silver hair, was an assistant trainer. He was good with gadgets, and he had helped make life easier for Miller's skate sharpener, having rigged the machine with parts from a vacuum cleaner to suck up all the dust and debris.

He was many valuable things for the team, but he was not a coach. Hull, with some smirking prompts from his assistants, asked Smith to map out what he thought would be the team's optimal line combinations. Smith smiled a bit and picked up the pen.

He wrote down a handful of names almost immediately, but then he stalled. The first few lines were easy—at least, they seemed to be. There were right-handed shots and left-handed shots, and there were players who seemed to play better with some than with others. Would the younger players be able to keep up with certain veterans, or vice versa?

"Larry," said Verner, the senior assistant coach, "hurry up."

Smith finished quickly. He handed the paper and then the pen back up the table.

Hull examined the suggestions. He looked at Smith as the pen arrived, a moment after the paper: "You won't need that again."

Everyone laughed, including Smith. It was only one loss.

●●●

For the second time in two days, Hull did not join the team for lunch. And for the second time in two days, Verner grabbed the head coach's vacant seat on the bus for the short ride to the restaurant. It was Sunday, and the Petes had a late afternoon game in Saginaw, the final stop on their road trip.

After clearing their gear from the arena, they stayed in Flint for lunch.

Dave Beamish, the team's studied bus driver, was not taking them back toward the airport. Instead, he drove the bus deeper into Flint. They rolled past more barbed wire and worn buildings, but now also a flat slab of concrete that seemed to stretch into the horizon. It had clearly once been the foundation of something, but whatever it was had been wiped clean, with nothing left behind.

Beamish made a left-hand turn and, after a few blocks, pulled into an empty parking lot in the middle of a quiet commercial strip. The assistant coaches and players stepped off the bus warily, crossing the parking lot to a drab grey building that housed an Italian restaurant. One of the adults wondered aloud, only half joking: Was this Hull's passive-aggressive punishment for how the team had played?

They walked inside. There was a bar and a jukebox and, over the table Hull had reserved for the team, a large television set. Framed photos of actors and athletes were splayed across the dark wood panelling. This place did triple duty as a bar, a lunch counter, and a family restaurant; it wasn't hard to imagine how the room might have felt a few decades earlier, the air blue with cigarette smoke and thick with beer fumes, filled with the voices of workers having wrapped their shift at Buick City, the assembly plant a few miles away. The last Buick rolled off the line in 1999, and the whole facility went dark in 2010, seven years before the Petes walked through the front door of this restaurant for lunch.

Timms, the 19-year-old defenceman just back from injury, looked around from his seat at the table and almost whispered: "It smells like a dead body in here."

Alex Black, the 20-year-old defenceman with dreams of becoming a firefighter, asked as politely as he could about the water, which had been poured into jugs on the table. The server did not miss a beat and assured him the water was safe—the pipes had been changed. The Petes filed toward the buffet line.

Many players opted for cola. Nick Robertson, the 16-year-old rookie centre from California whose parents had moved their hockey-mad sons to Michigan to hone their skills, did not like the idea of drinking cola before the game, but he was unmoved by the claims of water safety. Someone at the table offered him a bottle of brand-name water purchased before they left the hotel. He accepted gratefully.

Jonathan Ang, the 19-year-old forward from the Toronto suburb of Markham, became obsessed with what appeared to be a lottery game available at the table. Someone walked over to the jukebox and popped some U.S. coins into the machine. In an otherwise empty restaurant in the middle of Flint, the hockey team was suddenly listening to Tom Petty's "Free Fallin'." The choice was not universally supported.

"That's a fine," Timms said.

Logan DeNoble, the 20-year-old Petes captain, agreed with a smile. Some players started to sing along. The assistant coaches, sitting at a table over by the far wall, shook their heads.

The bus took a different route back to the hotel after lunch. It pushed deeper down the road past the restaurant. The challenges in Flint were not like the challenges most players could see out in the open at home. So they stared out the windows as two older men rode past on motorcycles clearly pieced together from spare parts. A woman drove past in a battered Dodge Ram van with a half dozen children in the back. There was an open-air market where vendors sold goods from the trunks of their cars. As the bus turned back onto the highway after driving past of a row of abandoned houses, one of the younger players said to another that he remembered seeing a neighbourhood like it before. On television. On *The Walking Dead*.

Their game in Saginaw was scheduled for 5:30 p.m., and they were quiet for the 45-minute ride north. The Saginaw Spirit—who were the North Bay Centennials until the franchise relocated 15 years earlier—were better than the Firebirds, but only a little.

The Petes were better, too, but only by a little. They gave up the lead twice, once in the first and again in the second. They attacked in a flourish late in the third period, but could not convert on a single shot attempt. They lost 3–2 and returned to the bus carrying a two-game losing streak. It was going to be a long ride home from Saginaw, so Hull ordered pizzas for the road, to be delivered right to the front of the idling bus.

"Well," said Verner, "back out of the top 10 we go."

Hull nodded. "Yup."

They had only been on the bus for a few minutes when the pizza delivery man arrived. A small handful of players were heard giggling about something as the first few boxes were passed back down the rows. For the coaches, the loss was still too fresh.

Duco shook his head. "These kids can't be fucking serious right now."

Verner turned around and looked toward the back of the bus. It was quiet again.

It was close to 9 p.m. when Beamish drove them down past Flint and then toward the border. Walser studied video from the game with Verner and Hull. Walser was still staring intently at his screen two hours later, when everyone else had already started *Happy Gilmore*, the Adam Sandler comedy, which was older than every player on the bus.

Walser was still glued to his screen after midnight, when the rest of the bus had moved on to *Billy Madison*, and he did not close his laptop until after 1 a.m., when they were through Toronto. Duco, sitting a row behind Walser, was fast asleep, even though someone had stolen his neck pillow. In the back, the veterans played cards quietly.

Nobody was throwing any candy as the bus pulled off Highway 115, past the site of the new casino and the Costco. Nobody had taken a bite of anyone's apple. Nobody was doing much of anything as the bus pulled into the parking lot at the Peterborough Memorial Centre.

It was 2:30 a.m. on a Monday in late October, and the Petes were a different team than the one that had left the Peterborough Memorial Centre six days earlier. That much would eventually become clear, but not as the players carried their pillows out of the bus in the still of the night.

ONE

THE PETES

It was just past 7 p.m. on a misty Thursday in September, two weeks before Peterborough's home opener, and a summer of anticipation was giving way to an autumn of promise. The Petes had swept two straight playoff series against Niagara and Kingston over March and April, going deeper into the OHL post-season than they had since 2006, when the team won its last league title.

They invited fans into the cafeteria at Thomas A. Stewart Secondary School that night for a barbecue and a meet-and-greet with members of this year's roster. Dozens of fans filled the lunch tables as players milled about wearing their team-issue jerseys. The mood was light as the meal ended and the next part of the program began, with team executives hosting a town hall in the auditorium.

First thing on the agenda was a video of a murder.

On the big screen before an audience of about 75 mostly older fans, the Petes, rather than relive their playoff victories, opted instead to show highlights of their third-round series against the Mississauga Steelheads. That one had gone differently. The Petes were outplayed, outmatched, and outscored 17–4 on their way to a four-game sweep, losing game four with a 7–0 collapse fierce enough to generate its own gravitational pull.

The video was set to up-tempo electronic music. Nobody applauded when it ended.

Greg Millen was the celebrity guest speaker. He had been a goaltender with the Petes in the late '70s, before his career took him into almost 600 regular-season NHL games and, in retirement, another sports-related vocation, as a broadcaster. He smiled as he picked up the microphone.

"Great things are to come, I would think this year, based on the team that is coming back," he said. "You all will be, I think, really thrilled to watch this season."

There was no reaction from the audience.

Dave Pogue, the team president, was fidgeting with a pen on the stage. Mike Oke, the general manager, was tapping away on his mobile device at the other end of the table. The video screen was behind them.

"Right from top to bottom, this organization now is back," Millen said. "If you walk around the rinks like I do, around the National Hockey League, I can tell you that people are impressed. And they're all saying the same thing now—something they didn't say as much the last number of years. They're saying: 'Wow—it looks like the Petes are back to the old Petes.'

"And for me walking around, that makes me stick my chest out a little bit, being a Petes alumni, and of course with Peterborough being my home."

Peterborough could be easy to overlook. From its perch atop Ontario Highway 115, it has a 45-minute drive through forests and farmland and windswept highway to protect it from the traffic along the 401, leading into Toronto. No two locals agree on which spot is the most treacherous on the 115 in the winter—the one with the blowing snow, or the one with the black ice.

A straight line drawn on a map from Toronto to Ottawa would take you through Peterborough, but most drivers take a different route: they trace the commuter rail path, which hems the shore of Lake Ontario, veering north well east of Peterborough. Finding your way into town, then, is more likely the result of a conscious decision than any happy accident.

In many ways, Peterborough has been a reflection of the country. It voted for the party that formed a government in every federal election from 1984 through 2015—a run of 10 straight. (It held an even longer run at the provincial level, extending it to 12 by sending Progressive Conservative Dave Smith to replace a Liberal MPP at Queen's Park in 2018.)

It weathered hard times, but never the boom-and-bust swings of other cities. It had government offices, but it was not a government town. It had industry, but never just one kind of industry. When one sector went down, there always seemed to be others around to help pick up the slack.

"I kind of compare us to the tortoise-and-the-hare race," said Ken Hetherington, manager of the city's planning division. "We're very much the tortoise, and we always have been since I've been here. We've been slow and steady. We haven't hit the peaks that the lakeshore communities have, but we haven't hit the valleys, either."

Slow and steady. A subtle stream of conservatism still flows through the city. Talk of extending a single roadway has been debated for a generation. When the Peterborough Memorial Centre started to show its age at the turn of the century, there was debate over whether it should be replaced; city council voted to renovate it instead. More than a decade later, with the arena falling even further behind its modern peers, council again resumed debate over whether the arena needed to be replaced.

Peterborough came by its pragmatic streak naturally. The city was not born of any romantic notions or entrepreneurial fancy. Nobody struck gold while panning in the Otonabee River. There was no oil rush, with hundreds of rugged dreamers pulled in from rugged towns across the region. Rather, it began as a solution to a problem.

In 1822, Ireland was a problem. It was a problem for the Irish Catholics who did not have enough to eat as the economy stumbled following the end of the Napoleonic Wars. They were just two decades from the Potato Famine, and they were a problem for the British, who wanted to avoid an uprising.

The British had another problem, across the Atlantic Ocean, in British North America: there were vast tracts of open and undefended land north of the 49th Parallel, and a war had just been fought with the country to the south of that line. They hatched a plan. With a reported budget of £30,000, the government would sponsor the relocation of 2,000 Irish Catholics to the area 150 kilometres northeast of what would eventually become known as Toronto. They would be removed from Britain's doorstep and used to colour in parts of an otherwise empty section of the map. Two problems, one solution.

Men over the age of 45 were not allowed to apply. They wanted strong, eager candidates who could not only survive the voyage but also thrive in the harsh conditions of the wilderness. Successful applicants were promised 70 acres of land. A handbill circulated in Ireland told them they would be transported to their new homes "wholly at the public charge," and that "provisions shall be furnished them during their voyage, and for one whole year" after their arrival.

There was no romance in the message. There was no mention of the verdant forests or the fresh water or the clean country air. Nobody was promising wealth or fortune or health benefits. It was a business contract, because the immigrants would be expected to work the land. And if they decided to leave the land for more than six months, the handbill made clear the government retained the right to reclaim all the land it had given them and hand it over to someone else. That was the very last line in the document.

For an impoverished Irish Catholic, it was tempting. The government had not just promised to transport them overseas and furnish them with more land than they had at home—the offer included the promise of a shanty on their new plot of land, as a kind of Irish-Canadian starter home. The government would also provide a cow and three bushels of seed. Approved candidates would receive a hammer and 100 nails, along with an axe and other tools. There were other provisions, too, that would help them get through that first brutal winter.

The handbill became popular, and 50,000 Irish applied for the 2,000 spots.

Peter Robinson, a 37-year-old politician and a veteran of the War of 1812, was put in charge. The son of United Empire Loyalists from Virginia, Robinson was responsible for selecting the passengers who would fill the nine ships set to sail out of Cork, in the south of Ireland. Robinson acknowledged the selection process was imperfect. "In a few instances," he wrote, "persons holding these Certificates sold them to others, who were perhaps, still more desirous of emigrating . . . but I believe, in no instance, did the deception succeed."

In 1825, the ships departed Ireland for the one-month journey across the Atlantic Ocean, ships with names such as *Amity*, *Fortitude*, *Albion*, and *Regulus*. The passenger lists were filled with a rainbow of Irish surnames: McCarthy and Murphy, Quinlan and Callaghan, Sullivan and Slattery. According to the *History of the County of Peterborough, Ontario*, published in 1884, the region at the time was "inhabited by but one family, that of Adam Scott, with a few workmen engaged as assistants at his mill." The area was thought to have 500 residents. Very quickly, the outpost became a community.

The Irish had struggled to get there, arriving in the summer in the unfamiliar humidity. Robinson was a vigilant planner—and an inveterate note-taker—but historians have noted even he "could not avert the effects of the fevers and sickness by which swamp and forest avenged themselves on their invaders." According to a letter from Robinson, referenced two centuries later in the *Peterborough Examiner*, 65 immigrants—or 3.3 per cent of the travelling party—died en route to their new home. Most of the dead were children under the age of 14, "including those just born."

Life was unpleasant even after they arrived. There was a cholera outbreak. Protestants in the area tried to intimidate the Catholic newcomers. The work was relentless, and the land was still wild. On the rare occasion they found free time in the winter, it was reported the Irish farmers would seek out a frozen pond clear of snow. With sticks fashioned from tree branches, they played a version of hurling they had played in Ireland. On the ice, it would have looked a little like hockey.

In 1826, the area known as Scott's Plains was renamed: Peterborough.

Peterborough became a lumber town, with the Otonabee River helping drive commerce into—and out of—the growing number of sawmills. That business hit its peak in 1860 and had basically evaporated by the end of the 19th century. By that point, Peterborough had already moved on. Local officials slashed tax rates to lure new business. In 1890, they offered Edison Electric a parcel of land and a decade free of tax to relocate from its base in Sherbrooke, Quebec. The company accepted, and in 1892 it made Peterborough the national headquarters of Canadian General Electric, with about 300 employees on staff. The town became known, at least locally, as the Electric City.

By 1920, the company had 2,000 on the payroll—or roughly 10 per cent of the town's population. (It would go on to employ as many as 6,000.) Other companies followed. The American Cereal Company, later known as Quaker Oats, was attracted by the railway and water connections. It established roots in 1902, with 500 employees. The Canadian Canoe Company opened for business in 1893. Outboard Marine Corp. opened a few decades later.

Peterborough became a blue-collar town. Its inhabitants worked on local shop floors, and at the General Motors plant in Oshawa. They made clocks and oatmeal and chainsaws. They could find a job with less than a high school diploma, build a life, and retire with the same company. And beginning in 1956, they could spend their winters watching the Petes.

The Petes arrived from Kitchener. They were part of the vast farm system the Montreal Canadiens had built on their way to becoming an NHL dynasty. In time, the Petes would grow into a dynasty in their own right. They became an extension of the city, producing hard-nosed, workmanlike players with the kind of skill the big league was looking for. The Petes would eventually send more players to the NHL than any team in junior hockey.

"It's an instant connection with anyone around the world," said Dan O'Toole, the long-time TSN anchor and the son of a local pig farmer. "If I say I'm from Peterborough, they say, 'Oh, the Petes!' Everyone in Canada knows that. That's our calling card: the Peterborough Petes."

The best teams had skill but also a willingness to punch opponents in the face, if needed.

"When you said 'Peterborough,' people knew what it meant," said Chris Pronger, who began his Hall of Fame career with the Petes. "If you said, 'I was in Peterborough,' it was, 'OK, I get it.' You didn't have to tell them any more than that. They knew you were going to be well coached. They knew what type of player you were going to be. They knew what type of people they brought in there to play, from a character standpoint."

The Petes rose to national power in the late 1970s. They played for the Memorial Cup in three straight seasons—1978, 1979, and 1980—and became the model for what a junior hockey franchise should be in Canada. They produced stars on the ice and innovators behind the bench.

That rise to national prominence coincided with the slow decay of manufacturing around the city. The clock factory closed, becoming a mixed-use office and condo building. Outboard Marine shuttered its operations and moved its remaining jobs to the United States and Europe. The final and most symbolic announcement was made in 2018, when General Electric revealed plans to close its operations, ending a relationship with Peterborough that had begun 125 years earlier.

Again and again and again, the city adapted. The local hospital became the largest local employer. Trent University and the school board were the next two in line. Peterborough, the average Canadian city, was just reflecting a broader trend, trading its blue collar for silver hair. In that sense, though, the city was superlative: it had the highest percentage of retirement-age citizens in the country, based on data from the 2011 census. Nearly one in five residents—19.5 per cent of the population—were over the age of 65. Retirement homes had become the new refrigerators, canoes, and breakfast cereals.

"One of our malls got turned into a retirement centre," said O'Toole, the TSN host—as had his old high school.

Grey hair had also become a marker for the hockey team's strongest constituency. Home games inside the Memorial Centre had largely become a gathering place for fans old enough to remember the glory days. There were still children and young families, but their numbers were dwindling.

Dave Pogue, the team president, prepared to field questions at the town hall, looking into an audience loaded with first-hand memories of those glory days. Most seats were filled by fans far more like to be drawing from their retirement savings than adding to them.

Pogue was a local entrepreneur who had worked in trucking, farming, radio, and real estate. He was born and raised in town and could never imagine living anywhere else—one of his family's farms had a deed that dated back close to the arrival of Robinson's poor Irish immigrants. (Robinson, meanwhile, had all but disappeared from local view—there is no statue or monument to him in Peterborough, and it is not even clear where he was buried after he died in 1838 following a stroke.)

For the assembled Petes fans, Pogue outlined some broad points around the team's finances, which had raised alarm during the inaugural town hall meeting the previous fall. He had admitted then that the team was losing money, and that its long-term viability in town would be in jeopardy without a revised arena lease with the city. The revelation was so shocking around town—how could the Petes possibly leave?—that the lease was ultimately revised.

There would be new LED lights inside the arena this season, he said. A new video screen would also be installed, allowing for more advertising and in-game entertainment for fans. Season ticket sales were up 12 per cent. The room was largely quiet until he reached one of the hot-button topics. It was not about a new coach, or a new player, or a new way to generate money.

It was about handrails.

They did not have handrails on the stairs leading to the seats at the Peterborough Memorial Centre, and it was not easy for the older fans to make it to and from their seats.

"I was on a roll," Pogue said as the audience groaned. "We'd almost succeeded on everything, hadn't we?"

There were more murmurs in the crowd.

"I didn't know everybody came for handrails."

It was an old building, he said. The city owned it, not the Petes, and adding handrails would not only be expensive, it would be costly: they would likely have to remove 200 seats to accommodate them, and they would leave some fans with an obstructed view of the ice. Besides, some of the staff had been trained to assist fans who had trouble navigating the stairs.

He fielded a question from the floor, from a woman who identified herself as Priscilla.

"Would you like me to volunteer to walk up to the top, where there's no railing, and I'll fall down, crack my head open, and we can have a lawsuit—and then we might get railings?"

There was laughter in the room as Pogue began to reply.

"I don't want that to happen," he said.

"You don't want that to happen? OK," she said.

Pogue wanted to add the railings. He wanted to add a great many things to the increasingly antiquated arena. It had charm, but that charm was getting in the way of progress. The bathrooms downstairs were small. The lines for food at intermission were interminable. The weight room needed updating. The front office was so cramped that if one worker developed a sniffle on Monday, everyone else was sick by Wednesday. Pogue wanted so many things. He wanted a new arena. But the Memorial Centre was a city-owned rink in a city that did not seem to make anything happen quickly.

"The paint on the steps going up and down is really slippery," another older fan said. "Can you not put some of that grit stuff on there?"

"We'll check," Pogue said, motioning to a member of the city staff sitting in the room.

The arena was so old, he could not imagine how many layers of paint had been slathered over those stairs. The Petes were the primary tenant, but they were not the only ones to use the rink, nor the building itself. High-level lacrosse was scheduled there over the summer. Beer league hockey players used the ice in the winter, sometimes an hour after the Petes played a game. Boxing and music and game shows filled the floor when it was free.

Someone else jumped in: "Can you not put some kind of a handle on some of the chairs? Like a bar that would go around, so as people go down—"

"Again," Pogue cut in, "I'm a guy up here, and I'm happy to be on the firing squad—I'm not the one making the decisions for the building, but when we sit down with the folks who are there . . . I'll pass that along."

A woman named Angela suggested asking local high schools for help. Students are required to log a certain number of volunteer hours, she said, so why not ask them to volunteer to help the elderly to their seats at hockey games?

"It's a great idea," Pogue said. "It's not something you see at arenas, and certainly in hockey these days. But we're in a little bit of a different situation than most places. We'll take a look at it."

One attendee finally had a question unrelated to seating accommodations: they wanted to know how the Petes planned to attract younger fans to the arena. Steve Nicholls, the team's coordinator of season ticket sales and service, stepped in to answer. The team, first of all, was going to host a night for Trent University, and another for Sir Sandford Fleming College.

"We recognize that we do want to get younger Petes fans, and for them to become Petes fans for life," he said. "That can start with the university and college crowd. And that's something we're definitely moving toward—with high school students and elementary, as well."

Pogue jumped in. "The challenge is, you almost have to go and pick them up at their dorm, take them to the game, and then take them back downtown after the game," he said. "They're willing to take the free ticket, but what we're finding is, they're not getting themselves to the rink." Eventually, they would have to.

The organization, Pogue said, loved the grey hair in the rink— those were the team's most loyal fans. "But when it comes to music and video and some of those things," he added, "we sometimes get complaints. For every person who thinks the music's too loud, there's somebody who thinks the music needs to be louder—and these are all balances we need to find."

On cue, another man spoke up with a comment, not a question. He was not as interested in attracting younger fans as some of his peers in the audience. He said he was a season ticket holder who gets to his seat before the game begins and stays there until the final buzzer sounds.

"But I never see the whole game," he said, "because people are running up and down the aisle, going up to get a drink or going to the washroom. It's usually kids. And they'll go up and down umpteen times, so I'll miss part of the play. You should police that a little bit better."

The Petes were trying to modernize. They had overhauled their front office and tried to change the way they had been doing business, to catch up to the modern trends they had been ignoring. The team knew it needed to find a way to get younger fans into the building, or face the possibility of weakening its tether to the city. The Petes had to find a way to become more relevant.

There were long-term concerns. In the short term, though, there was one possible solution. They could win.

TWO

THE NEW FACE

Mercedes Robertson went into labour one night in September, and that was not a good thing, because she was not due until December. She and her husband, Hugh, had three other children together—Michael, Jason, and Brianne had all arrived as easily as any child possibly could. This time, it was different. This time, everything seemed wrong.

They called the ambulance. Mercedes was admitted to Huntington Hospital, not far from their home in Pasadena, California, just after midnight. It was affiliated with the University of Southern California, and it was where the most challenging cases were sent. They rushed Mercedes into surgery.

Doctors told Hugh the situation was even worse than he feared. They told him they had to remove the baby in order for his wife to survive. Their third son, Nicholas, was brought into the world with lungs that had not matured enough to survive outside the womb. Nicholas weighed only three pounds.

Doctors asked Hugh if he wanted his son placed on life support —the baby's lungs were not functioning, and there was a possibility the newborn had not gotten enough oxygen to his brain. With every update, the news seemed to get worse. One thing was clear: without life support, Nicholas was going to die.

With Mercedes still in critical care, Hugh assented to any means doctors deemed necessary to keep his newborn son alive. Doctors told him of a "miracle drug" that could be used to jump-start his son's lungs. They administered it once, to no effect. They tried it a second time. Nothing. They could not get the newborn's lungs to function properly.

Doctors asked Hugh if he wanted to take his son off life support.

"Can't do that," he said. "Let's just roll the dice, and let's see what happens."

It was creeping toward dawn. It was now the morning of September 11, 2001.

●●●

Hugh was raised in Michigan but moved to Southern California, where he would build his law practice and assume control of a money management company that once worked with Hollywood royalty, advising the likes of Elizabeth Taylor, Humphrey Bogart, Rock Hudson, and Audrey Hepburn.

Mercedes was born in Manila, where her father worked as an attorney. The family left the Philippines, which was then still under the rule of dictator Ferdinand Marcos, and settled in Los Angeles. She met Hugh while working at his law firm. They were married in 1997.

They did not waste time in building a family; there's a one-year age gap between each of their four children. They have baby pictures of all but one. It was difficult to take any pictures of Nicholas—Nicky, to his father—because, for the first two and a half months of his life, he was hooked up to machines that were keeping him alive.

Hugh had to scrub in to visit Nick inside the neonatal intensive care unit. Later, on some visits, when he was washing his hands, a priest would be washing up next to him. It was one of the grim rhythms of hospital life: if a priest was scrubbing in, it meant a baby somewhere in that unit was being taken off life support. It only had to happen once to be seared into Hugh's memory forever, but the scene repeated over and over and over. He would be looking down at Nicky, tethered to machines. He would hear the monitor beeping, just as it beeped on all the monitors around the room. When a priest was there, it usually meant one of the monitors would sound a final, long beep over one of the other newborns in the room.

"The parents are crying, the mom's hysterical, the priest is giving last rites," Hugh said, his voice trembling. "And I'm sitting here watching my kid."

At the end of the first night, Hugh went home to change his clothes. It was near sunrise, and he was going to head back to the hospital. Someone called him to say they were going to have to cancel the meeting they had planned for later on—it was not the day to meet, not with everything happening in New York City, where it was closing in on 10 a.m.

That was how Hugh found out about the terrorist attacks.

He dressed and returned to the hospital. Doctors suggested Nick would need a transfusion, and Hugh would have to supply the blood. He had to go upstairs to donate, but with the panic and uncertainty on the other side of the country, donors had begun lining up in Los Angeles, just in case there was another attack.

There might have been 100 people in line ahead of Hugh when he arrived. In his head, a clock kept ticking: every moment that passed without a transfusion would be another moment that weakened his struggling newborn. Around him, everyone was talking about the planes and the World Trade Center.

Hugh joined in. Eventually, he shared the story of his night.

The person in front of him let him take their spot in line. And then the next person let him pass, and then the next, and the next. In short order, all 100 people let the tired, bewildered father pass to the front.

The Robertsons did not live far from the hospital, which was only about 15 minutes from downtown. It became a second home. Hugh stopped in every morning on his way to work. He would visit Mercedes, and he would visit Nick, who was improving but not yet healthy. It was still not safe for the father to hold his son. So he read to him. Every morning, Hugh would read something to his newborn. At 4 a.m., he would be reading stories about baseball, about home-run heroes and do-or-die moments that were really only life or death in the safe, simple context of sports.

One day, back at work and speaking with a client, he learned that a close friend had a son who had been born premature. Not only had the son survived, but he grew up to be an athlete. He went to Princeton, where he played hockey. That one stuck in Hugh's mind. If Nick could get far enough to get into hockey, it would mean he'd made it. He would have gotten strong. He would have lived. It was a thought that Hugh would keep close.

That November, over Thanksgiving, they were finally allowed to take their newborn home. He had been in the hospital for the first two months of his life, and he brought some of it with him. Nick Robertson had an oxygen tank for his underdeveloped lungs, and he had a heart monitor. The monitor was attached for the first month Nick was at home. Sometimes, it would go off overnight.

"It's not like feeding a baby in the middle of the night," said Hugh. "It was like, maybe the baby died."

Life went on like that for six weeks. Slowly, Nick grew stronger. His survival was no longer a question, but it was not clear what kind of life he would lead. They tested not just his reflexes but his cognitive development. For a while, doctors could not say for sure whether he would ever walk.

Eventually, the family was put in touch with a physical therapist. For two or three years, they worked to get Nick walking properly. At one point, the therapist pulled the parents aside—there was one quirk in Nick's stride they might never be able to correct, and it was a mystery: Nick had developed a habit of walking on his tiptoes, the therapist told Mercedes and Hugh. Neither of the parents had noticed it.

They were discussing it when one of Nick's older brothers walked into the room. Michael, the eldest, was walking on his tiptoes. They looked at Michael, then they looked at each other.

It was hereditary.

"It was just how they comfortably walked," said Mercedes, smiling. "It's just, when they're strolling, they like to be on their tippy-toes. Kind of like to look up, to see what's going on. That's their way of seeing the world."

More than a decade later, Hugh and Mercedes were sitting in the mezzanine of a hotel in Chicago. It was the official hotel of the NHL leading up to the 2017 draft. Agents and prospects and executives were mingling with each other down below. Reporters from across Canada and the United States were circling the crowd, looking for stories and sources and ways to fill the time until the first name was called at the United Center.

It was a hockey convention, both for those who had already made it and for those who were just on the cusp. Hugh and Mercedes had never set out to become a hockey family, but here they were, on the brink of becoming NHL parents. It was expected that Jason, their middle son, would be selected at some point that weekend—likely sooner rather than later.

Brianne, their daughter, played volleyball. The boys had started playing Little League, which Hugh coached. There was a basketball net in the driveway. Then they found hockey.

It started with a trip to see the Mighty Ducks of Anaheim. They went because of the movies. When the Los Angeles Kings moved to the Staples Center, Hugh bought season tickets. The kids were small, so they might only get a period out of them. They were good seats, though. Close to the ice. The kids would bring their foam mini-sticks to the arena. Intermission became their time to play. They would head into the concourse and take shots on each other. Before long, regulars began to recognize them.

They became entertainment for fans in the beer line, but Michael and Jason were not playing for fun, not even at intermission. They were pint-sized versions of the men down on the ice, moving hard and fast and aggressively at each other.

The Detroit Red Wings were in town to play the Kings one night. Michael was taking shots when a Wings fan in his mid-20s walked up. He loudly suggested to Michael that they play "real hockey," and that Michael should take a shot at him. The fan was holding a beer when he stepped into the line of fire.

Michael took his shot.

"Hits him right in the nuts," Hugh said with a belly laugh.

The fan's beer went flying. The Kings fans cheered.

Nick, the boy who had to learn how to breathe before he could learn how to walk, would become an especially quick study when it came to hockey.

●●●

They have hockey arenas in Southern California, but they also have traffic, which can make it difficult to reach those arenas. As the boys grew into the game, Hugh and Mercedes had to develop plans to get three minor hockey players to and from practice while somehow avoiding the worst rush hour gridlock. So they hatched the most sensible plan they could: they bought an RV.

The day would begin when Mercedes drove the children to school. She would pick them up in the new purchase—a "little 25-foot RV," Hugh said—and drive them to the rink, a half-hour away. The parking lot of the arena would become home from about 4 p.m. until 9:30 p.m.

They were not all the same age, which meant they were on the ice at different times. One would go in for practice while the others sat in the RV and did homework. Mercedes would make dinner in the RV, feeding the children around their hockey schedules. One would leave, then come back for homework and dinner as the next went into the rink.

Eventually, the family's hockey ambitions outgrew Southern California. Michael was offered a spot on Little Caesars, a renowned youth hockey program based in Detroit. It was early August, in 2010, and Hugh and Mercedes had a decision to make. Would she be willing to take the children halfway across the country so her son could join a minor hockey team?

Her answer came quickly. The next thing Hugh knew, he was at the airport with his wife and children and three pieces of luggage.

By the end of the month, Mercedes had taken all four children to Michigan. They did not have a place to live, so they spent three or four weeks at a Residence Inn. It was furnished, which was nice. By October, they had settled into a home in Northville, about a half hour's drive west of Detroit.

Hugh was born in Detroit, but his family moved away in 1969, and they had no relatives left in the area. Mercedes, on her own during the week, home-schooled the children. One was 9, the next was 10, the next was 11, and Michael, the eldest, was 12. All week, every week through the winter, she was alone with four children. Sometimes, she felt like the star in an episode of *Hoarders*, buried and helpless in the whirlwind of kids and belongings.

The only way to do it, she said, was to not think too hard: "Because if you stop and think about it, you won't do it."

Hugh commuted to Detroit on weekends. He usually tried to catch the 11 p.m. flight out of Los Angeles on Thursday, which would put him in Detroit around dawn. Mercedes and the kids picked him up at the airport. Hugh would then drop Mercedes back at home and attend to the needs of minor hockey. There might be a skating lesson in nearby Ann Arbor, followed by a session with a stickhandling specialist. If there was a quiet moment between sessions, Hugh would try to have a nap back at the house.

Michael eventually drifted away from hockey and toward academics, enrolling to study business at the University of Southern California. His two younger brothers stayed with the game, which moved them even farther away from Los Angeles: eventually, they decided to leave Michigan and move across the border into Canada.

Jason played minor midget triple-A—the season he became eligible for the OHL draft—in Toronto, with the Don Mills Flyers. The Flyers are part of the Greater Toronto Hockey League, the largest minor hockey organization on the planet, with roots dating back more than a century. It boasts more than 500 teams at the single-A, double-A, and triple-A levels. It's unusual to find an NHL roster without at least one GTHL graduate. Connor McDavid played for the league's Toronto Marlboros. P.K. Subban played with the Markham Islanders before graduating into the OHL with the Belleville Bulls. John Tavares (Marlboros) and Tyler Seguin (Toronto Young Nationals) played in the league, too, as did Mitch Marner, who graduated from Don Mills, the team Jason Robertson moved to Canada to join.

In 2015, the Kingston Frontenacs took Jason in the fourth round of the OHL draft, 62nd overall.

Nick, the youngest, was determined that, when his turn came, he would be drafted higher. It was not just a family joke—it became a guiding principle. The brothers were friendly, but they were also pathologically competitive, whether on the ice or in the family garage, where they would play ball hockey well past sundown. The noise from their games echoed through their neighbourhood in Pasadena.

Nick followed his brother to the GTHL, putting up 36 points in 32 games with the Toronto Red Wings in his OHL draft year. The Petes had concerns about his size—he was still small, even for a 15-year-old—but his skill was undeniable. And he had the tenacity of a kid brother.

The Petes granted his wish, taking him in the first round, 16th overall, in the 2017 draft.

Nick had dark, intensely expressive eyes. He always maintained eye contact in conversation with adults, which impressed scouts. He had a vise-grip handshake and an uncommonly singular focus on hockey. He was also still only 16 years old, and capable of endearing lapses into innocence.

On the first drive to Peterborough, when Mercedes had fallen asleep and Hugh was at the wheel, something seemed to be troubling Nick. He was not nervous, at least not about rookie camp and not about joining a new team in a faraway city. But he still had a problem: he told his father that he had to be better than his older brother Jason, the established OHL forward. It was not a want; it was a need.

The Kingston Frontenacs had drafted Jason in the fourth round. The Petes took Nick in the first. So that was good. But now there was talk that Jason could be taken in the first round of the NHL draft.

"Well," Hugh answered, "I hope so."

"But Dad," Nick said, "what if, by some chance, Jason got picked first overall in the first round? How do I get zero?"

●●●

Chris McNamara, the director of scouting in Peterborough, knows about undersized players. He played at a decent level of junior hockey growing up in Nova Scotia. His rise up the ladder slowed as it started to become clear that, while his opponents were growing, he was not. It would be hard to make a living as a stay-at-home defenceman forever frozen at 5-foot-4.

He went to university and eventually settled in Toronto, where he was running a training centre for some of the most talented teen-aged hockey players in the city. He has also watched between 350 and 450 minor hockey games every season in his role with the Petes, driving to games and tournaments in North Bay, Ottawa, Windsor, and all points in between. He usually makes it into the United States for tournaments and showcases five or six times a year.

"I probably go to the extreme with how many games I watch," he said, speaking with the thin gloss of a Maritimer's accent that has survived life in Southern Ontario.

He is single.

"If I was married with three kids"—he shrugged—"it'd be tough."

Tournament weekends can be marathons. They open on Friday, and McNamara can spend 12 hours inside the arena. He returns on Saturday for another 12 hours. It gets easier on Sunday, championship day—he can usually escape after only about 10 hours.

"There's many, many Fridays and Saturdays when you walk into the rink when it's dark outside," he said, "and you walk out when it's dark outside."

The culinary options are limited inside the rink, and snack bar coffee brewed by bored teenagers is not typically the height of luxury. But there are benefits. Scouts have the freedom to design their own work schedules. They know they operate as the eyes and ears of a franchise, and that the clarity of their vision can shape how a team performs on the ice. A diamond found in the rough of old coffee filters is still a diamond.

And while he might not wield the same power as a general manager, like Peterborough's Mike Oke, McNamara gets to avoid the headaches.

"I have a lot of respect for Mike and what he does, just because I know how difficult the GM side of it is, dealing with parents and the coaching staff, agents," he said. "The scouts? I get to go to a rink, I get to watch hockey—I'm getting paid to watch hockey—I get to pick the players I want to pick. The buzzer goes off in the third period, and you can leave. You don't have to deal with crazy parents, you don't have to deal with coaches and all this stuff. It's fun."

As an observer, he has seen the business of the game evolve. Training has become specialized, and it has become expensive. The stakes are higher, and at younger ages. Players in Toronto can be directed into elite-path programs as young as five, with private companies that promise skills development and extra ice time. Those companies do not operate as charities.

At the Canadian Ice Academy in Mississauga, near Toronto's western border, McNamara worked with 40 to 60 of the most promising triple-A players in the area. They were usually dropped off at 7:30 a.m. and would stay at the centre until about noon, skating in the morning and then working out in the gym. After lunch, a school bus would pick them up and deliver them to their regular school classes.

They would usually spend about 40 weeks with McNamara. Over that time, he would learn everything there was to know about them. That could be good, and that could be bad. One player in particular stood out for the latter, and it still made McNamara shake his head. He would not name the player, but nor would he ever forget him.

The player was at the rink one day when he formed a small group with his peers. Together, they set out to jam all the drains in the shower room. The child—he was still only 14 or 15 at the time—executed the final stage of the plan. He turned on all the showers and left the scene. By the time the adults caught on, there was already a foot of water in the basement.

McNamara said it was not the only incident.

"I walked in the dressing room one day, and he was pissing all over the walls," he said. "Pissing all over the walls. Just so undisciplined, and disrespectful to the instructors. Our instructors would kick him off the ice on a daily basis."

The child, who was from a well-to-do family, fell into a pattern.

"He would write an apology letter, and then do the same thing two days later," McNamara said. "And his parents would continuously bail him out, bail him out."

A first-round draft pick can be both a gift and a burden to an OHL executive. The players at the top of the developmental pyramid have skill, and that skill has been scrutinized at length. What can be trickier is what happens off the ice. Is the prospect stubborn? Can he be coached? What about the parents? Are they going to be an issue? Will the kid flood the shower stalls and piss all over the walls?

A first-round draft pick is also a major investment. Junior teams are responsible for room and board, but they are also required to fund an education package if the player enrolls in university or college after his time in uniform. McNamara said the tab could end up at $60,000.

Screening out a potential problem child was part of his job. McNamara and Oke interviewed their top prospects before the OHL draft. They would sit at the family's kitchen table like a pair of detectives on *Law & Order*, taking note of every detail and every tic, looking for clues.

"Nine times out of 10, the parents want to do all the talking," said McNamara. "They want to answer for the kid. We're like, 'No, no, we're asking little Johnny here—he's the one who may play for the Peterborough Petes one day.'"

Anything can be a sign. If the prospect lets the parent do all the talking, it can suggest the kid lacks confidence or intelligence or both. If the prospect asks his parents to leave the room, or asks for them to be quiet, it can be taken as a mark of agency and confidence.

The prospects are still only 15 years old.

Some of the children have been so good for so long, they might only know what it is to live in an environment of praise and deferential adults. They know they are outliers, part of the tiny fraction of minor hockey players with the natural skill to make it this far. They know they are special. "There are some of those kids," McNamara said, "and you walk away thinking, 'Oooh, he may be hard to coach.'"

Some, though, can be self-aware. They know they are special, but they also know they will be competing against other special players, and that only a tiny fraction of their own tiny fraction will get to move on to the final stations on the hockey map.

It's both an art and a science. McNamara knows some of the teenagers have already been coached on what to say, either by their parents or by their agent. And like any job interview process, there are also those who might present well but then play terribly. There are great players who might present badly.

Nick Robertson could do both. He was the best player on a bad triple-A team, and he was small. But his older brother had grown, and the family seemed grounded and reasonable about what they saw as an OHL career trajectory.

So the Petes drafted him.

●●●

It was a half hour to puck drop at the Peterborough Memorial Centre, and Nick Robertson was walking the upper concourse in a suit jacket that made him look even younger than he did in equipment. And he looked very young when he was in equipment, his helmet and shoulder pads never quite able to conceal the fact he was a 16-year-old waiting impatiently for a growth spurt.

He was 5-foot-7 and 143 pounds. He looked so small and frail that it seemed irresponsible of the Petes to put him on the ice. But he was fast and tenacious and skilled, with 10 points in his first 12 games, to rank alongside the most productive rookies in the league.

It had taken eight games to score his first goal, but even that made sense, knowing his propensity for late starts. He scored the winning goal in a mid-October game at home against the Kingston

Frontenacs, and was named the game's first star while his older brother Jason, playing for the visitors, was forced to watch.

Robertson was flourishing despite surprisingly stringent limitations from his coach. Hull had adopted a tough-love approach with his ascendant forward. He was sparing, almost fickle, with ice time. An older player could turn the puck over in the neutral zone and not miss a single shift; Robertson could be held off the ice until the end of the third period as punishment for doing the same.

Perhaps with that in mind, he approached a visitor on the concourse and produced an iPhone from the breast pocket of his blazer to explain his absence from the evening's game. He had been involved in a collision during practice earlier in the week, the team's first since its unexpected stumble during its Michigan road trip. His face bore the brunt of the impact: his gums had been driven lower beneath his bottom teeth. He showed the photo on his iPhone, revealing the damage not clear to the naked eye.

Through the stitches and the brace behind his lower lip, he declared: "I'm not a healthy scratch."

His tenacity had become a running joke around the rink. Robertson took online correspondence classes, and he would do that work at the rink. He was the first on the ice and the last off, every day. He would sometimes plead with Duco to stick around and help him polish his faceoff technique, or to teach him how to shield the puck from a defender.

A member of the team's staff wondered how Robertson would adjust socially, having not been exposed to much of a life outside the arena, or to other children his age at school. Hockey was all he knew, all he wanted to do, extending into his leisure time. At home in California, Hugh would place a sheet of plastic near the couch, and whenever Nick and Jason were in front of the television, they had hockey sticks in their hands, a small ball on the floor, stickhandling as they watched. It helped to teach them to play with their heads up.

Nick could skate and he could shoot. Even on a team with NHL-drafted players, he had the unique ability to place the puck not where his linemates were skating but where they should be skating. Though he was usually the smallest player on the ice, he was fearless.

He bickered with opponents. He drove through players twice his size in the offensive zone and, when he yelled for a pass, his voice cut through the arena like a siren. Robertson started life too early, and he was not going to slow down now.

THREE

THE LIFE OF NOBBER

It always sounded like Logan DeNoble was nervous, or maybe just a little bit cold. There was a tremor in his voice, a little catch as he spoke in the hallway outside the dressing room, or in the hotel lobby, or in an appearance on the local television station, facing square to the interviewer with his hat backward.

He was not the biggest forward on the roster, nor was he the fastest. There were others who could fire a puck harder, pass it more creatively, or see the ice a little crisper. DeNoble had joined the Petes almost as an afterthought, having been drafted 242nd overall four years earlier, or 223 spots below where Mitch Marner, the future Toronto Maple Leafs winger, was selected.

As the Petes stumbled away from their trip to Michigan, DeNoble's was among the team's most important voices. He had worked diligently after the draft, playing with the lower-level Lindsay Muskies for parts of two seasons until Peterborough management was finally compelled to promote him to the roster. He scored 20 goals in his first full OHL season, and had 34 in his second as the franchise went on its deep playoff run. When that run ended in Mississauga, it was DeNoble who was chosen to sit next to coach Jody Hull at the table in the interview room. That was one of the early signs he was going to be named captain, and it was a role he took seriously.

DeNoble was born and raised in Peterborough, and he came from a line of Petes players. He was an avatar for the town itself: others might be flashier, but he could do a little bit of everything, and he would work hard while doing it, even if it meant he had to bleed.

Other players would move away after their junior hockey career. A lucky few would sign professional contracts. Many would enroll in university. Others would just return home, whether it be to Brantford, Toronto, or Moscow. To them, the Memorial Centre would become a version of high school, home to a handful of fond youthful memories, where visits would be confined to reunions and special invitations.

DeNoble thought he might move away for university—the Maritimes sounded nice—but he would return. Peterborough was his home, where he could get to a lake or a golf course in less time than it would take to battle 15 blocks in a city like Toronto. For him, the Memorial Centre would remain a part of everyday living. Old-timers used the ice for shinny after Petes games. Children skated there. DeNoble would still be walking the same hallways, past the plaque showing the name of every captain in franchise history, and past the rows of carefully mounted team pictures. Whatever story the photo of this season's team would end up telling, it would repeat it to Logan DeNoble every time he visited, for the rest of his life.

There was no reason to panic yet. Peterborough still had more wins than losses, and the team was still safely near the top of the

OHL's Eastern Conference standings. The cracks were spreading, but they were not irreparable. The Petes ended October with an 8–3 romp over the Hamilton Bulldogs, and DeNoble was named the game's third star after scoring twice and adding an assist.

They beat Barrie in overtime a few nights later, but they started losing players to injury. Forward Zach Gallant, the Detroit Red Wings draft pick, hurt his knee. Two-way winger Nick Isaacson hurt his shoulder. Adam Timleck, the quiet 19-year-old winger, was lost to an undisclosed malady. And DeNoble joined them on the injured list.

None of them were in the lineup for the game in Mississauga on the first Sunday in November, when the Petes fed rookie goal-tender Hunter Jones to the sharks. They were outshot 23–7 in the first period, and that was probably the best they played all game. Jones ended up facing 62 shots that afternoon, en route to a 9–2 loss. Jonathan Ang was ejected for cross-checking in the second period, and defenceman Cole Fraser was sent off in the third for punching an opponent who never dropped his gloves.

Though calm on the surface, Dylan Wells was struggling. But, rather than offer him rest, the Petes threw him back out under the lights. It was a tactical error. He allowed three goals on the first five shots he faced. Jody Hull pulled him before the game was eight minutes old.

They fell 4–0 to Hamilton a few nights later. And 24 hours after that, they lost 4–1 to Oshawa at home, Peterborough's fifth loss in its last seven games. Over that stretch, with some of their most important veteran players sidelined by injury or suspension, the Petes had been outscored 38–20.

Nick Robertson, the promising rookie from California, went five games without a point and was often punished for mistakes, left on the bench as a harsh lesson from Hull. Ang was held to a single assist through six games. Wells had faced 40 or more shots more often than anyone would have liked, and he allowed a few more goals than anyone really expected.

DeNoble knew it was a low point in the season. But it had to get better. The Petes were too good of a team for it not to.

He'd returned from the injured list for the game against Oshawa after two weeks of watching from the sidelines. He saw the Petes struggle to stem the tide of shots against them, and he saw how bedraggled they were on defence. On the power-play, the Petes seemed to have developed the unusual nightly tradition of allowing at least one short-handed breakaway.

It was hard to pick out just one problem, so he did not try. DeNoble instead dipped into the universal hockey captain's thesaurus and pulled out a handful of trusted bromides. The Petes would have to develop more of a physical presence, he said. They would have to be "tough to play against," which meant they would have to be willing to go to "the dirty areas" of the ice.

"I've been through losing streaks every year," he said. "It's not time to panic. It's November."

●●●

One of the only truly intimidating Petes players was smiling sheepishly from his chair on the dais, his smooth features softening to appear almost gentle. Cole Fraser had been taken 131st overall in the NHL draft, and he walked into the interview room at the United Center in Chicago with a new Detroit Red Wings baseball cap to match his new team-issue jersey.

It was the second day of the draft, which is far more businesslike than the opening night, when all the top prospects are showcased and celebrated on national television. The second day moves quickly, and without nearly as much fanfare. Teams have to grind through six rounds of drafting on day two; they make 186 picks without commercial interruption. Near the end, it starts to feel a bit like the last day of school. People have flights to catch.

Fraser was not expected to be picked, or at least not as high as he was. The NHL's central scouting service had listed him as the 206th-best North American skater six months before the draft. Peterborough had four players on that list. Fraser was ranked lowest. He moved up on the final list issued in the spring, all the way to number 197.

"I wasn't really sure what to expect," he said, his broad smile revealing the small gap between his front teeth. "Like, I was going to the washroom when I got picked."

The Red Wings did not draft him hoping he would score goals, run the power-play, or contribute in any significant way on offence. They picked him because of his mean streak, because of his willingness to block shots and maybe scare an opponent or two. Tyler Wright, Detroit's director of amateur scouting, told the team's website the Red Wings hoped Fraser would "make life miserable" for anyone wearing the wrong sweater.

It was exactly what the Petes needed from him, too. Fraser was big, but not a cartoon version of big. At 6-foot-2, 195 pounds, he had broader shoulders than any other player on the roster. Peterborough had largely moved to embrace skill over muscle; if anyone on the team was going to fight to frighten, or hit to send one of hockey's unspoken messages, it would be the 18-year-old from Carleton Place, Ontario.

"I'm definitely going to make a big hit when I have the chance, to get the guys on the bench going," he said. "Because I know, when I see a big hit happen, that's something that speaks to me, that's something that gets me going. And I know, for the guys on the bench, it kind of gets some laughter out of the bench, and it gets us all pumped up and more ready to go."

Even from the depths of their November slump, everyone in town knew the Petes would ultimately score their way out of trouble. They had too many skilled forwards with NHL aspirations to be held off the scoresheet. And as soon as Dylan Wells regained his footing, they knew they had one of the best goaltenders in the league, if not the country.

It was the defence that was a concern; the team had lost two of its key blueliners to graduation after its playoff run the previous spring. Former captain Brandon Prophet was at Queen's University. Kyle Jenkins, who led all Peterborough defencemen in playoff scoring, was now in the arts program at Wilfrid Laurier University.

Matthew Timms was back this year, but he broke his foot shortly after the season opener. He was only 19, but at 5-foot-9, he had long since accepted the reality that an NHL career was not in his future. Timms had the ability to both run the power-play and drive team management into fits of forehead-slapping. He was a risk-taker, which sometimes led to chances at either end of the ice. None of those risks were to blame for the broken bone in his foot: that happened when he dove into the water at a pool party designed to foster team spirit. It was described as a fluke injury.

Alex Black was another veteran returnee. Tall, with an easy smile and a shock of red hair, he was in his second year with the Petes, having been acquired in a trade with Sarnia the previous December. He was a so-called over-ager, turning 20 a week before the season began. Teams are permitted three over-agers each, and Black, DeNoble, and Nikita Korostelev were the designated elders in Peterborough. Black adored playing hockey, but part of him could not help but look ahead. He was a serviceable defenceman, but it was clear he was not going to play professionally. With any luck, he would be enrolled in university the following season, playing with men his age rather than mixed in with teenagers away from home for the first time, guided by early curfews. After graduation, he would be a firefighter.

Black and Timms were both useful veterans in certain roles, but neither fit the mould of a Chris Pronger, that looming tree of menace who could play 30 minutes a night. It had been years since a Peterborough coach had a player with that kind of skill on the blue line, though not for lack of trying.

General manager Mike Oke had a working understanding of what the team's fans were saying in the online forums—he would have heard the talk around town before training camp: *What is Oke going to do about the defence?* He made his biggest splash two weeks before the Petes drove into Michigan, trading two fourth-round draft picks for Austin Osmanski, a tall defenceman with the Mississauga Steelheads. Osmanski was a 19-year-old from the Buffalo suburb of East Aurora. He had some of the size and some of the menace everyone thought the Petes were missing. The Buffalo Sabres thought enough of his potential to pick him in the seventh round of the 2016 NHL draft, 188 places behind first-overall pick Auston Matthews.

Osmanski was one of only two U.S.-born players on the roster, and it took time for the staff to figure out what made him tick. During a brief conversation between the three coaches early in the fall, one coach shrugged and told the other two that Osmanski was "the unknowable American."

Declan Chisholm was the best skater of the bunch, a 17-year-old heading into his NHL draft year. He could fly up the ice, but he was still learning parts of the game, along with some of the responsibilities that went with being a full-time hockey player. Coach Jody Hull scratched him from a pre-season game in Buffalo after he overslept. His roommate made it on time.

Fraser could not skate like Chisholm, and he could not create offence like Timms. His specialty was in being unpleasant. Fraser could skate and he could shoot well enough, but he was no artist with the puck. He typically expressed himself by blocking shots, and by shoving or punching opponents. Sometimes he would do all three in the same shift.

The challenge for the Petes was in anger management. Fraser was at his best when he flew around the defensive zone with the bomb doors open, ready to explode on an opposing forward foolish enough to carry the puck for too long. He was Peterborough's nuclear deterrent, with the only catch being nobody was ever sure exactly when he might detonate.

There was a switch, somewhere. Fraser could seem so gentle in the Memorial Centre hallway after a game, when he would laugh and tell the crowd of friends and family that he let his girlfriend cut his hair. He was so playful at the team's Christmas party, when coaches and players competed together in an annual holiday-themed trivia contest; seated at a table with assistant coach Andrew Verner—an avowed trivia expert whose expertise, according to murmuring rivals, was actually rooted in his ability to check Google on his phone without detection—Fraser was a quick study, smirking as he tried to check his phone for an answer. He blushed when he was caught.

And then there were times when the light seemed to leave Fraser's eyes. He would grunt a salutation in the hallway, his head tilted to the floor or to his phone. And he was never more unpredictable than when he was on the ice. Fraser could be goaded. When the switch was flipped, no one could turn it off.

Jake Grimes was one of the only coaches who seemed to know where the switch was even located. He had been one of Hull's assistant coaches the previous two seasons, before he left for another OHL job. A former OHL forward with more than a decade of experience on the bench, Grimes was affable without being too chatty, and he'd had a rapport with Fraser. But Grimes was gone now; over the summer, the Petes had offered him only a one-year contract. By his way of thinking, the only thing less respectful than a one-year offer was no offer at all. He moved to work with the Guelph Storm. He did not leave behind the operational manual for Fraser.

Opponents soon realized how easy it was to stoke a fire: a hit, a colourful word or two. They could get him to turn his head, to speak back in anger. Sometimes, he would follow the offending player after the whistle to continue the conversation. Even from the stands, it was clear when the temperature rose.

Fraser exploded in the blowout loss to Mississauga that led to his November suspension. The Petes were down 8–2, en route to their second loss in three games. They had been picked clean, thoroughly humiliated. On television, the play-by-play announcer joked that a long shot taken from beside the Peterborough net might have been the toughest the Mississauga goaltender had faced all game. Hunter Jones, the rookie making his fourth start in net for Peterborough, faced more shots than in his previous two games combined. He would make 53 saves, and he would still lose.

Mississauga was the same team that had ground Peterborough into a fine powder in the playoffs the previous season; this was supposed to be the year the Petes avenged those losses. They were supposed to be the ones delivering those blowouts. As the time ticked down in front of the nearly empty Hershey Centre stands, the frustration on the ice was nearly audible.

The Petes were already short-handed when Fraser went into the corner to clear the puck. Steelheads forward Michael Little was on his knees, and the two collided. Fraser was knocked down, but it was nothing out of the ordinary until he turned around. He shoved Little and, as the two regained their feet, he cross-checked him.

And then he dropped his gloves like they were on fire. He hammered Little, landing three devastating punches, at least one square in the face. Little did not have time to block the punch. He had not had time to drop his gloves. It was not clear that he even wanted to fight. Fraser did not seem to care, and he did not give him a choice. The assault—from first contact to last punch—lasted five seconds.

Little skated slowly back to the bench, blood dripping from his face. Mississauga players raged against the silence of the arena. Fraser disappeared quickly down the tunnel toward the visiting dressing room, and would not return to the ice for almost three weeks.

●●●

In 2013, the Toronto Maple Leafs qualified for the NHL postseason for the first time in nine years, and they did it by outrunning their destiny. The schedule that year was cut short by a labour stoppage: teams had time to play only 48 games, rather than the usual 82.

The Leafs finished the shortened schedule fifth in the Eastern Conference, with a six-point cushion in the playoff race. At the same time, a fast-growing subset of mathematically inclined hockey fans had examined the data and concluded the success was a mirage: the Leafs were not as good as they looked in the standings.

It was based around a concept known as Corsi, developed by a Chicago financial analyst as a means of quantifying which team controlled the puck during a game. The statistic itself is not so complex: it takes a team's shot attempts—those that make it to the goalie, as well as shots that miss and shots that are blocked en route —and measures it against those of the opposing team. The final number is expressed as a percentage. A team with a higher percentage is generally regarded as being better with the puck. More shot attempts suggests more time with the puck, which usually leads to scoring chances.

The Leafs did not have a good Corsi that season. In fact, they had one of the worst in the league. After losing their first-round post-season series that spring, the team failed to qualify for the playoffs in each of the next three seasons. It seemed to reinforce a cold, mathematical reality: it's possible to outrun the numbers in a sprint, but they'll almost always catch up eventually.

Like the Leafs in 2013, the Petes likely would not have been a strong Corsi team the year they went deep into the playoffs. The OHL does not publish all the statistics needed to formulate Corsi, but during the regular season, Dylan Wells faced the second-most shots in the league. Peterborough went on to be outshot in 8 of its 12 playoff games.

It was happening again this year. Something seemed structurally wrong on the ice. Opposing teams seemed to know precisely where to pressure the Petes, as if there were a button they could tap to open a trap door underneath the neutral zone. Peterborough skaters would flail as they fell, turning the puck over and leaving their goalie to deal with the consequences. Their swashbuckling play of early October had lost all of its swash, and they mostly just buckled.

The coaches said they were preparing the players. They showed them video—sometimes projecting it on a dressing room wall, which they did in Flint—and laid out strategy. In private, they were starting to wonder whether other teams had come to realize Peterborough forwards were not what they once were, that they were not cut from the same tough cloth celebrated in the banners above the ice. On defence, they wondered if the team had the foot speed to keep up. Their guys needed help, and it was not clear if any was coming in the form of a trade from general manager Mike Oke.

The captain tried to set minds st ease. "You have to remember: it's November," said DeNoble. "The season's not won or lost in November."

Nobody called him by either his first or his last name, at least not around the Memorial Centre. He was Nobber, and he was from a line of Nobbers, with a family tree that was sunk deep in the soil around the Otonabee River.

The team was in his blood. His maternal grandfather, Ron Chittick, had spent six games with the Petes 50 years earlier. His great-uncle Perry Chittick appeared in 71 games over two seasons, including one in which he overlapped with Ron. DeNoble also had an uncle on the other side of the family who made the team: Jeff DeNoble had a two-game cameo in the 1980s.

Logan DeNoble was born in October 1997, a year after Peterborough hosted the Memorial Cup for the first (and, so far, the last) time. He missed the glory years by more than a decade. The Petes had never finished first in the OHL standings in his lifetime. They had never won the Memorial Cup, and they had made only one appearance in the tournament. The flow of players to the NHL from Peterborough had slowed to a trickle.

When he was growing up in town, the Petes were about more than just what happened on the ice. They were a way to connect with family—and, in his younger days, to stay up past his bedtime. His aunt had season tickets, and he had vivid memories of straining against sleep until the moment her car pulled into his parents' driveway on game nights to take him to the arena. The sound of the engine was a shot of adrenaline, jolting him awake as they started the familiar journey down to Lansdowne.

Becoming captain meant something to him—he had been working at it long before the Petes stitched the *C* onto his jersey. Playing for the Petes turned him into a representative for all of Peterborough, wearing a logo that was more closely associated with the city than anything else. A fellow tourist in a beer garden in Europe might not know about the area's wealth of natural beauty, but there was a damned good chance they would know about the Petes.

Being from Peterborough was different, too. The city had a downtown strip, a mall, a Costco, and a ring of suburban housing, but it would never be as big or as bright or as electric as a metropolis like Toronto, and DeNoble saw in that a virtue rather than a drawback. Peterborough was smaller, but he believed that was part of what made it superior: the scale made it easier to pull tight the threads of community, especially in times of crisis. He had witnessed it with his own eyes.

His mother, Jodi Chittick-DeNoble, led the city's emergency management department. She was on call 24 hours a day. If a resident was ever the focus of those calls, it usually meant that person was having an extraordinarily bad day. When the river rose too close to the banks, she was in charge of placing the sandbags. When there was an emergency at the airport or a chemical spill in the local water supply, her phone would ring.

One day during the previous season, she and Logan were together in the car when her phone rang. A family's house had caught fire. Instead of heading home, his mother raced to the scene. It felt like she stayed on her phone for hours. She was managing a crisis, but she was not alone.

"It was so cool to see how many people took time out of their day to help this family," he said. "I think that's kind of what Peterborough's about: a tight-knit community where, if anyone needs anything, you can call anyone and they're there for you, and there to help you out."

He tried to carry that part of Peterborough with him into the dressing room. In 2015, the Petes drafted a centre from Finland named Jonne Tammela. He was a teenager when he arrived in town, and he arrived without the use of a car. DeNoble arranged to give him an extensive tour, pointing out all the sights and landmarks during a 90-minute drive. When it was finally over, he made a promise to his new teammate: "If you need anything, just text me and I'll come pick you up."

In August, the Petes contracted a sports psychologist, and she was holding a seminar in the Pat Casey Alumni Room during a break between sessions at training camp. Veterans and rookies listened as the psychologist informed them that the formula for success was 30 per cent talent and 60 per cent mental toughness, with the remaining 10 per cent left up to luck.

Fifteen minutes into her presentation, she said she had a game she wanted to play. "All right, now we're going to do something a little bit crazy," she said. "I'm going to need somebody who is really going to be very brave, who's willing to come up here in front of everybody."

Several of the rookie players, only hours into their OHL careers, looked down at the floor. Some of the veterans smiled. A few giggled. And then there was a moment of awkward silence. It was far too early in training camp for anyone to volunteer for potential humiliation. There were still too many strangers in the room. It was the first day of school.

"You guys are all looking at me like I'm crazy right now," she said. "I wish I could show you your faces." She coughed. "I don't want you to be scared. I'm really not that scary. But I'm going to get somebody to come up here and help me out with something."

DeNoble raised his hand.

"OK, awesome," she said, surprised. "Remind me your name again?"

"Logan," he said.

She asked what made him volunteer.

"Uh, no one else was really saying anything," DeNoble said. "Take one for the team."

The other players chuckled. The psychologist had no game to play. She only wanted to see if anyone was willing to stand up and take a risk. She gave DeNoble a crisp new Petes baseball cap as his reward.

"You were actually pretty quick," she said. "Sometimes, when I'm with a group—usually bigger than this—literally nobody comes up."

Whenever the role of a captain comes up in discussion during a difficult stretch of the season, it usually involves his soft skills. A captain cannot help the goaltender make a critical save in the third period. A captain cannot turn a struggling team's Corsi rating around by himself, and he cannot fix a wonky power-play. The expectations of a captain often cannot be quantified. They can seem almost mystical. But a captain can be judged by how cohesive a team appears off the ice—if a room filled with two dozen teenagers can remain cohesive in any meaningful way.

DeNoble hoped to rely at least partly on a tradition. After practice every Tuesday night, it was Petes custom to go for dinner at Riley's Pub, two kilometres up from the Memorial Centre on George Street. It was a long-standing reservation, and the servers had pitchers of cola and water on the tables for 5 p.m. After dinner, players would head en masse to the movie theatre two blocks north. If nothing of interest was playing, they would retire to a player's house to watch the Maple Leafs game.

"You just hang out, and get to know guys," said DeNoble. "You get more comfortable with everybody, and I think that's a huge key."

Cliques were bad. The team had cliques during his rookie season. He said the Petes had worked hard to change that culture over the last few years. It just required effort. The team had four Russian players on the roster, for example. On the road, he said, the Russians would stick together—"for obvious reasons. But even last night, at dinner, we were like, 'OK, Russians, you're sitting at different ends of the table, just for something different.'"

The thing with being a captain, though, is that the test never comes when the seas are calm—it's when the water gets choppy.

FOUR

THE FLAG-BEARERS

Everyone has a breaking point, and Rob Wells reached his 16 months after becoming a father. His issue was not with the child—the bright, green-eyed boy he and his wife had named Dylan. It was with a purple dinosaur whose eyes were dead and dark, and the Christmas video it had unleashed on the world. Dylan loved Barney, and he insisted on watching that video again and again, and again and again.

Dylan was still in diapers when Rob took a stand. He seized Barney and forcibly removed him from the video player for something he thought they both might enjoy. Rob was a musician, a drummer who had opened a recording studio a few months before Dylan arrived. He made sure his son owned his own kit, with a little tom-tom drum and a hat box set up on the living room floor.

Barney was not much of a musician. On the day of the rebellion, Rob made a calculated risk, slipping a copy of Peter Gabriel's concert video *Secret World Live* into the player. The lights were bright, and the music was a bit more percussive than traditional dinosaur fare. Dylan was mesmerized, and within a few minutes, he seemed to zero in on the drummer, mimicking what he saw on the screen with the instruments in front of him on the living room floor.

Rob had scaled back his touring commitments after Dylan was born, and was teaching at a music store in St. Catharines, Ontario. He believed anyone could learn to play the drums, but he also knew there were limits to the powers of instruction. Some people were born with ability that could never be taught. And it looked like Dylan had been born with such a gift. Long before the first day of elementary school, the son would accompany the father to the studio.

Dylan could barely reach the pedals on the big drum kit up on the second floor. He sat near the edge of the seat, almost standing, but he could play. He could hold time, lay down a groove, and execute a basic fill. Which is what he was doing the afternoon a session band arrived for work.

Two of the professional musicians were lugging some of the gear up the stairs toward the studio. From the sounds of it, another professional drummer was already hard at work. By the time they reached the door, though, all they could see was a small, blue-eyed child by the kit. Where was the drummer?

They were stunned.

It was about a month after his fourth birthday when the tiny drummer developed a new obsession. The Salt Lake City Winter Games were becoming famous for moments of triumph and scandal and several areas in between. Canadian figure skaters Jamie Salé and David Pelletier were robbed of a gold medal by the nefarious voting of a French judge. Speed skater Catriona Le May Doan won her 500-metre race to become the first Canadian to defend their Olympic title. Then there was hockey, where the Canadian women overcame historically awful officiating to beat the United

States for global supremacy. Just as he had with the concert video, Dylan developed a specific fixation amidst all the noise.

He kept watching Martin Brodeur, the goaltender on the Canadian Olympic men's team. Brodeur had a set of white pads with a scythe of red slashing through the middle. After becoming the starter, he lifted Canada to its first gold medal win in a half century. Not long after the tournament, Dylan's parents found him drawing pictures of goalies and their pads.

Barb and Rob never expected they would become goalie parents. There was always a suspicion they were going to raise a drummer, but neither of them had any experience in net. They had both dabbled in sports as children, but there was no rich vein of goaltending lore coursing through the bloodlines. In fact, they both seemed normal and well adjusted—traits traditionally antithetical to goaltending.

That Christmas, they bought him his own set of goalie pads. It turned out to be a dry winter, without much snow on the ground. A puddle of standing water had turned into a small patch of ice on the driveway, though, and as soon as he could, Dylan strapped on his new pads and went sliding outside.

They signed him up for ball hockey. Dylan turned out to be pretty good, and other parents began asking where he played in the winter. He had not been playing anywhere, in part because neither of his parents were fluent in the seasonal rhythms of hockey registrations and sign-ups. They bought a set of ice hockey gear, and they registered Dylan for the local minor hockey program.

He was seven years old.

One of the coaches was apprehensive, bordering on concerned. Players at that age usually take turns in goal. Depending on the personalities in the dressing room, playing net could be like jury duty: it had to be done, but that did not mean anyone had to enjoy it. And here was Dylan, volunteering to be a goalie moments into his minor hockey career. The coach rolled his eyes, suggesting it would all go sideways.

Rob and Barb picked a spot close to the bench, near the coaches, for Dylan's first game. One of the kids got a breakaway, moving in all alone on a little boy who, up to that point in his young life, had only seen a breakaway on television. It was new to all of them.

Nobody seemed quite sure what to make of what happened next. Dylan went down in the full splits to make the save. It would not be the last time that season, either. His team advanced to the championship game at the end of the year. It went to a shootout. A girl from Dylan's class was the goalie at the other end of the ice, and she was a star. None of the first five shooters from either team could sneak a shot behind the goaltenders. Neither could any of the following five. The coaches went through their entire benches without finding anyone who could beat either tiny goaltender.

Finally, on the 15th or 16th shooter, someone scored on the girl at the other end of the ice. Dylan was a champion.

Minor hockey coaches started calling the Wells home that spring. None of them were rolling their eyes anymore—they were asking if he was available to join their teams. There was a coach from single-A and another from triple-A, the highest level in the system. Rob was still trying to digest the terminology and the layers of implications attached to any decision. Mostly, he was trying to figure out why there was such interest in his plans. Dylan was only eight.

●●●

Whatever plans the Petes had for the 2017–18 season, they began with Dylan, now a fourth-year veteran starter. He was not tall by modern goaltending standards, but he was tall enough, at 6-foot-2, and he was athletic. He had to be, because the team in front of him tended to bleed shots on net, keeping him busier than most of his peers.

The previous spring, Wells faced more shots per game than any other OHL goaltender who appeared in 10 or more playoff games. He played in 12, and he was exceptional, fighting through screens and using his athleticism to cover for his team's defensive miscues. He nearly stole a game against the Steelheads in the conference final, serving as the only breakwater between the Petes and total humiliation, facing 55 shots in game three and allowing only two goals. It went into overtime, but they still lost, 2–1.

By game four, he was spent. He allowed a goal on the sixth shot he faced, and was beaten six more times as the Petes were swept out of the playoffs in front of a nearly empty arena in suburban Toronto. Wells had been abandoned on an island with nothing but his gear to protect him.

If there was a fire that burned within him after those losses, it was protected beneath layers of hardened serenity. When he walked onto the Peterborough bus after their awful loss in Flint, he bore the same air of calm and vaguely bemused smile as he had after their win in Windsor two days earlier.

His mother, Barb, insisted on that. She had played a little baseball growing up in Thorold, not far from St. Catharines, and played basketball and volleyball in school. She was the youngest in a family of six, so she knew about competition, and she knew about sportsmanship. She told her son to be humble when he won and humble when he lost. She also threatened him. It was not a hollow threat: if she ever saw her son throw a tantrum on the ice—tossing his stick, or smashing it over his net—she would walk onto the rink and pull him off by the ear. She did not specify which ear, which was the only part of the threat left to the imagination.

Dylan was still in minor hockey when Barb was diagnosed with breast cancer one year just before Christmas. It was his minor midget season, the year of his OHL draft. Rob had begun working with a local country music artist named Tim Hicks, and the light on the horizon of his drumming career had never seemed brighter. When Barb got her diagnosis, everything suddenly seemed jumbled. It was just the three of them, after all. Rob, remembering the moment, shook his head: "You just don't know what's up or down anymore."

The Petes took Dylan 21st overall in the OHL draft that spring. At 16, he would have to move to a new city and a new school, into a new home with a billet family he didn't know, all while his mother was battling breast cancer at home. She endured radiation, as well as surgery to remove the cancerous growth, and the treatment continued when Dylan arrived in Peterborough for his first season with the Petes.

Doctors told her they'd caught it early, and they gave her a promising prognosis. Midway through that first season, Dylan unveiled an addition to his mask: he had a pink ribbon painted onto the back of his helmet, and he told the *Peterborough Examiner* he wanted it on the back because he wanted his mother to "know she is always in the back of my mind."

Barb had been declared cancer-free more than two years before her son entered his final junior hockey season. She was making the three-hour drive to Peterborough as often as she could to watch him, in what was shaping up to be perhaps the most transformative year of his life. Edmonton had selected him in the fifth round of the NHL draft a year earlier. He signed his first professional contract in the spring, a three-year entry-level deal worth

$2.825-million (U.S.), and put some of it toward a shiny (but used) Audi.

With the world junior tournament, the OHL playoffs, and the potential of a trip to Regina for the 100th Memorial Cup in May, his recently purchased car was going to be the first in a trophy case full of rewards by the end of the season.

●●●

Hockey has a storied tradition of eccentrics. Sidney Crosby will not walk past the visiting dressing room before home games. The goaltender Patrick Roy held regular conversations with his goalposts on the ice. Darcy Tucker had a phase where he would drink a toxic-sounding cocktail of coffee and cola before the puck dropped. Stan Mikita, the Original Six star, always made sure that whenever he finished a cigarette, he flicked the butt over his left shoulder rather than his right.

The Petes had Jonathan Ang. He was one of the best pure skaters in the OHL, and possibly in all junior hockey. He was also an enigma for coaches and teammates. Coaches struggled with his enormous gifts, with the speed and skill and aggression that could materialize and disappear on the same shift. His teammates, meanwhile, were mesmerized by his cascade of personality quirks.

It would take him a half hour to tape his stick, where it took most only a few minutes. If at any point the tape job was not to his satisfaction, he would start again from the beginning. Inside the dressing room, he positioned his stick to his left side, making sure the blade faced a certain way every time. Sometimes, if he left the room, a teammate would move it, just to see what he would do. Every time, Ang would move it back into place, because in his mind, that place was where it belonged.

Then there was the tic with his skates. Ang would slip his foot into the boot, then pull it back out and rub his foot over the ground. Sometimes, teammates caught him tugging the collar of his jersey, and it looked like he was spitting, except he was not spitting—for reasons that were never understood, Ang was sending short bursts of air into the front of his collar, as if he were trying to blow away a mosquito. One teammate called him "twitchy," though quickly clarified they didn't think "he was a weird guy or anything."

There was more. If a teammate ever playfully poked Ang, he would have to poke the teammate back, or brush his hand over the spot the teammate had poked. One of the assistant coaches had also noticed that whenever he patted Ang on the shoulder during a game, Ang would wipe a hand over the spot the coach had just patted.

Did he have superstitions?

"Some of the guys in the room might say I do, but no," Ang said with a shrug. "I just try not to think about it, honestly."

"He's got so many," said DeNoble, the captain. "If he doesn't want to talk about them, I'd feel bad about giving them away. But I think he's probably one of the most superstitious guys I've ever met in my life. And he's been like that since day one."

Ang was one of the reasons so many people expected the Petes to succeed. He was a veteran now, a 19-year-old forward with an NHL future: the Florida Panthers made him a mid-round pick in 2016, taking him 94th overall—or 93 spots behind the Maple Leafs' Auston Matthews.

"He's got some quirks to him," said Bryan McCabe, the director of player personnel with the Panthers. McCabe is a retired defence-man most famous for his time with the Maple Leafs. Despite his on-ice credentials, and despite his role with the Panthers, he found it took a couple of years to build a sense of trust with Ang.

McCabe had made a handful of trips to Peterborough. He took Ang out for meals and discussed what he would have to do to succeed when he left junior hockey. His skating was a gift from the heavens, a natural skill that could never be taught. If he could add a bit of weight, the Panthers projected him as a potential middle-six player, meaning he could slide up and down the lineup as a utility forward.

"He kind of walks to his own drum, a little bit," McCabe said. "But he wants to be a player. He puts the time in. He does anything you ask of him."

For the Panthers, there was no rush. There would be time to iron out the wrinkles in the way Ang played. They could work with his body language, which sometimes telegraphed his frustration in the middle of a shift with the Petes. They could help shorten the length of his shifts, which left him exhausted at critical moments during games. Their coaches would be able to underline the importance—the necessity—of harnessing his raw talent all game, every game, in the NHL.

The Petes did not have the luxury of time. Ang was a first-line forward and part of the team's top penalty-killing unit. For them to get where they wanted to go, he was going to have to score goals, but also use his speed and veteran experience to help patch some of the leaks on the blue line.

There had always been flashes, glimmers of an NHL-ready teenager who could skate and score and be a force in the defensive zone. They were usually only flashes, though. There was a pre-season game in Buffalo where Ang seemed to be floating above the fray, drifting above the ice in some kind of out-of-body experience while the Petes played the Kitchener Rangers down below.

It was a neutral site game on a mild September afternoon at Harborcenter, Buffalo's shiny new downtown arena built as part of a hotel complex across from where the Sabres play. The stands were sprinkled with friends, family, scouts, and hockey executives when Ang suddenly went down in the offensive zone. There were 19.9 seconds left to play before first intermission.

Someone yelled down from the stands, near where some of the Petes supporters were sitting: "Hope your mom has a good dental plan."

Ang had taken a puck to the face. He left the ice but returned for the second period, and it was clear he was ornery. He took a cross-checking penalty five minutes after the faceoff. A few minutes after the penalty expired, he took his first shot of the game and scored. He was still flying in the third, setting up a goal, scoring another and taking control of a game that only mattered to whoever was making money at the concession stands.

Ang kept burning rocket fuel as the regular season began. He had a goal and two assists in a romp over Oshawa. He had another three-point game four nights after that in a rout of Niagara. Peterborough was flying, and he was at the controls. Ang had 13 points in 11 games when the team hit the road for its trip to Michigan, ranked among the hottest teams in Canada.

He was held without a single point on that trip. By the end of the first week of November, with injuries creeping deep into the roster, the Petes would have to ask even more of Ang. And for one night in particular, Wells would need him, too.

●●●

It was only the second Thursday of November, but a winter travel advisory had already been issued for Owen Sound, Ontario, a small town at the mouth of an inlet leading into Georgian Bay. Within three hours the main road home would be covered in ice, the wind whipping the snow into a blinding froth for 50 kilometres. And still Rob Wells stood, leaning against a railing inside the arena, with a coffee. Arena coffee—he'd drunk many gallons.

Dylan Wells and Jonathan Ang had been called away from the Petes to play for a team of OHL all-stars in an exhibition game with a junior team from Russia. It was part of a series, with the Russians playing teams from all three divisions in the Canadian Hockey League—the OHL, the Western Hockey League, and the Quebec Major Junior Hockey League. The game in Owen Sound was going to be carried on Sportsnet, beaming the players into more households than they'd almost ever reach at home, as regular-season junior games were typically broadcast on local-access cable.

Russia had split its first two games in the series, outscored 10–4 by the Western Hockey League. Dylan Wells was named the starter for game three. His father was overlooking the ice, the traffic from the arena's concourse moving along slowly behind him. When Dylan was in tyke, at the very beginning of his minor hockey career, he wanted his father to stand right at the glass, where he could see him. Gradually, Rob worked his way up into the stands.

It started well. Canada took a 1–0 lead on a penalty shot 36 seconds into the first period. The Canadians were carrying the play and outshooting the Russians. It was an unusual pace for Wells, who could face more than a dozen shots a period at home with the Petes, even when they were winning.

The pace was slowed even more by the television timeouts, a feature of being broadcast on a major cable network. Suddenly, with all the extra time between shots, Wells had to find ways to keep his mind occupied. It took the Russians more than seven minutes to get two shots on net. Back home in Peterborough, the Petes could surrender two shots before the game began, before the anthem singer finished the second bar of "O Canada."

On their third shot, the Russians scored. They won a faceoff in the Canadian zone, with the puck zipping back to the defenceman along the boards. With a quick look, he relayed the puck over to his partner for a shot on net. A Canadian forward made an awkward attempt to block the shot but missed. Wells had plenty of time to adjust but could not get his pad over to the far post. It was a soft goal.

He was expressionless as he watched the replay on the screen above the ice. Off to the side, along the railing, his father continued to quietly chew his gum and drink his coffee. His son looked calm. It was a personality trait, and his father figured it was a benefit for the team. If a goaltender is losing his composure, it can be jarring for teammates trying to play in front of him. Dylan looked almost serene, even though his father suspected his mind was racing.

Canada continued to dominate the play, leaving Wells alone with his thoughts. This was going to be the winter when he cemented his name as a national brand: signing an NHL contract, then taking the Petes back to prominence, with a role in the world junior championship appearing as a highlighted line on an impressive resumé.

It just felt like he needed a bounce, or a helping hand, to get back on that track.

Ang had been used sparingly at even strength. The Canadian coaches seemed intent on seeing how well he could use his speed on the penalty kill. With about four minutes to play in the first, he got another chance, sent onto the ice with the Canadians down a man.

Russia gained possession of the puck. They made four passes on their side of centre ice, looking for an opening, finally finding a small one along the boards. Ang tried to pressure but circled back to the neutral zone after that outlet pass. And then, as three

Russians broke across the blue line against two Canadian defenders, Ang stopped moving his feet. He was coasting back, watching the play in the far corner instead of communicating with the defencemen or picking up the extra forward.

He did not move his feet once—not a single stride—inside the Canadian blue line. When the pass finally came across, Artyom Manukyan was wide open at the far post. It might have been the easiest tip of his calendar year. Wells had no chance to get across in time, and was left on his own as Russia took a 2–1 lead into intermission.

Wells would allow two more goals, but the first two were the most easily preventable. One was his fault, and the other was on Ang, his teammate from Peterborough. Canada went on to lose 5–2.

"It's one of those things you wish you had back, you wish you could do a couple of things differently," Ang told a small group of reporters near the stands. "It sucked."

● ● ●

Every loss, even back in October, was met with a performative mourning that made it seem like someone in the family had died. There was a grim ritual in what coaches and players expected to see and hear from each other in defeat. Conversations were held to a minimum, especially if they were all on the bus after a loss on the road. Laughter was absolutely forbidden. Coaches adopted the look of parents who would say they were not upset but merely disappointed. Players were expected to look like they were always lost in deep thought over the consequences of their actions—or inactions, depending on the nature of their defeat.

Some losses required more post-game penance than others. On a Friday night in Oshawa, the Petes suffered one of those losses.

They were still trying to shake off whatever sense of doubt had crept into their minds during their back-to-back losses in Michigan. Doubt was not healthy; it had a habit of spreading, like a virus. Doubt could metastasize into hesitation, which could evolve into fear of making a mistake. The longer doubt lived in its host, the more drastic the cure would need to be.

The injuries on the roster were not limited to the metaphysical. Nick Robertson was still sidelined with his grotesquely damaged gums. Head coach Jody Hull had a head cold, and his voice sounded as flat as the Petes' performance on the ice in Oshawa. They lost 4–1, their third loss in four games.

The Generals seemed to have identified a weakness. They targeted defenceman Matthew Timms early, and pounded him into the boards as quickly as possible. It seemed to make him jumpy. He started to hurry his passes in the shadow of Oshawa players storming the Peterborough zone. Some of the passes were risky. Cole Fraser was not easily intimidated by anyone, but he was missing passes as well. The Petes got no help from their forwards, either, who never got a foothold in the offensive zone. The assistant coach with the most difficult job that night would be the one in charge of finding a single redeeming quality in how Peterborough had played.

Andrew Verner, the senior assistant, shrugged a little. His staff had shown the players the film they needed to see. The coaches were confident they'd told the players what they needed to hear, and prepared them for what the Generals were going to do. The staff knew what was coming. They believed there was a disconnect with the players, and it was likely somewhere between their ears.

The players held their ritual parade of silence back to the bus. They slung their equipment bags over their shoulders and stared at the bare concrete arena floor along the way to the loading bay.

Hull was least happy of all. He was one of the last to cover the 100 yards from the dressing room to the bus, and he felt most players had not put in enough effort. Worse, he felt some players had put in almost no effort at all.

His team was in a rut.

It was just after 10 p.m. when Hull took his customary seat in the first row. The door closed and the bus backed out through the bay door into the eerie quiet of downtown Oshawa. They were only 45 minutes from home, and only a few days from more trouble.

FIVE

THE PRIDE OF PETERBOROUGH

There was not much hockey where Dallas Eakins grew up, north of Tampa in Dade City, Florida. His family lived in a trailer near the Green Swamp Wilderness Preserve. His mother kept a .22 nearby for when a curious snake needed shooting.

He turned eight the season the family moved north. His step-father was a Canadian who drove a truck for a living, and they were going to resettle in Peterborough, roughly 2,000 kilometres from the reptiles and swamps of their home state. When they arrived in the fall, one of the first things Eakins noticed out the car window as they approached the new family home was how so many of the children seemed to be out in the street.

They were driving past free-flowing, unsupervised games of street hockey. Eakins had seen the game on television, but Florida was still 20 years from its first NHL expansion team. He had played baseball at home. He was aware of hockey, but he was nowhere close to conversant.

The weather began to turn weeks after his family arrived. His stepfather built a rink in the backyard, and Eakins started learning how to skate. Soon, he was registered in house league hockey. As it happened, the childhood athleticism that had served him so well on the baseball diamond helped him on the ice, and he continued to improve. More than that, he met friends and neighbours through hockey, and learned about his new home through his connection to the game.

"A lot of communities are built on church," Eakins said. "Some communities are built on a company. And I always felt, in my heart, when I really look back over my life, that Peterborough, Ontario, was built on hockey. At least, it was for me."

In Peterborough, the higher-level minor hockey teams are also known as the Petes. There are peewee Petes and bantam Petes and Petes who are even smaller than that. An 11-year-old can wear the same jersey and the same number as their favourite player on the big team. Eakins wanted to wear one of those minor hockey jerseys: "The Peterborough Petes—that was it, man."

The kid from Florida was born with many of the attributes they prized in Central Ontario. He was wiry and he played the game as hard as a coffin nail. He made the youth travel teams, an immigrant who became a name in local hockey circles. When he was old enough, the big team picked him in the sixth round of the draft. Eventually, they would make him captain.

Eakins spent four seasons in the Memorial Centre. He played a style of game that was low on goals and high on penalties. He finished his OHL career with 20 goals and 504 penalty minutes. He almost certainly punched many more faces than he did scoresheets.

In the mid-'80s, Peterborough was a junior hockey hotspot, and not an outpost. Eakins lost count of how many times he would run into a rival from another team over the summer, and they would ask him if he could put in a good word for them back in Peterborough. They played with the Oshawa Generals and the Soo Greyhounds, but they all wanted to play for the Petes. They wanted membership in the mafia.

The Petes were not merely relevant—they were a model franchise. They capped the 1970s with three straight league championships and won their national title in 1979. Even in their leanest years in the 1980s, they could still reliably be counted on to win at least one playoff round. Missing the post-season never occurred to anyone.

The Petes landed on the city's doorstep from Kitchener in 1956, and they only failed to make the playoffs three times over their first 47 seasons. At first, they were called the TPT Petes, thanks to a sponsorship agreement with the Toronto Peterborough Transport Company that might have been worth about $2,500 a year. (That would be the equivalent of about $23,000 today, which would only cover part of the team's stick budget.)

They won nine league titles. More Peterborough graduates have moved on to the NHL than any other team in the OHL. The list is so long—more than 245 and counting—that it could fill every spot on the active roster of 10 NHL teams. A third of the best hockey league in the world would have ties to Peterborough.

Their visages still monitor the Petes from the framed team photos that line the hallway outside the home team's dressing room in the Memorial Centre. The hairstyles and the equipment changed over the years. Some of the hairstyles even changed back, after a decade or two. But the one constant for so many of those teams was that they won. And for decades, they did so without anybody really knowing who even owned them.

Dave Lorentz spent three seasons as a forward with the Petes before returning to town after university and eventually joining the team's board of directors. And even then, as an executive, he was not sure who owned the team. Many people around town assumed the city owned the Petes. It made sense. As a former history major at the University of Waterloo, though, Lorentz was curious. He started digging through the archives, which were just documents scattered across old filing cabinets. He spent a summer poring over ancient contracts, records and minutes from management meetings.

The Petes were not owned by the city. They were a private, non-profit company that, technically, was owned by the members elected to the board of directors. As Dr. Bob Neville, a board member, joked at the town hall: "It costs you a dollar to join—you get your dollar back when you leave."

There are no term limits. Pat Casey, a former player, served for a record 37 years before he retired in 2016. A dozen other directors sat on the board for at least a decade, including two current members: Neville, a local family doctor, and Ken Jackman, a retired police officer.

The five directors generally meet once a month. They discuss the business matters around the team, and they also wield the final say on hirings and firings on the hockey side. If the general manager wanted to fire the head coach, for example, it would have to be cleared through the board ahead of time. When a board member resigns or retires, the team advertises the opening, then interviews the potential replacements. There is no record of any woman having served on the board.

If the team were to lose money and exhaust its reserve funds, the five directors would technically be on the hook to cover any losses. Lorentz, the principal at Adam Scott Collegiate Vocational Institute, smiled when asked what would happen in that scenario: "My wife would be divorced."

Lorentz was raised in Kitchener, two hours to the southwest, where the local junior hockey team is also steeped in tradition. Like the Petes, the Rangers are controlled not by a single wealthy owner but by an elected board of directors. They play in an older arena, in the shadows of championship banners. (The Petes have made more appearances at the Memorial Cup, but the Rangers have more titles, with two.)

Still, for Lorentz, it's different in Peterborough. Players from his era tended to settle in town after they finished playing. Peterborough is where they met their future wives, found job leads, or discovered a community and lifestyle that suited them more than their hometown's. It was difficult to explain what it meant to have played for the Petes. It was almost like marrying into a family of 80,000.

Five or six years earlier, members of his team had a reunion. Some of his old teammates were apprehensive about coming back —they were convinced no one would remember them 20 years into retirement. Not all of them made it to the NHL. Not all of them got famous after they left town. Who remembers a junior hockey player from two decades ago, anyway?

Andy MacVicar was one of the apprehensive teammates. He was coming in from Halifax for the event, not sure how long he was going to stay. MacVicar spent three seasons in Peterborough, during one of which he scored 30 goals, but his career stalled on the way up the professional ladder. He played in a few American Hockey League games, but quietly disappeared into the professional fringes.

MacVicar ended up cancelling his flight in order to stay an extra two days. "He said it was unreal," Lorentz said. "He said they were walking through the arena, and ushers came up to him and knew him by name." And so he lingered. He went to visit his ex-girlfriend. She was married now, but they still had a nice dinner, and they caught up and reminisced. He went to visit his old billet's house. Two decades after he had left for other places, Peterborough embraced MacVicar like a beloved son.

"This organization made me who I am," said Lorentz. "Even in my job now, as a principal, I have people who come in—grandkids with grandparents—and it's, 'Oh, Dave, I remember when you played.'"

The community remembers.

●●●

There was no way Chris Pronger was going to report to Peterborough, even after the Petes picked him in the sixth round of the OHL draft. He was going to follow his brother's footsteps and go to school in the United States—he had even planned out his five college visits. That was going to be his path to the NHL, without a question in his mind. The OHL was a league for barbarians. And besides, what was there to do in Peterborough, anyway?

It was hard to get information in Dryden, near the end of the road in Northwestern Ontario, about what Peterborough could offer. There was no Street View function on Google Maps—there was no Google Maps, no internet at all. In 1991, what he had was a weekly hockey digest that was delivered to the front door.

All he knew was that the Petes wanted him, and they wanted him bad enough that they offered to send a plane to fly him across the province for a visit. The pilot was a friend of Dick Todd, the Petes coach, and he did not exactly arrive in Dryden with a passenger jet.

"It was a little tiny one," Pronger said with a laugh. "I can't remember if it was a two-seater or a three-seater. It was small, though. We had to stop to gas up."

They showed him around the city. They showed him the schools, took him to his potential billet's house to meet the family. It was a lot for a 16-year-old to process: "I was pleasantly surprised."

It was a calculated courtship. The Petes knew Pronger still had another year of high school to finish before he could enroll at a school in the NCAA, which meant another year of playing in a low-level junior league. It would be another year of playing for coaches who might not be able to help him blossom into an NHL-calibre defenceman. It would be another year of skating with players who were never going to advance further in the game.

The Petes continued to play their cards with expertise. They offered Pronger a substantial education package, which would cover the full cost of his post-secondary schooling. The caveat: they would only have to pay if Pronger actually went to university.

He was 6-foot-5, and not just tough but country tough. He signed with the Petes.

He enrolled at Thomas A. Stewart Secondary School. He joined the field lacrosse team and helped it to a title. He tried to get to know his fellow students. Quickly, he felt at home in Peterborough.

"You're a superstar," he said. "Kids who are playing minor hockey, they want to be a Pete. They want to get to that level. I think with the background of the city and the history of the team, that plays into the players. The types of players that come out of Peterborough, a lot of them are well rounded, well schooled, and well versed in the game. And I think the Petes are a big reason for that."

Everybody knew who you were when you played for the Petes. "And that was good and bad, because there was no hiding," Pronger said. "Dick knew everything that was going on at all times."

Months before he arrived, the Petes had finished fifth in their division and were promptly swept in the first round of the playoffs. With Pronger in the lineup as a rookie, Peterborough finished first in the division and won a playoff round. In his second season, the Petes made it all the way to the Memorial Cup. Pronger had 40 points in 21 OHL playoff games. They would be his last in Peterborough. The Hartford Whalers took him second overall in the 1993 NHL draft, and they had him in uniform that fall.

Pronger did not forget about his teammates, though, nor a vow he had made to them before the Whalers drafted him. For all that he enjoyed about Peterborough, there were still some shortcomings, and players confronted one of those every day during the season. It was the sound system in the dressing room. It was awful, with two ancient speakers that might have been installed before any of the players were born. The only thing that seemed to drown out the distortion was the static.

When he turned pro, Pronger had promised, he would buy a new sound system. After he signed in Hartford, he sent instructions back to Peterborough, sending a team staff member out to buy a new CD player, an amp and "at least four speakers—so you've got one in every corner."

●●●

"My first-ever date was at a Petes game," said Dan O'Toole, the TSN host who grew up on a pig farm just outside town. It was in middle school, he said, in grade seven or eight. "I got to hold hands and everything," he said. "And that's where you would do it: at a Petes game."

He paused a moment, then rephrased. "You wouldn't have sex. That's where you'd hold hands. When I said 'do it,' it sounded like I meant having sex."

O'Toole found his way to the Memorial Centre even on nights when he did not have a date. A Thursday night in Peterborough was hockey night, and it was where he could go to meet up with friends, pick up a cheap snack at the concession stand, and wander the narrow concourses in a herd until game time.

He went to St. John Catholic Elementary School, on Park Street South, three blocks and one parking lot from the Memorial Centre. There were dedicated seats, but he preferred the benches up above the home team's net. It was a space that seemed set aside especially for children, opposite the giant portrait of the Queen and separate from most of the adults.

Up in what they called "the greys," it felt like recess. Children were allowed to be children. "Parents would send their kids up there," said O'Toole. "They're playing ball hockey at the top. Teens who wanted to hold hands and stuff, they'd go up there. It was a great place to just see a hockey game in the background, and be a kid and just soak it all in."

Sometimes, he would sit in the "good" seats, near the adults. He was there during one game when he heard a voice in the crowd yell "look out" as the puck left the ice during play. It was the era before protective netting above the glass.

"I felt something," O'Toole said. "Like, 'Whoa, that puck's around here somewhere.'"

Seconds later, he got another hint: a trickle of blood was snaking down his face. The puck had smashed into his head, and he was still in shock. Staff rushed him out of the stands and got him ice for his wound. When he returned to his seat, they handed him a souvenir.

"I got to keep the puck," he said. "Someone behind me took it in the knee, I think. But I took it off the head."

He paused a beat. "I took a slapshot off the head at a Petes game."

●●●

The Petes gave something else to Gabe Robinson. He was a few years behind O'Toole, and he was still learning about life in Peterborough. He had been born on Vancouver Island to parents with no ties to sports and no interest in developing any. The kids he'd met in grade four played hockey and then lacrosse in the spring. "Their names were Kevin and Paul and Joe," he said. "They weren't Gabriel and Flower Child, like my family. Everybody had a Petes jersey that they wore to school like it was normal clothing."

Robinson would eventually find his own sport. He was big and strong and fast and smart, and he went to the University of Toronto, where he played football. In 2003, he signed with the Toronto Argonauts, and in 2004, he won the Grey Cup. Back in grade four, though, he was still only learning about sports.

The Petes ran a program in the local schools. Students who volunteered to be crossing guards—who got to wear the little orange safety sashes—were rewarded after five weeks on the job with a voucher for a ticket to watch the Petes at the Memorial Centre. Robinson's parents would drop him off at the arena. He went to the games by himself.

He started playing soccer with other children in the playground, but watching the Petes, and watching how the fans interacted with the team and with each other, was his real introduction to the sport that mattered most around town. It was inside the arena, for example, that he got to see the grown man who carried a donkey-headed stuffed animal with him, bellowing "hee-haw" whenever the referee made a questionable call.

Robinson grew up with granola bars and basmati rice as prominent pillars of his diet, but for two dollars at the arena, he could sample exotic fare such as hot dogs and chocolate bars. The rink was where he learned what seemed to bond the town together. It was a tutorial for life in Peterborough.

●●●

It has been a long time since Dallas Eakins visited home. The Washington Capitals took him in the 10th round of the 1985 NHL draft, launching a career that would be spent on the fringes. He played in Baltimore and Moncton, in Cincinnati and New Haven, Connecticut. Using what he learned in Peterborough, he fought and scratched his way into the NHL, appearing in 120 regular-season games with eight different teams. Later, he would become a coach, working with the Toronto Maple Leafs and the Edmonton Oilers. His most recent job has taken him to Southern California, where he is head coach of the San Diego Gulls, the AHL affiliate of the Anaheim Ducks.

His mother died in 1995, and while he has some cousins and friends around the city, Eakins admitted he was not up to date with the latest news around Peterborough.

"Is it the same now? I hear maybe things aren't as great as they used to be when it comes to attendance and the following, and the Petes' effect and influence on the city," said Eakins. "But that could be all bullshit, too. I'm just hearing it."

SIX

EMBRACING AN ECHO

In 1979, the year the Petes won their first—and only—Memorial Cup championship, a rising literary figure in Quebec was living in the first house he ever owned. He had his first child, and his first car was parked outside. All Roch Carrier needed was for his income to keep pace with his ascendant profile, because it felt like he was still at a point in his life where he was ready to do "anything that would bring money."

His first novella, *La guerre, yes sir!*, had drawn praise when published a decade earlier. It explored difficult themes reflected in contemporary Quebec, in particular the frayed relationship between the English and French, and it established him as a cultural commentator on both sides of that divide. When the CBC Radio station in Toronto called him about writing an essay, he accepted eagerly. All he was asked to do was address a single question: What does Quebec want?

Carrier started writing, but the words that landed before him were not the ones he wanted. The text felt dull and unnecessarily heavy. Worse, it felt worn, like the ashes of something that had already burned through in the pages of the local French-language papers. He wrestled with the typewriter, but the typewriter kept winning. Nothing seemed to work, and his deadline was looming.

He called the station to apologize. It was late in the week, Thursday or Friday, and he was conceding defeat. He could not answer their question, at least not with the tone or the flair he thought it deserved. The person at the other end of the call was unmoved. They had time set aside for Carrier on the Monday morning show. "So," they told him, "write whatever you want."

Suddenly, like a photographer's flash, an idea struck. Carrier wrote quickly and he wrote longhand. It was the story of a young boy in a small Quebec town. The boy loved Maurice "Rocket" Richard, like all the other local boys. And he loved the Montreal Canadiens. Hockey was the heartbeat of all childhood activity.

One day, the boy's mother decided his beloved Canadiens sweater was too tattered to continue wearing in public. She wrote to a national department store chain in her finest cursive, requesting a replacement. When that replacement arrived, it sent the young boy into a spiral of existential despair. It was not a Canadiens sweater but a Toronto Maple Leafs sweater.

The story was about more than a sweater, and about more than just a game. Carrier historically has downplayed the political symbols sprinkled through his story, but it nonetheless highlighted tensions in the power dynamic between French and English Canada, when so much influence seemed to rest in the streets of Toronto.

He was invited to read the story in towns across Canada. Once, in Ottawa, a bookstore manager assigned a security guard to watch over Carrier in case the bustling crowd got a little too bustling. During that stop, a tall man approached with an old copy of the book. He requested an autograph, and as Carrier was signing, the man produced a new copy of the book. Again, he asked for an autograph. The old copy was for him, and the new copy was for his son. At some stops, expectant parents would ask Carrier to autograph the book for children who had not yet arrived. He would smile warmly and nod and sign: "I don't know your name, but all the best."

There was another reading in a library somewhere in Western Canada. Carrier remembered seeing an imposing figure listening carefully from the back of the room. By now he had grown accustomed to hearing the personal connections readers made with his story, but he never tired of them. Something about the man in the back of the room that day kept his attention, though—he did not look like the typical library patron, at least not to Carrier's now experienced eyes. But the author could tell the man wanted to join the conversation. It was also clear that he felt too out of place to jump in by himself.

So Carrier opened the door. He motioned for the burly, hardened man to speak. The man declined at first, but then he opened up.

"You know, it's difficult for men to talk," the man told him. "Women talk a lot, but it's difficult for men to talk. And if you have a son, it's tough to talk to your son."

The man had an eight-year-old son at home. When neither of them could find the words they wanted to say, or find common ground on which to meet, Carrier's story became a bridge. There was a connection somewhere in the lingua franca of hockey, or winter, or the sum of both, in the shared experience of being Canadian. Sometimes, the man said, he would tell his son, "Bring the book."

"He brings the book, and we look at the pages," the man told Carrier. "Sometimes, the boy tells me: 'Dad, I bring you the book?' And I say, 'Yes.'"

Carrier's work became a beloved cultural touchstone. Teachers built "The Hockey Sweater" into their curricula. The book that the story became would go on to sell more than 300,000 copies in Canada, where the National Film Board also commissioned an animated short film, with both French and English versions. For more than a decade, a scene inspired by the story even appeared on the back of the five-dollar bill.

In the final frames of the film, the young boy is shown praying in the quiet of a small-town church. He requests delivery of 100 million moths to eat his Maple Leafs jersey. And as the organ music swells, an apparition appears over his shoulder to shake his hand: it is Rocket Richard.

Carrier was once visiting a school in the United Arab Emirates when the film was screened for students. He fielded questions afterward. One stood out, from a child who asked, "Sir, at the end of the film, the man in the cloud, is it your god?"

He paused and thought about it for a moment, then smiled: "Yes.'"

●●●

Hockey had been good for Nelson Riis, in the way anything can be good for a Member of Parliament seeking national attention. He had been a teacher once, with a background in geography, but it was hockey that earned him mention in the *Washington Post*, the *New York Times*, and the major wire services during a normally quiet period of the Canadian summer in 1988.

On August 9, the Edmonton Oilers traded Wayne Gretzky to the Los Angeles Kings. The transaction also included four other players and $15-million (U.S.) in cash, but it was that one name that seemed to grind a vacationing country to a halt. Trading Gretzky to a team in the U.S. seemed preposterous, as impossible as trading the Canadian Shield. He was part of Canada, and part of Canadian hockey.

Riis, a member of the third-place New Democratic Party representing Kamloops, B.C., quickly issued a media release: "The Edmonton Oilers without Wayne Gretzky is like apple pie without ice cream, like winter without snow, like the *Wheel of Fortune* without Vanna White—it's quite simply unthinkable."

He had a plan: "I figure the federal government could purchase Gretzky's contract and then resell him to a Canadian team. The bottom line is that we have to keep Wayne in Canada where Canadians can see their greatest hockey player ever on a regular basis."

In the end, no government intervention could stop the Oilers from exporting Gretzky. But a few years later, as a sovereigntist movement swelled in Quebec, Riis found another way to convert hockey into headlines. It would become more than a simple publicity stunt. Some argued it was a means of helping save Canada.

By April 1994, Canada was teetering on the edge of a crisis. The Bloc Québécois had earned 54 seats in the federal election six months earlier, meaning a party dedicated to redrawing the country's borders stood as the official opposition in Parliament. Riis introduced a private member's bill, which is not a document that typically makes the news across Canada. This one did: it sought to formally declare hockey as Canada's national game.

"I was concerned," he said years later, "like everybody else at that time, and part of the motivation was to say, 'There are all kinds of commonalities here, and we should just remind ourselves.'"

Facing a real threat, Canadian politicians turned to hockey for help. It was—and is—unusual for a private member's bill to advance through the House of Commons. That spring, with the NHL playoffs getting underway, Bill C-212 became a popular document.

It was getting late on a Wednesday afternoon when Riis rose to speak in the House. Almost everyone in the room, he said, could skate before they could tie their own laces. Everyone remembered the moment they first learned to raise the puck, watching its flight and listening as it slammed against the boards.

"It is safe to say that hockey matters to all of us, in Quebec and the rest of Canada," he said. "It is part of our culture. It is key to the understanding of Canada. It is the perfect game on the perfect Canadian medium in the perfect Canadian season.

"We are a northern people and hockey is a northern sport. It is certainly fair to say it is much more than a game in our country."

Dennis Mills, the Liberal MP from Toronto, rose. Hockey, he said, "pulls us together, not only as a House of Commons, but as a country."

Antoine Dubé, a member of the Bloc, supported the bill as well, but was careful to add: "Nothing prevents two countries from sharing the same national sport."

Following an amendment to also recognize lacrosse as an official sport, the bill passed. It only took about 90 minutes. Bob Kilger, the deputy speaker, happened to be a former NHL referee. "I remember going up and talking to him a number of times," said Riis. "There were some people who were against it, for odd reasons." A number of his opponents were trying to get to their feet to say something. By what he could only assume was coincidence, Kilger, the deputy speaker and former referee, "just didn't quite see them."

●●●

Roch Carrier grew up in Sainte-Justine, Quebec, about 90 minutes outside Quebec City. He had six siblings, and while not all
of them played hockey, they would all gather around the radio
every frozen Saturday night to listen to the Canadiens. Carrier
was five when Maurice Richard cracked the Montreal roster as a
rookie in 1942.

A hockey stick then cost 69 cents. Carrier served as an altar boy,
reporting for duty at 6:30 a.m. to help the priest prepare for mass.
He received 10 cents for his efforts, which would have allowed
him to buy a new stick every seven masses. The children used catalogues for pads—the nice, thick ones from the Eaton's mailing list,
or the thinner ones from a regional chain. They would all walk
home from school, snatch the pair of skates that was waiting for
them, and head down to the rink.

"It's a common experience," Carrier said. "A common experience of the climate. A common experience of growing up. A common experience of having friends, and having enemies, and how
to deal with enemies. And how to grow. How to challenge yourself, how to do something that is very difficult to do. Because
playing hockey, it's trying to improve yourself."

There was symbolism even in the ice itself, outdoors and exposed
to the elements. No ice machine was idling beyond the boards,
waiting to clear the surface before shinny. Players had to earn their
ice, had to clear it off themselves. Sometimes, the parish priest
would join them, pulling up his cassock and grabbing a shovel to
move the snow. Playing hockey was more than just a way to connect with friends and classmates: it was divine privilege.

When the Second World War ended, a handful of veterans
returned to Sainte-Justine without a place to land. They had no jobs
at first, and no clear entry point through which to rejoin society.

They found a home at the hockey rink, when Carrier and his friends were in grade four or five.

"Big guys, strong," Carrier said. "They were playing with us. But I think they were educating us, at the same time." There were lessons the younger ones would carry with them: how to be tactical, to consider problems from a variety of angles, to collaborate with teammates with a common goal in mind.

One of the veterans reminded him of Dick Tracy, the tough-minded police detective who rose to fame as a newspaper comic-strip hero during the Great Depression. Carrier saw a resemblance somewhere in the chin, strong and square, like a safe.

Carrier took a hard shot off his leg during a game one day. He was wearing pads, but they were thin. It hurt. He wanted to cry. He needed to cry. But he could not cry, because Dick Tracy was standing there, and there was no way he was going to cry in front of Dick Tracy.

Lessons, for better or for worse.

●●●

Nelson Riis grew up in Longview, Alberta, an hour south of Calgary. His father worked in the oil business, building the old wooden derricks, having immigrated to Canada with his wife from Norway. As the son of immigrants, Riis found an easy way to connect with children of families who had deeper roots in the area.

"Every boy played hockey," he said. "It wasn't as though it was a choice, or you even thought about it." Hockey was just part of living in that part of Southern Alberta, in the foothills, in a town with 500 or so residents. Riis does not remember exactly how old he was when he started playing, cannot recall how he got his first pair of skates or who introduced him to the customs of life at the rink. All he knows is that he was very young, and very much in love with hockey. "As soon as you could kind of walk around, or waddle around, you had skates on."

Their sticks were wooden, with straight blades. They tied their skates inside a wooden shack with a 45-gallon drum stove. It would be red hot by the time the sun set and the temperature plummeted outside, and the tiny players would huddle inside to get warm. The magazines they stuffed down the fronts of their jeans for protection served a dual purpose: they used the pages as toilet paper in the outhouse near the rink. They would play all winter, and they would play for as long as they could.

On Saturday night, they would listen to other people play hockey. They huddled around the radio to listen to *Hockey Night in Canada*. And once television arrived, they would migrate to whichever house had a set, and they would cluster around the fuzzy black-and-white images beamed from Maple Leaf Gardens in Toronto.

Some weekends, there might be six people around the television. On other weekends, the number might be double. There was never much thought of doing anything else, Riis said: "It was just part of what you did when you were growing up."

● ● ●

It was a mild July afternoon, with the remnants of a summer downpour still flowing down the street in front of his Montreal home. Carrier sat in a comfortable brown chair in the front room, talking about hockey. He was no longer talking about the idyllic version from his childhood. He was talking about the modern game.

"I see a lot of kids going to play," he said. "At any time of the day, you see buses coming, kids get down from the bus, waiting for the luggage."

He called it "luggage" because he could not believe the size of the hockey bags the children carried to the rink every day: "I was leaving for a boarding school for a year, I didn't have as much stuff as they have to play a game.

"I see them with the mother," he said. "The kid looks mad, and the mother is mad because the kid is not nice this morning. I don't see many kids carrying their own stuff. They go to a job that's dull. And there is the competition between the parents. It's not beautiful."

Carrier's home was not all that far from the grave of the Montreal Forum. The rink had been gone for almost 20 years, replaced with a mall that was largely empty except for spectral reminders of its former tenants. The Canadiens logo was painted and brightly lit in the centre of the main promenade, with a sliver of a grandstand off to one side. A statue of Rocket Richard sat next to the arena seating, surveying a row of movie theatre kiosks across the floor. Two decades-old arcade games were also in the statue's line of sight, with Ms. Pac-Man (released in 1981) and California Speed (1998) awaiting the attention of anyone looking to fill some of the time between downpours outside. Nobody approached either machine.

A shop dedicated to Canadiens memorabilia was one of the few with its lights on. The stencilling on the window offered to buy, sell, or trade. Replica Stanley Cup banners hung from the ceiling, with jerseys of retired stars such as Bert Olmstead and Larry Robinson on the wall. A black-and-white photograph of Richard glared back out to the concourse. There were no customers inside.

Carrier never got to watch Richard play in person, though the two did meet several times before the star winger died in 2000.

"The heroes are not the same," Carrier said, then paused with self-awareness. "I'm this old guy complaining now."

He had an admission to make: he barely watched hockey anymore, rarely bothered to even check the scores in the newspaper.

Grassroots hockey had gotten too expensive, too exclusive. The NHL players were no longer like the Maurice Richards of his day. Now they were millionaires, and multi-millionaires, who drove fancy cars and moved in social circles alongside the city elites. They were not the everyday working heroes of his youth.

"Those players and the organization belong to a new caste," he said. "That's OK. Let them enjoy their millions. But I'm thinking of the people. It's difficult to connect. And it might explain why, in places like my village now, soccer is very popular."

Riis, the politician who made hockey Canada's official winter sport, said his two granddaughters were also deeply in love with soccer. They had been to watch the Ottawa Senators, but they had no real ties to the game. He was not sure either of them had ever held a hockey stick.

Riis reclined in his seat on the patio of a roadhouse in the Glebe, the Ottawa neighbourhood where the OHL's Ottawa 67's make their home. It was sunny and mild with a light breeze as he considered the fate of the game over a couple of beers. "For some people, hockey remains an important part of their life," he said. "But certainly, it's diminishing in significance."

Like Carrier, he pointed to the cost. There is equipment to buy, registration fees to pay. And that's just to get in the door. Children cannot find their way into hockey by stuffing department store catalogues down the front of their jeans.

"There wasn't much of a class feeling," Riis said. "Most people were working-class people. And most people had the same kind of income. Most people's mothers stayed at home. Most guys had a half-decent job and made a half-decent living."

"There was always sort of a managerial group in the community, but it was very small. We were all poor, if the truth were to be known. But nobody knew it, because everybody was poor. Nobody could afford real equipment, so it was never really an issue."

He wondered about the physical nature of the game itself, how the blood-and-guts image that is so often celebrated—the toothless Stanley Cup photographs—might look through the eyes of a parent who is new to Canada. Children grow only so many sets of teeth, after all.

"I think the violence in the game, which hockey players generally support, just doesn't fit in with the Canadian modern-day world," said Riis. "It must be a complete shock to people who see it for the first time."

There was an example from Alberta, where he grew up. "It's a bit like watching the Calgary Stampede," he said. "If you haven't been brought up in that mode, I think it looks like a pretty peculiar experience for most people—I would think certainly for most newcomers, if not for most Canadians today."

Hockey is not there yet, he said, "but it would hold a certain strangeness to people."

Riis, 76, is five years younger than Carrier. They grew up in small towns separated by three provinces and more than 3,900 kilometres. One family had established roots in Canada, and one family was new to the country. And yet for all their differences—English and French, Albertan and Québécois—one experiential thread was woven through both childhoods.

They played on outdoor rinks for as long as it was cold outside. They had makeshift equipment. They found through hockey a connection to their peers and neighbours. And they would both help to define what the game meant to generations of Canadians —one through literature, one through legislation.

And both have noticed a shift in how Canadians relate to the game that shaped not only their childhood memories but also their professional legacies. Riis believes Bill C-212 would pass if forwarded to the house today—no Canadian politician is going to vote against hockey—but he wonders how much it would resonate.

"I think the legacy still continues to this day," he said, "but probably diminishing each year."

SEVEN

A FRAYED TETHER

In the first week of December 2017, James Bradburn decided he was due for a haircut. It was hockey season in Peterborough, and the Petes were wrestling with the broad existential questions that usually arise when a team suddenly seems to be not very good at the sport it plays. There would be plenty for Bradburn and his barber to discuss.

They got onto sports soon after he walked in the door, but not the sport he was expecting. His barber had Italian heritage, and the family had season tickets for Toronto FC, the 10-year-old Major League Soccer franchise. The games were held 140 kilometres from the barbershop chair, a 90-minute drive even under perfect conditions; she'd be making the trip in a few days to see Toronto FC host Seattle for the league championship. In the middle of hockey season, in the middle of a Canadian hockey town, hockey suddenly felt less than essential.

Bradburn, the pleasant, bespectacled married father of three, was volunteer president of the Peterborough Hockey Association.

The association formed the bedrock of local minor hockey, administering programs for the house league and travel teams across the city. He had won his position not thanks to his vision for the future, though, nor over pressing concerns about the present. It was not an election at all: Bradburn was the only board member who eventually raised his hand for the job.

Minor hockey needed the help. Registration was eroding. Two years earlier, 1,349 youth players were registered to play in both the house league and rep programs. That number dropped the following year, to 1,241 players.

It was down again this year, to 1,146 players. The association was losing about 100 players a year. He could only imagine the numbers plummeting even further over the next 10 to 15 years.

He was in a booth by the window at a Tim Hortons on Lansdowne Street, near the edge of the known world. A few blocks to the west, past the last Shoppers Drug Mart and the Beer Store, the city ran out of blocks. It was where Peterborough conceded to the open road and the farmers' fields; to the kind of landscape that conjured snow-globe dreams of winter days spent on hidden frozen ponds.

The reality of modern minor hockey was less romantic. It was expensive to play, and that cost was not just in cash, but in the time parents had to invest in driving to practices, games, and tournaments in and out of town. Retention rates were weak, and it was hard to convince newcomers to fill some of the empty spaces. Children had more options; they did not have to fill their winter schedules with hockey to connect with friends and neighbours.

Bradburn grew up playing hockey, with his father taking him to the Memorial Centre for early-morning practices on Sundays, and then sometimes returning to watch the Petes host their matinee game. As he drove those same streets now, he was more likely to see a basketball hoop at the end of a driveway than a hockey net. There was a thriving cricket scene in town, too—Sir Sandford Fleming College was preparing to host an indoor tournament for the first time that March.

Bradburn's kids were Raptors fans—they liked the action of the sport. Registration for the local basketball house league was still relatively small compared to hockey, but it was growing. The last Bradburn had read, enrollment was now above 400. It did not seem like long ago, he noted, when only 200 children were registered to play basketball.

He suggested money played a role. Signing up for house league hockey could cost around $500, and that did not factor in the equipment, which could end up doubling the price. Joining the basketball league, on the other hand, would work out to less than $300—and they gave you a ball. The math made sense to him: if you're a new family coming to Canada and you don't have the funds, you're looking at basketball, soccer, and other low-cost sports.

Some of the hockey association's biggest losses were in the older age groups. Players at the bantam and midget age groups—starting at age 14—were leaving the game altogether. It was not just an issue at the house league and rep level, either: local high school hockey was also shrinking, down to 10 teams from 14 a season earlier.

Children at that age have homework. They have part-time jobs. They have girlfriends and boyfriends. It is also the age when it becomes painfully clear who still has a chance to move on, and who has climbed as high as they can up hockey's ladder. Without the hope of reward, the risk of being hurt playing with full contact becomes more unattractive.

Teenagers in the lower levels of rep hockey still play with body-checking, which is, in Bradburn's eyes, a significant part of what eventually chases them away from the game. And as a parent, do you want your son or daughter risking a concussion or a broken collarbone and being out of commission for six weeks?

●●●

When the two Canadian hockey missionaries stopped in Peterborough, they chose to spread the gospel of the game in a school only 950 metres from the Memorial Centre. Scott Carlow and Ryan Hurley were visiting a class at St. John Catholic Elementary School, and they asked the same question they asked of all the classes they visited: By a show of hands, who was playing on a hockey team this season?

The children were eight and nine years old, and if they walked a block north on Park Street, they could see Jody Hull's massive Hummer parked against the arena wall. If they walked a little farther north and turned left onto Lansdowne Street, continuing past the Home Depot, the Imperial Tandoor and a Tim Hortons, they would reach the Evinrude Centre, a more modern facility with two sheets of ice. Hockey was all around them.

Not a single child raised their hand.

"That school was the first where we had a class that had no one," said Carlow, bearing both a hockey player's build and accent. "And that's where it kind of shocked me."

It would not be the last. Carlow and Hurley were travelling across Ontario as part of Try Hockey, a program under the Hockey Canada umbrella. Funding came from the proceeds of the 2015 world junior hockey championship in Toronto and Montreal, and the idea was born from a creeping realization: Canadian hockey was showing signs of losing market share at the grassroots level.

Carlow and Hurley were travelling the province on a mission to convert the curious, the indifferent, and the lapsed hockey children. They had a trailer full of hockey equipment they hauled behind a big black pickup truck. After coordinating their visit with each school, they invited the children to the auditorium for an assembly and a chance to play floorball. If they liked the presentation, the children were invited for another session at a local arena, where they could try the real thing with the equipment stored inside the trailer.

Just before Christmas, they were sitting in the concourse of a busy downtown Toronto office building, killing time before a meeting at the National Hockey League offices. They needed funding to expand the program, because they knew that two men and a pickup truck were not enough to reverse a national trend. Their program needed more helping hands, more equipment, and more visibility.

Try Hockey launched in 2016, and they visited 22 schools across Ontario that year. They saw another 22 schools the following year, interacting with more than 3,000 children. The plan the coming year was to get into 12 schools in three different communities. All of the children received a Hockey Canada jersey to keep, and they used one of the 65 pairs of skates Carlow and Hurley towed in their 16-foot trailer.

Their superiors had committed to running the program through 2020. The two men wanted not only to extend it but to expand the initiative across Canada.

A few months earlier, they had been standing at the front of a small conference room in the basement of a suburban Toronto hotel. They were pitching their services to minor hockey executives from across the province, having been invited to speak during the Ontario Minor Hockey Association's annual meeting. They laid out their most frightening numbers.

"Nine out of 10 kids—aged 4 to 19—don't play hockey," Hurley told the room. "One in 10 play hockey. When we heard this stat, it was astonishing to us."

That was across Canada.

"When I heard that, I questioned it, but I let it sink in," he continued. "And in my opinion, it's kind of a scary stat."

Carlow picked up where his partner left off, saying that one in five Canadians was foreign-born. And in some jurisdictions, such as Brampton, Ontario, that number could be much higher. Immigration helped grow Canada's population, which made stagnating hockey registration statistics more concerning: they were not keeping pace with the country's rate of growth.

"One study showed that hockey is the fourth-most-played sport among our youth," Hurley said right after that. "And on the female side of the game, hockey didn't show up in the top 10."

Petes general manager Mike Oke was sitting in the audience during the meeting. He rose to speak near the end, urging the minor hockey executives in the room to call Carlow and Hurley that summer and arrange a visit to their towns. If the phone was not ringing off the hook by the end of the weekend, he said, something was wrong.

The phone did not ring off the hook. It rang twice, once from Newmarket, and once from Bradford, a smaller town 16 minutes away.

"I think there still is a hesitance," said Carlow. "And I think we have to remember that all of these minor hockey associations are volunteer-run, and their time is stretched as is. They might feel bringing in another program like this, while it might help, is another constraint on their time."

Their help seemed urgently necessary. To that point in December 2017, only 6 per cent of the children that Carlow and Hurley had met played hockey. Their visits were concentrated in lower-income regions of the province, but not exclusively. One visit to Brampton, where income is not generally an issue, they had 103 children on the ice—and 90 of them were wearing skates for the first time in their lives.

Out of every 100 children they met, though, only six played hockey. Many more raised their hands for ball hockey (about 36 per cent), but the more familiar version was entirely foreign to the majority. And only about half (54.5 per cent) said they watched hockey.

They spent two days in Kitchener, about an hour west of Toronto. On the first day, they had 112 students come through, and only one played hockey. On day two, 161 children passed through, and not a single one played on a hockey team.

"A lot of people don't know hockey as a [children's] sport," said Hurley. "They turn on *SportsCentre* and see the big hit, a fight and a nice goal, and they go, 'OK, I don't want my kid to get in a fight. I don't want my kid to get hurt. So I'm not going to put them in hockey.'"

"Oh, we find kids all the time," said Carlow. "We were in a school not too long ago, and a kid came up to me at the end of the day, when we invited him to our on-ice session: 'Oh, I can't go to your on-ice—it's too dangerous.'"

"Being a kid today is different than it was back then," said Hurley. "I mean, even when I was a kid, you come home from school, and as long as I came home when the streetlights were on, that was fine. But now, kids don't have that same freedom, they don't have that same flexibility to come home from school and go climb a tree and fall and hurt themselves, and realize it's not that bad.

"Parents are protective—which is great—but at the same time, it takes away some of that freedom of kids learning how to be kids and get their basic, fundamental movements in, like climbing and throwing."

Carlow pointed out that some communities have banned street hockey.

"Playing hockey in the street is inherently dangerous, by putting two nets out in the middle of the street," he said. "But even us, as kids, we didn't have a problem—when a car came, everyone yelled, and you moved the nets and shuffled them off."

Carlow grew up outside Peterborough, and Hurley was raised in Markham, just north of Toronto. Both played hockey.

"I think a lot of us who did grow up and play hockey, we kind of take it for granted," said Hurley. "Now it's not the norm."

●●●

Glenn McIntyre had a story that made seasoned hockey administrators gasp. He was general manager of Brampton Hockey, the governing body of minor hockey in the suburb northwest of Toronto. It used to be a sleepy bedroom community, but its population had nearly doubled over two decades, with more than 590,000 residents now calling it home. That number was forecast to grow to 750,000 within another decade.

McIntyre rose to speak in the small conference room where Carlow and Hurley had just finished their presentation at the Ontario Minor Hockey Association's annual meeting. Two decades ago, McIntyre told the room, there were about 4,200 registered players in Brampton. Now, despite the population explosion, it was down to about 2,000.

Several of the volunteer executives in the room drew a sharp breath.

"Every year," McIntyre said, "we've seen a decline of about 100."

Brampton's minor hockey association had four full-time employees and about 130 teams that played out of 12 ice pads across the city. Players entered the system as young as four, and they could continue playing to their juvenile season, as 20-year-olds. Girls had a separate league, but many still played in McIntyre's association.

He suggested part of the decline was due to "misconceptions" over the price of hockey. It cost $520 to register, and for that a child would receive 24 weeks' worth of practices and games. With two hours on the ice every week, it worked out to about $11 an hour, which seemed like a pretty competitive price.

"Getting that word out, and doing all that, is a tough thing," he said.

Cost is not always the largest barrier to entry, though, especially in Brampton, which swims in an ocean of detached suburban homes that start at $500,000 and reach as high as the imagination pleases. Having no fluency with the game is another invisible barrier: What equipment is required to play? And how does it work? Do the shin pads go on before the pants?

The minor hockey infrastructure had not kept pace with the change in the city. Immigration had been a driving force behind Brampton's population growth, with more than a third of residents coming from South Asian families.

McIntyre's father was the son of Scottish immigrants, but he still found his way into a pair of hockey skates at a relatively young age. That tether new Canadians once had to the game had frayed in Brampton, and McIntyre suspected it was because the minor hockey association had not nurtured its ties to those communities. (Many of those families had now been in Canada for generations, he said, and they had still not found their way into hockey—and minor hockey executives had still not found a way to sell the game to them.)

"We've seen the same people in the same meetings, every single night—the same people making the decisions," he said. "And the only reason why they're making those decisions is because we can't get others in the room."

There might have been 600 people in the room during the main reception at the OMHA meeting that spring, he said, and he had seen many of those same faces year after year. They needed new blood on their board, but they were having trouble generating interest.

In Brampton, the minor hockey association had a nine-person executive board. A few years earlier, there had been a realization: not one of the board members had a child left playing minor hockey —they had all aged out of the system. And this was the cohort still making all the decisions for the league. They wanted to embrace the new and growing communities, to invite them into the arena. They were struggling to find an entry point where they could make their case and break down some of the barriers—be they concerns about cost or safety or anything else—that had grown like a wall around the game. That wall had not seemed as high when his own father learned the game as a first-generation Canadian.

"I don't really know what's changed," he said. "The ball hockey league in Brampton has grown. The ball hockey league is separate from the minor hockey association. We have a lot of similar members. But then they have a whole pile of members that we haven't even trapped yet. They love to play hockey. The South Asian community loves that game." He said he had also noticed an uptick in road hockey around town. "It's the skating part that's slowing them down," he said. "Most of their parents have never been on skates."

●●●

In 2008, Eamonn Nolan transferred from the uptown Toronto arts school where he had been teaching for the better part of a decade. He said he based his decision on what he described as "an early midlife crisis."

Nolan requested a placement at Sir Sandford Fleming Academy, in a lower-income area of the city touched by gun violence. He taught drama.

"It was a Toronto I'd never seen," he said.

The school ranked high on the Toronto District School Board's so-called Learning Opportunities Index, which attempts to take stock of things that might work against student success in the classroom. Some of the forces included in the evaluation were the median income of residents, the percentage of parents without a high school diploma, and the number of students living in a single-parent household.

"I taught a kid from Afghanistan who had witnessed his uncle beheaded in his home," said Nolan. "The Taliban crashed into their house looking for the father, who was long missing. And this kid saw his uncle executed, and watched his aunt scream her lungs out." The student was a sweet kid. "They dealt with all kinds of abuses and horrors that come with poverty," he said. "And you can't deny that. It's real. If you're poor, you're dealing with shit that you and I don't deal with."

Nolan was born in New York City, but his parents were from Limerick, a town with its own reputation for violence. (A "tough, tough city," Nolan said, a bit wide-eyed. He remembered visiting his grandparents when he was a child, and homeowners still got their heating coal off a cart pulled by a donkey.) He was four when they moved to Canada. The family did not have a lot of money. For the longest time they did not even have cable television.

But Nolan always had hockey. They played ball hockey until it was time to play soccer. His friends were immigrants, too: kids from Turkey, from Nigeria, and Nolan said their common bond—other than all being "fresh off the boat"—was the game.

"Hockey was my thing," he said. "It was my access to my new friends in Canada."

He brought it up one day early in his first year at Sir Sanford Fleming. "When I opened up the discussion about hockey, they were like, 'Well, hockey's not for us,'" Nolan said. "That really rubbed me the wrong way. Not just as a hockey-lover, but as a dude. It was like, 'Come on, man, there's enough barriers here—if you want to play hockey, let's go.'"

Baycrest Arena was right next to the school, close enough that it was almost as easy for him to park in the arena parking lot as it was to park in the faculty lot. To the students in his class, though, it might as well have been on the other side of town. It was completely inaccessible. And the realization bothered him.

Nolan called the arena management and found out he was eligible for an educator's rate. An hour of ice was available for as low as $70, which meant it was practically free by Toronto standards. He brought it to the school principal: open an hour of ice time to the students, between 3 and 4 p.m., once a week.

The principal consented immediately, but that was the easy part. Nolan, a married father of two, had to find equipment for students who had never set foot on the ice. He scavenged the lost-and-founds in arenas around the city. He pestered friends and teammates from his beer league teams. He accepted any piece of gear he could find. No elbow pad was too worn, no glove too smelly.

The program was free, and it was open to the whole school. When he started, Nolan had 18 regulars.

"The kid who witnessed that horrific thing in Kandahar played with no gloves," he said. "Like, ice hockey with no gloves. Bare hands. It was fucking wild."

Not all of the children were new to Canada, but they were all new to the game. Nolan hustled to keep it going. He had never had the most expensive equipment when his family was new to Canada, but he always had enough to play. He spent the following summer driving around for more gear for his students. They would need to upgrade. Eventually, having children playing hockey with bare hands and skateboard helmets was going to result in an injury.

The hunting had become difficult. Nolan had pestered all of his friends, and he had emptied all of the lost-and-found bins. Someone told him the NHL Players' Association operated a charitable outreach program that provided equipment for those in need. He checked the website, and the fine print warned the process would take three months. He did not have three months. He scoured the website for more contact information, and he called them out of the blue. When a voice answered at the other end, he laid out his case: the principal was paying for the ice, but the kids were playing in skates from the 1970s.

His request was approved before the call had ended. The NHLPA's Goals & Dreams program pledged to send 25 brand-new sets of equipment to the school. The children would also be invited downtown to visit the Hockey Hall of Fame.

Nolan has photographs of the day the equipment arrived: a mountain of cardboard boxes by the wall, towering over a vast field of discarded plastic wrap and hockey bags that had been opened for the very first time. Children were trying it on right there in the room, wearing real shoulder pads and real helmets with facemasks.

"It was almost like building a time machine, saying: 'Here's what hockey was like 30 or 40 years ago, and it can be like this for you, too,'" he said.

Nolan later moved to another inner-city school on the other side of town, where he launched a twin program, with another 25 sets of equipment from the NHLPA. It led to a friendly game between the two schools, featuring guest appearances from then–Toronto Maple Leafs players Luke Schenn and Tim Brent. Nolan has a picture of a smiling Steven Stamkos in the dressing room from that day as well.

The students were smiling, too, with their new skates and crisp white hockey socks. It turned out that hockey was indeed for them, but only with the direct intervention of a teacher set on breaking down the economic barriers with his own hands.

"We have the hockey model backward," said Nolan. "From the earliest age, kids are told, 'You gotta train hard.' Parents are involved, all of the sudden. They're fucking breathing on the glass. They're pounding on the glass, and they're shouting over the glass. My parents? I don't think they ever saw me play hockey. They were working."

He paused and smiled. "Or drinking."

●●●

A button on the TCU Place website advertised tickets for the Hockey Canada Foundation gala, an event that promised to turn downtown Saskatoon into an early summer hockey carnival. Mike Babcock, the prodigal son and coach of the Maple Leafs, was an honorary co-chair for the event, a fundraiser to help strengthen "the bond between Canadians and hockey."

They would be taking over the local convention centre one night, then move off to a local golf course for a round the following day. The button for tickets redirected the user to Hockey Canada's website, but no tickets could be found. It turned out there was a reason: there were never any tickets to sell.

It cost big money to celebrate hockey in Canada for one night, bond or no bond. The gala was not open to the media and it was not open to individual ticket sales. It cost $5,000 to buy a table, which was the lowest point of entry advertised on Hockey Canada's website. For $5,000, you would receive a mention in the gala program, as well as space for 10 guests. You would not be invited to play golf the following day, and you would not have a celebrity guest seated at your table.

The glory was saved for those who bought the so-called Platinum package. For $70,000, you would be guaranteed prominent display around the event as a sponsor, not only for the gala but also for the round of golf to follow. You would receive a full-page advertisement in the gala program. You would have 24 people on your gala guest list, and room for 12 players at the golf tournament. The tables would include celebrity guests.

After launching in Toronto in 2004, the gala moved across the country. Calgary hosted it three times, and it had also made stops in Halifax, Montreal, Ottawa, and Vancouver. The most money it claimed to have raised was in Edmonton in 2010, when it said it generated $796,000 to help fund hockey-related projects around the city, including an outdoor hockey facility. (It would later claim to have raised more than $650,000 in Saskatoon, with money earmarked for an on-ice festival for entry-aged players, among other causes.)

Barry Lorenzetti, an insurance magnate from Montreal, was serving his term as the foundation chair. A few months before the gala, a Twitter account bearing his name posted a photograph of U.S. president Donald Trump speaking with dinner guests, under the caption: "Enjoying a beautiful evening with my wife at Mar-a-Lago."

In November 2015, during the run-up to the U.S. presidential election, the account tweeted "Good luck from Canada" after Trump landed in New Hampshire. Five months earlier, Trump had claimed Mexico was "not sending their best" to the United States: "They're bringing drugs. They're bringing crime. They're rapists. And some, I assume, are good people."

According to the Hockey Canada Foundation website, "many new Canadians are not naturally drawn to the game," and part of the foundation's mandate was to remove "barriers to the game."

Tom Renney had silver hair, glasses, and the comportment of a popular sociology professor. As the chief executive of Hockey Canada, he was speaking at a news conference inside a small downtown hotel conference room a few hours before the gala. As one of the only public events tied to the proceedings, it had to cover a lot of ground.

They acknowledged those who would later be honoured behind closed doors. Scotty Bowman would be receiving the Order of Hockey in Canada, and he also sat at the front of the room. Murray Costello, the long-time amateur hockey executive, shared the dais with Bowman. Fran Rider, the heralded builder of women's hockey, was the only woman to be feted.

Before long, the focus shifted to the ostensible reason everyone had assembled: growing concern over the state of grassroots hockey. It was getting too expensive for many Canadians to play. Some of those who had the means did not want to commit the time to an endless stream of practices, games, and skills development camps. Other sports were starting to siphon young athletes from the talent pool that had once belonged solely to hockey. Accumulating scientific research painted a terrifying portrait of what could happen to a young brain subjected to repeated head trauma. Waves of new Canadians were not finding hockey as easily as their predecessors. Climate data suggested that within a generation it would become more difficult for most Canadians to access natural outdoor ice surfaces.

Renney, the 62-year-old from Cranbrook, British Columbia, joined Hockey Canada after a decorated career as a coach. He won a Memorial Cup with the Kamloops Blazers, led a patchwork team of Canadians into the 1994 Winter Olympics, and spent the better part of a decade working in the NHL, with stops in Detroit, Vancouver, Edmonton, and the New York Rangers. Now his organization was responsible for the big picture: assembling the men's and women's Olympic teams, and selecting the world junior teams, in which two dozen teenagers would be thrust onto a nationwide stage for a month of relentless scrutiny. And yet it was obvious Renney had a passion for the game at the grassroots level as well. He could talk about it—the challenges, and his ideas to address those challenges—for an hour straight without once breaking eye contact. At the news conference in Saskatoon, he added one of his growing concerns to the list of pressures that was starting to suppress participation: technology.

"We recognize that, by drag-and-click, or pressing a particular button, you can get just about anything you want, at any time you want," he said. "And unfortunately, that's at the expense of activity, and the development of our population."

About half of Canada's hockey-playing population was based in only one province, with 43 per cent of all registered players classified under one of Ontario's three governing bodies. As executive director of the Ontario Hockey Federation—the largest of the three bodies—Phillip McKee oversaw more than 200,000 players.

McKee was raised in a hockey family. His father, Don, was a long-time hockey coach who worked in junior hockey and Canadian university hockey before venturing into the fringes of the pro ranks. The son aspired to play hockey, but his growth spurt had other plans. Phillip McKee was a forward, and a pretty decent one, too. He played double-A, but he was small—just 5-foot-4, 100 pounds—in what would have been his OHL draft year.

He was never drafted, but he was also never 5-foot-4 again. That growth spurt finally arrived at the end of his teens. The undersized forward was suddenly 6-foot-3 and 170 pounds, and he was out of hockey. McKee found his niche in volleyball, which he played in university.

Hockey was what pumped through his veins, though. It was his father's game, and it had been his game until he was forced elsewhere. McKee was also making his first steps into the game as a hockey parent, and he was doing it at a time when fewer and fewer Ontario parents were making the jump.

Overall, he said, the OHF had seen an annual 2.5 per cent decline since 2008. The federation had also seen a decline in the number of coaches and officials willing to participate.

"We're great program developers," McKee said. "We're not great business people."

For generations, hockey had a marketing plan that was devastating both in its simplicity and its effectiveness: open the arena doors. "It's like *Field of Dreams*," McKee said. "If you build it, they will come. That's been our marketing plan."

But minor hockey associations were only as strong as their base of volunteers, and not every volunteer had a comprehensive background in modern marketing strategy. In Peterborough, James Bradburn raised his hand to become president only because nobody else wanted the job. In Brampton, where the association was desperate to make inroads with a growing community of new Canadians, Glenn McIntyre sat at the head of a table surrounded by faces that had been there for years.

They were all well-meaning but not necessarily well equipped to deal with a challenge that was tormenting minor hockey executives like it never had before. There were success stories—strong participation in the Lower Mainland, in British Columbia, and exploding registration lists southwest of Toronto in Milton—but many volunteer executives were wrestling with the notion of how best to market a game that had never needed selling.

"They don't have the skill set, they don't have the knowledge, or, it's occasionally a white guy like myself going, 'How in the hell am I going to get a new Canadian involved in this game?'" McKee said. "We're trying. But right now, we've got a shotgun approach."

There were a handful of programs designed to increase the game's reach, like the travelling roadshow Carlow and Hurley were taking around Ontario. But there was no uniform marketing plan.

Part of the problem was structural. Hockey Canada was the sport's governing body, but it did not speak directly with players or their families. A message—about a rule change, or a policy tweak—would pass through a handful of channels, like a slow-moving relay race. There were provincial federations, then regional associations, local associations, local executives, conveners, and coaches. News did not always flow cleanly downhill.

McKee offered an example. The Greater Toronto Hockey League had Maple Leafs tickets and decided to stage a contest. It was going to invite young players to submit 100-word essays about why they wanted the tickets. The winners would get a free trip to what was then the Air Canada Centre to watch a game. All for a 100-word essay.

"You would think lots of kids would want to apply to win Leafs tickets," McKee said, then paused a beat for dramatic effect. "How many entries do you think they got?"

More than 40,000 children played in the GTHL, so probably quite a few.

"Three," he said.

Three essays.

"No one passed it on," he said, shrugging.

The problem lay not with the intent, but with the structural experience. McKee said the executives in power often began as volunteer coaches 20 or 30 years ago, when the draw of hockey was unassailable. As tastes evolved, those minor hockey executive boards did not.

McKee knew minor hockey desperately needed new voices, but the governance model discouraged new thought. To get a seat on the provincial board, you would first have to volunteer with your local association. After five or six years with your local board, you might progress to a regional board, where you might spend another six or ten years. By the time you reach the provincial board, you have already spent the better part of two decades in the system. Your new ideas are no longer new.

"We're in a democratic society, but we have built our system of hockey on the communist structure of assimilating them to our program and our thought process," McKee said, shaking his head. "It's a bad way to look at it, but it's the truth."

●●●

Long before he began his career in education—both in hockey and in the conventional setting—Paul Carson frequented a pair of outdoor rinks in Calgary. There was one at the high school, and there was one at the foot of his street, which had a hot stove in the middle of the shed, with a man who came to stoke the fire every night. "We scraped the ice ourselves," Carson said.

They played outside all winter. Even their organized league games were outside. They only went inside for the playoffs, when the conditions were too unpredictable outdoors. Legends were made outdoors, in games that could be 3-on-3 or 10-on-10, depending how many children showed up that day.

"I can't really recollect who would be the person who would decide, 'Hey, there's too many of us here, so sticks in the middle, and let's pick teams,'" Carson said with a chuckle. "Sometimes, you'd even have guys show up with goalie equipment."

More than anything, he said, it was a place for children to play. They fought their own battles on the ice and they honed their own skills. There were no adults to howl and bellow from the stands or to bark orders from the bench, demanding children dump the puck in deep or bounce it to safety off the boards. It was just about playing. It was pure.

"Anybody can go," said Carson, now vice-president of hockey development with Hockey Canada. "If I had a new friend at school who'd just moved here from an African country, and it's a kid you're really starting to connect with, you'd do what you could to find a pair of skates for him, so you could include him in the activity." Outdoor hockey, at its best, was once a radical act of inclusivity.

According to the International Ice Hockey Federation, there are roughly 5,000 outdoor rinks in Canada—more than double the number of outdoor rinks around the rest of the world. But that global dominance is no longer a birthright, with climate change turning many of those rinks into mid-winter marshland: the *New York Times* sent a correspondent to survey the damage in 2018, and his findings were published under the headline "Canada's Outdoor Rinks Are Melting. So Is a Way of Life."

The reality has been looming much longer. Two researchers from Montreal—from McGill University and Concordia University—examined weather data from 1951 to 2006 and concluded the conditions needed to create natural skating surfaces in most Canadian cities would disappear within a generation. Minor hockey has already moved indoors.

"It's exclusive," said Carson. "And the only way to become a part of it is to get in that cattle-car line and register and get the necessary equipment and follow the schedules and pay the fees. There's too much of a jump."

Hockey requires an investment, with each level giving rise to another barrier. Want to play house league hockey? There is a cost to register, and a cost to outfit the child from head to toe, from skates to stick to helmet. What equipment does the child need? In what order does the equipment go on? What if it turns out the child does not want to play all winter?

"We often expect people to leap the Grand Canyon to get to the other side and say, 'I want to do this,'" said Carson. "And the gap is far too wide."

●●●

In grassroots hockey, there is only one force of nature stronger than a force of nature: hockey parents.

On a cold night in the middle of December 2017, Scott Oakman, executive director of the Greater Toronto Hockey League, took up position along the glass inside the main rink at Scotiabank Pond, a gleaming, privately owned arena in the north end of Toronto.

Some of the best 15-year-old players in the city were on the ice, skating in an exhibition that had playoff intensity.

The game had its own title sponsor: the 9th Annual GTHL Top Prospects Game, Powered by Under Armour.

Connor McDavid had played in that game, as had Mitch Marner. These were players, at the time, on their way into the OHL draft and, possibly, to the NHL. Outside, luxury cars twinkled like stars under the parking lot's light standards. The stands were filled with serious-looking men and women wearing team jackets.

"On the negative side, people see this, and they think this is the whole hockey system," Oakman said. "It's not representative of the whole hockey system. It's the highest-profile of the hockey system, because of events like this, and because of where many of these kids are going to end up one day."

Six months after the top prospects game, in the same rink where Oakman was standing, former Maple Leafs defenceman Carlo Colaiacovo would be chased off the ice after losing track of the time during a skills development camp he was leading. He scrambled to collect the pucks and the training equipment as the ice resurfacing machine revved its engine in the distance.

It was early June, and he had to make way for a team of seven-year-olds who had booked the ice for a practice. Parents had paid $600 for the spring hockey season, which included 10 practices and two tournaments—both of which began with games on a Friday, during school hours.

"Bobby Orr is my guy, he is the hero of my life," said Oakman. "And in every interview you've ever heard from him, he learned to play the game on a pond, and not by somebody teaching him in a rink.

"I don't think we can go back to that, but I think the system has evolved to where parents think they need to give their kids these things in order for their kids to be successful. And I think it's our responsibility to show them that they don't need that."

He told the story of a friend who had three sons. The friend had always planned to allow his children to play hockey through the winter, but then to toss the gear into the basement each spring. The change in the seasons would signify the change in sports. His boys would spend their warm-weather days on a soccer field or on a lacrosse floor. Oakman said his friend had felt strongly about this point.

Then his eldest son turned nine and, when he reported to his hockey team that fall, he was well behind the teammates who spent the summer on skates. Oakman tried to ease his friend's anxiety —"he'll catch up"—but it did not help. The next summer, the children were skating.

"I understand, as a parent: I wanted my daughters to have everything so that they could be successful," said Oakman. "I think there's more and more evidence to show that overexposure hurts their long-term success."

It can also create an arms race in minor hockey dressing rooms, where parents are confronted with the fear of allowing their children to fall behind without additional training. That arms race can lead to yet another barrier, with parents who cannot afford the extra expense eventually migrating away from the game.

Oakman relayed something Paul Carson had told him about the cost of playing hockey. Carson said the cost to parents should be broken into three tiers. The first tier was the most sensible, which covered only the basics: the puck, the stick, the equipment, and the ice time.

The second tier was where things started to straddle the line, with practices, games, and tournaments. It was in the final tier that the costs started to get out of hand, with expenses such as private lessons and off-ice training.

"The hockey system doesn't control that," Oakman said. "That's parent-driven."

Pamphlets and posters for power-skating and skills development camps decorated the main concourse outside the arena bowl where he was standing. Oakman conceded the "existence of hockey outside the structured system—hockey schools, private lessons—is still growing at an unbelievable pace."

They were never going to shutter the businesses growing adjacent to minor hockey, and Oakman was not sure that they should. The economy of the specialized skills coaches, skating instructors, and high-level hockey schools had already grown too large to be controlled. What was left, Oakman said, was the power of perspective. "I think our role is to educate parents on the path their child should take in order to achieve whatever it is they can achieve in the game of hockey."

●●●

Tom Renney had a cold. It was a bad one, leaving him raspy and coughing in the lobby of a downtown Buffalo hotel. He was in Western New York for the world junior hockey championship, weeks before a critical series of meetings to discuss who would play on the men's Olympic team, with the NHL staying away from the 2018 PyeongChang Winter Games.

A blizzard had paralyzed the city a day earlier. Jeff O'Neill, the former NHL winger working as an analyst with TSN, was sitting across the lobby by the front door. He was still wide-eyed at what he had seen, saying it was like watching a skit on television with the actors trying to walk against the wind and the driving snow, and losing.

The sun was out now, though, and the air was crisp and still. It was an afternoon right out of the memory bank of Roch Carrier, or a Nelson Riis speech during a crisis in the Commons—a moment indistinguishable from the collective Canadian memory of a time when the game was a pastime, an obsession, and a universal bonding agent.

Reporters asked Renney, in the face of the modern barriers to the game, if that time might be gone forever.

"It might be," he said. "But I can tell you right now, they still learn about it through the mechanism of television, or through the digital age. They can still identify with the world junior, or the National Hockey League, or how important it is for us at the Olympic Games.

"Canadians still very much embrace the game."

Are Canadians still connected to it in the same way as before?

"You see the Canadiana of it all," said Renney. "You see how important it is, and how passionate Canadians are, and how emotionally connected we are to the game through that same mechanism."

He had a plan to change the way Canadian children connected with the game. It would be a difficult sell—not to the children, but to many of their parents—but he felt it was a critical step in drawing more young players back to the sport, and keeping them there longer. It would be known as "modified ice," a concept that would become far more volatile than it sounds.

"I don't know that I've got enough time to change this myself, as much as I wish I had," he said. "For me, this is now philanthropy. This is my job in life. And my job in life is to make sure the hockey experience is of more benefit than any other activity that a child participates in.

"That's what's critical for me. I think that we have to change why we play hockey."

EIGHT

LOST IN THE SNOW

I f the bodycheck had been any more violent, it could only have happened in a cartoon. Nick Robertson, the tiny American rookie, was skating along the boards in the third period of the pre-season finale when an opponent barrelled into the frame. The opponent was older. He was also 11 inches taller, and when he hit Robertson, it looked and sounded like an anvil crushing Wile E. Coyote into the canyon wall.

Robertson nearly disappeared from view, with only his skates and gloves visible from beneath the mass of humanity. His chin slammed into the glass and the rest of his face quickly followed; nobody had ever hit him that hard in minor hockey. It was only an exhibition game, held on an unusually muggy September night in 2017, but the Petes were playing the Oshawa Generals, which meant the air was always going to crackle with electric malice.

Petes captain Logan DeNoble was kicked out for fighting. A line brawl threatened to erupt a few minutes after that. The teams combined for 14 penalties in the third period. Fans roared for more, their blood lust echoing off the walls of the community arena in Bowmanville.

"It started with a skill game," Robertson told reporters afterward. "But once it got closer and closer to the end of the game, I think it got chippy, and I think they used more of their bodies than their mind."

The rivalry between the Petes and Generals was never intellectual—it was primal, rooted deep in the soil of cities bound by geography, economy, and antipathy. Two of the oldest junior hockey teams in Canada had spent half a century playing 45 minutes from each other's arenas: the Petes had been affiliated with the Montreal Canadiens; the Generals with the Boston Bruins. The Petes had Steve Yzerman and Chris Pronger and Roger Neilson. The Generals had Bobby Orr and Eric Lindros and John Tavares.

Oshawa hosted the Memorial Cup in 1987. Peterborough hosted it nine years later. The Generals had made 12 appearances in the Canadian championship tournament to the Petes' 9. Evidence of the mutual dislike was reborn on the internet, with grainy VHS tapes digitized and uploaded as the Zapruder films of winter hatred; generations of fights, brawls, and full-blown melees were only a keystroke away.

Durham Regional Police were called onto the ice to help break up a brawl between the teams during an early-round OHL playoff series in 1981. Oshawa coach Bill LaForge got into a fight with Peterborough counterpart Dave Dryden near centre ice before the puck dropped. The players followed their lead. One report in the *Globe and Mail* described what ensued as "a donnybrook." The OHL announced it would suspend LaForge through January of the following year, making it the longest suspension in its history.

In a regular-season game seven years later, the teams combined for 192 minutes in penalties—including 22 fighting majors.

Defenceman Brent Tully spent four seasons with the Petes in the early '90s, and, according to long-time junior hockey journalist Sunaya Sapurji, his mother refused to attend games in Oshawa —the fans were too intense when Peterborough visited. One of the greatest scandals in modern history happened a few years later, when Generals head coach Bill Stewart ordered his players off the ice before the post-game handshake after Oshawa had eliminated Peterborough from the playoffs. You can still find people who talk about that breach in etiquette today.

Lately, though, the rivalry was starting to feel imbalanced. The Generals had won the Memorial Cup three years earlier and were still sending players and coaches to the NHL with some regularity. After leading Oshawa to the title, head coach D.J. Smith joined the Toronto Maple Leafs. A handful of players on the championship roster would eventually wear an NHL jersey. Oshawa had won two Canadian titles since Peterborough won its only banner in 1979. The Generals also had a modern downtown arena, opened in 2006 at a cost of $45-million. It had a main bowl and a secondary sheet of ice for more hockey. It had a multi-level restaurant, wide concourses with attractive concession stands. Players had space of their own in a new, comfortable dressing room.

Peterborough, meanwhile, had spent millions to renovate its old rink rather than build something new, and now the roof was leaking and damaging the concrete beneath the ice surface. Players had to warm up in the concourse. After home games, the room where coach Jody Hull conducted his post-game interviews was next to a washroom. Sometimes, when the door was left open, sounds of washroom use were audible in the background as Hull spoke with reporters.

By the time the teams met in the middle of December, months after that pre-season scrap and days before the league-mandated holiday break, they were finally back on equal footing: they were both standing on shaky ground.

The Generals were sputtering on offence, having been shut out twice in their previous five games, and held to just a goal in two others. The Petes had lost five of their last six games, and their only win was in a 5–4 overtime squeaker against the Sudbury Wolves, a team destined for another last-place finish.

Dylan Wells was starting in goal. The injuries that had ravaged the ranks of the players skating in front of him seemed to have eased. Robertson was back from a concussion. DeNoble and Adam Timleck were back in uniform and on the top line with Jonathan Ang. The defence was more or less intact. This was the time the Petes needed to rediscover whatever they had lost on that October trip to Michigan. They were sinking down the division standings, suddenly threatening to settle near the bottom with the other wrecks.

A light afternoon snowfall had intensified as the sun dipped below the horizon. It was no longer falling onto cars as they approached the arena—it was blasting across the windshield like bristles in a car wash. An hour before the game was scheduled to begin, the snow was ankle-deep outside the arena in Oshawa. Puck drop was delayed 15 minutes, but entire sections in the main bowl remained fallow.

The Petes guided the hearty attendees through a condensed tour of their season that night. The soaring promise of the early moments gave way to a series of confounding decisions. Someone got hurt, and a dizzying blur of anger and exasperation swept across the bench. Once it started, nobody could stop it.

Peterborough had a power-play early in the first period, and 51 seconds after it began, Oshawa took a second penalty. Hull suddenly found himself with a two-man advantage and the chance to send his five most dangerous skaters onto the ice. The Petes had taken to using four forwards and one defenceman with their top power-play unit. It was both a testament to an unyielding faith in the power of their scorers and an indictment of the team's depth on defence, with the coaching staff never quite as confident in using two defencemen on the point. Matthew Timms, the undersized 19-year-old, was the only defender they sent over the boards.

He skated the puck deep into the offensive zone by himself and looked up to pass. He spotted Ang by the blue line. Ang was back in uniform a day after being cut from the Canadian junior team selection camp, having been invited to try out for the group headed to the world championship. It was the camp Wells had been expected to attend, but after the Petes tumbled down the standings, and after he struggled in the exhibition game against Russia, management never extended an invitation.

Ang accepted the pass from Timms, but he was too casual with the puck and too slow to read Oshawa's defensive coverage. A penalty-killer seized the opening to pop the puck off his stick and race down the ice on a partial breakaway. Timms raced back in coverage to prevent a clean attempt on goal, but it was another tremor rattling under a brittle team. They had still somehow given up a breakaway with a two-man advantage.

Despite all of their offensive firepower, and all of the NHL prospects on the roster, the Petes seemed fragile. They had made plenty of mistakes during their playoff run, but those were discarded and dropped out the window as the forwards shot back up ice. Now whatever was left in the rearview mirror was always closer than it appeared, and it was always a looming sense of dread.

Austin Osmanski, the lumbering American defenceman acquired in a trade two months earlier, helped reacquaint the Petes with that feeling a few minutes after the breakaway. He sidled up behind Oshawa winger Hayden McCool near centre ice as the puck skittered away. Osmanski placed his sizable left leg behind McCool, slipped his stick across his opponent's stomach, and then twisted, wrenching McCool to the ice. Not only was it judged to be an illegal play, it was judged to be badly illegal—he was assessed a five-minute major and a game misconduct for a slew-foot.

The Petes were down to five defencemen on the bench, but only for the time being. It would get worse.

Oshawa scored on the power-play, but the goal was waved off because of goaltender interference against Wells. It was only a temporary reprieve. The Generals scored one that counted a few minutes later, and it was against the best line Hull could throw on the ice. Ang lost a faceoff in the defensive zone, and a shot from the point deflected off his leg and into the corner. When the pass came back out, it got past both Ang and Timms, finding an Oshawa forward alone in the slot. The Petes were down 1–0, but it seemed clear something had already cracked.

They were being outshot again, a sin the hockey gods will only forgive for so long. Upper management figured an unholy combination of injury and bad luck was behind the slide. Quietly, they were also starting to wonder where coaching fit into the mix. They weren't alone: on social media and around the arena, fans were starting to whisper about Hull's job security. The Petes had signed general manager Mike Oke to a contract extension but did not do the same for their coach, who was now heading into the final months of his agreement. The less time that was left on the deal, the cheaper it would be to fire him. The coaching staff, for their part, also grumbled quietly as the team stumbled. The injuries were an issue, but only because they further exposed a defence too slow for the modern game. They wanted better players, and they wanted the general manager to find reinforcements.

If anybody had been coming to help, they wouldn't have been there in time for the second period in Oshawa, anyway. Peterborough tied the game at 1–1 with three seconds left in the first, but the hope was just a bolt of lightning, gone an instant after it appeared. The ice was still clean after intermission when Zach Gallant started skating into the Oshawa zone with the puck on his stick. The Petes forward had his head down, which was a mistake, because if he had looked up, he would have seen Generals defenceman Alex Di Carlo working through the mathematics of what was to follow. Di Carlo considered the angle, calculated the force, then drove his hip into Gallant with enough ferocity to generate a buzz inside the half-empty arena. Gallant was lucky he tied his skates as tightly as he did, or they might have gone flying off his feet and landed somewhere in the third row.

That hit turned into another link in the chain of events that led to Peterborough's downfall. Defenceman Cole Fraser was sent over the boards moments later, and he had revenge on his mind. He tried to land a bodycheck of his own and missed, giving the Generals an easy path across the blue line. Hull gave his rookies a rare shift, putting Robertson and John Parker-Jones on the ice, but they struggled to get control of the puck in their own end. Fraser, back in position, tried to clear the puck with a backhanded flick, but it was too weak. The Generals sent it back behind the net with Fraser in pursuit. An Oshawa forward got the puck, spun away from Fraser with ease, walked in front of the goal, and fired high past Wells for a 2–1 lead.

Two and a half minutes later, the game was over. The Peterborough forwards were playing high in the defensive zone—not quite at the blue line, but also not close enough to dig the puck loose— and left their defencemen alone on an island. Timms had to fight off two Oshawa forwards in front of the net, and he could only fight one at a time. The second forward took a pass from the corner and fired into an opening behind Wells to make it 3–1.

Everything that followed added another layer of sediment that archeologists would have to dig through when they sought to unearth the truth about Peterborough's season. Gallant lost his stick and his glove during a wrestling match in the corner, and the Generals scored on an odd-man rush to the net. Fraser was hurt at some point in the second period, and he was not on the bench for the third. With Osmanski having already been banished for his slew-foot, the Petes were down to their last four defencemen. The burden shifted to Timms and Alex Black, the veterans, and to rookies Adrien Beraldo and Gleb Babintsev.

The Generals, the biblical rivals, did not slow down. They used their bigger bodies to forecheck hard, to mash any remaining resistance into the glass like a fine paste. Timms started to sag under the work, and the Petes went careening further down the hill. They lost 6–3, and they left the ice bewildered and angry.

"Fuck you, too, buddy," Black bellowed into the stands as he entered the tunnel leading to the dressing room.

Forward Bobby Dow took a dozen steps toward the dressing room before he stopped to snap his stick over his knee. Hull was a few paces ahead and looked over his shoulder at the sound. He did not say a word. Wells was waddling toward the dressing room when, without warning, he reared back to swing his stick at the doorway, only to pull back when he saw there was glass inside the frame. He took six more steps and slammed his stick against the cinder block wall outside the dressing room instead.

Osmanski, already showered and changed after his game misconduct, was sitting on his equipment bag in the hall, indifferent or inured to the simmering rage of his teammates. The 19-year-old American was tapping on his mobile phone until Declan Chisholm, the injured defenceman, hobbled by on crutches.

"Are you going to challenge it, Oz?" he asked.

"Did you get two games?" another teammate asked.

Osmanski glanced up from his phone to answer just as Fraser limped past. He had also showered and changed back into his suit.

"What happened to you?" someone asked.

Fraser was returning to the trainer to get more ice for his leg before the ride back up the 115 to Peterborough. Dave Beamish pulled the team bus into the arena through the big bay door and turned off the engine. He and the bus both stood silently as players fumed inside the dressing room 50 yards away.

Black was literally spitting mad when he emerged from the room in his suit, doing so twice in silence as he walked toward the bus. Silence was a requirement. No player spoke on the walk back to the bus, all staring at the same invisible path in the concrete floor.

It was not their worst loss. They had been eviscerated in Kingston (7–1), shut out in Hamilton (4–0), and bleached straight off the ice in Sault Ste. Marie (8–3). The worry in Oshawa was not the final score but how dramatically the team had stalled. Nothing was happening when they pressed the accelerator. And no one seemed to know how to fix it.

"At this point, it's tough to pick out one thing," DeNoble said later. "I'm at a loss for words, to be honest."

He shook his head. There was no reason, with the talent on their roster, that the team should be where it was in the standings. And yet the Petes were getting outworked. They were losing one-on-one battles. They had watched video, seen the breakdowns on their end. They'd come up with new ways to correct their lapses, and then nothing would change. For whatever reason, they just weren't good enough.

Hayden McCool scored three goals for Oshawa, more than doubling his season total; he'd had two goals in 23 games before facing the Petes that night. It was the first hat trick of his OHL career, and it would be one of only two multi-goal games he would enjoy all season. (The other would come against Flint, the second-worst team in the league.)

The Generals were going to make the playoffs, but they were far from the heights of their former glory—they were just another team somewhere in the middle of the standings. And the Petes had made them look like champions.

It was late on Friday night, 10 days before Christmas. The Petes still had one game left before the 10-day holiday break, a road game in Hamilton on Sunday. After that, the players would be set free. They would get a break from the riddle nobody could solve: What was wrong with the Petes?

DeNoble thought the break could be restorative—it would be good for the guys to go home, spend some time away from the rink, maybe hit the reset button. He didn't know if it would work that way, but things could hardly get worse.

It was 10:30 p.m. when Beamish backed the bus slowly through the bay door and into the crisp dark silence of downtown Oshawa. As the giant bay door closed behind them, the Petes inched north, back home through the snow.

NINE

THE GLORY, THE ANCHOR

Two days after Christmas, after city snowplows turned parts of the Memorial Centre parking lot into a mountain range, Petes general manager Mike Oke was trying to get some work done in his office. He was sitting behind his desk, near his space heater, as a worker on a stepladder poked around in the ceiling tiles by the door. The heat hadn't been working for a while now, and with the temperature dropping below minus-10 degrees Celsius, things were getting frosty.

His office window looked onto the parking lot, where the wind whistled through the snowbanks. Maybe the frigid conditions in Oke's office made sense: given how the team was playing, most of the building's heat would have been one door down, squarely under Jody Hull's chair.

"There's enough heat to spread around," Oke said with a smile. "Trust me."

Oke did not keep his desk quite as tidy as his coach. There were cheques and papers and invoices strewn across the middle, broken up by a pair of scratch lottery tickets. They had not made him a millionaire—not yet, anyway—so he kept focused on the matter at hand: fixing the Petes.

The team had six games in the next 10 days. The OHL's annual deadline for trading players would toll after that sixth game, meaning Oke had a little more than a week to decide the fate of the season. A strong run out of the break could signal that the Petes were back, and that whatever ailed them after the trip to Michigan had finally been cured. If they continued to falter, he would have to follow the kind of plan that had seemed unthinkable in early October, when the Petes were being mentioned among the very best teams in Canada. A few more losses and Oke might write off the entire season, move some of his players for pieces to help in the future. They would have to wait, and then try again.

It used to be that the Petes never had to wait for the playoffs. The team missed qualifying for the OHL's post-season in 1976, but did not miss again for a generation. For 28 years—from before the Toronto Blue Jays played their inaugural game until a decade after their back-to-back World Series titles—the arrival of spring was always met with playoff hockey at the Memorial Centre.

They won the Memorial Cup in 1979, with future Hockey Hall of Fame inductee Larry Murphy on the blue line. They won the OHL title again the next season, with future NHL coach Mike Keenan working behind the bench. A few years later, a teenaged forward named Steve Yzerman would score 42 goals in 56 games and still not lead the team in scoring, with that honour going to fellow future NHL forward Bob Errey, who had 53 goals. For a long time during the streak, even if the Petes were not contenders, they were at least still in the neighbourhood.

Their streak finally ended when they missed the playoffs in 2004. Then they missed again in 2007.

And again in 2011.

And in 2012.

And once more in 2013.

For half a decade after the turn of the century, the Petes were among the very worst teams in Canadian junior hockey. Their best players were no longer moving into the NHL with fluid regularity. It became a damaging cycle: top prospects did not want to play on a team that could not send them up the ladder, and the prospects who did report soon grew frustrated with the inertia and the losing.

Ryan Spooner was leading the team in scoring a month into the 2010-11 season when the constant burden of defeat prompted him to request a trade. He was 18 years old, recently drafted by the Boston Bruins, and he went home to Ottawa to await reassignment. Spooner was the second player to request a trade that week; defenceman Chris Buonomo had also asked for a change of venue.

That was the first of three straight seasons the team would miss the playoffs. Matt Puempel, a forward destined for the NHL, requested a trade in the spring of 2012. Another coveted prospect asked to leave the following season: defenceman Slater Koekkoek publicly complained about a "negative attitude" in the room five games into the season, having grown tired of the constant losing. The Petes granted both players their wish.

Prospects who had better options simply refused to report, telling the Petes not to waste their draft pick on them. One of the most embarrassing refusals came in 2012, when Derek Schoenmakers, a marginal veteran acquired in a November trade, refused to set foot on the Memorial Centre ice. The Petes tried to coax him to Peterborough, talking with his family and offering to meet anywhere he wanted. He would not be swayed. Two months later, the team sent him to the Kitchener Rangers, his hometown team. He reported, and he finished the season in uniform.

The Petes finished that season early, missing the playoffs.

Everywhere around the province, there were signs the game was changing; one of the first was in London, Ontario, when Mark and Dale Hunter bought into junior hockey. The former NHL forwards, both known for being ruthless on the ice, purchased the Knights and their aging home rink for $3.8-million in 2000. The London Ice House had opened in 1963, making it only about nine years younger than the Memorial Centre. Within two years, the Knights moved into a new downtown arena modelled after what was then the Air Canada Centre, where the Maple Leafs played their home games. It could accommodate more than 9,000 fans for hockey. The Knights did not have any national championship banners to move into their new home, but they found a quick remedy: they won the first Memorial Cup in franchise history five years after the Hunters took over, then another in 2016.

Patrick Kane spent a season with the Knights. Nazem Kadri and Mitch Marner became stars in London before the Leafs made them first-round picks in their respective draft years. The franchise turned into a factory floor, taking raw teenage material and shaping it into ready-made NHL players. The Knights became the luxury sport-utility vehicle of the OHL. Other teams tried to follow the model, with modern arenas opening in Windsor, Kingston, St. Catharines, and Oshawa.

Teams were no longer owned by local lawyers (Oshawa) or doctors (Belleville). They became part of a big business. There was money to be made, especially in the large markets. In 2017, an Ontario Superior Court judge certified a $180-million class-action lawsuit against the OHL from players asking for back pay, as well as remuneration for overtime and vacation. (A TSN report revealed the Niagara team was leasing four BMWs in 2016, presumably for adult use.)

The Petes were not generating that kind of revenue, claiming losses of six figures in seasons in which they did not make the playoffs. Part of the blame lay with the Memorial Centre, which the Petes did not own. And part of the problem might have been with the ownership structure, and the culture it fostered.

Peterborough was not controlled by a swashbuckling sole proprietor. There were wealthy people in the city, but none of them could ever own the team outright. The Petes were controlled by an elected board of directors responsible for charting a course into the new world. There were no term limits. Five directors had spent 20 or more years on the board.

Sam Cosentino, the long-time junior hockey analyst with Rogers Sportsnet, suggested that was part of the problem. Embracing the past is one thing, but shackling an organization to the ghosts in the rafters can be costly.

"It seems like, so many times, the undercurrent of what's gone on is that it's always tied to the past," he said. "I think it's really hard for a community-owned team, especially when you sit in the building and you look at everybody there, and how old they are. That's what they gravitate toward: the past. They don't want to see change. They want to see the same old colours, the same old square boards, the same old seat when they walk into the rink. They want to see the same old guys behind the bench. They want to make sure that there's some tie to the past. It's almost like they're afraid to let go."

The Petes were attacking a new landscape with an institutional line of thinking.

"The thing that helps move an organization forward is divesting itself a little bit from the past," said Cosentino. "The game has changed so much. The business part of it has changed so much."

The players had changed, too. The Knights had become a success in London because they built a solid program that identified strong prospects, developed them toward their potential, and assimilated them into a team that won games. Those London teams became popular, drawing crowds into an arena with modern amenities. It became a place players wanted to play. Their success became a self-fulfilling prophecy.

Peterborough had drifted to the other end of the spectrum. The Petes played in a small market, in an old arena, as part of a franchise that had not won a meaningful game in a decade. The team struggled to attract stars, and when it did, it struggled to keep them. That problem, in some ways, also became a self-fulfilling prophecy.

"Players have choices now, and they have more choices than they've ever had before," said Cosentino. "The first thing that's going to draw me to a program is probably my playing time, because we're in the 'me, me' age.

"The second thing that's probably going to draw me is: 'Am I going to a winning program?' And part of that is: 'Is that guy going to develop me into an NHL player? And can that coaching staff support me enough to become an NHL player?'"

Instead of changing, he said, the Petes seemed tethered to the glories of their past. Mike Oke joined the team while his father, John, was on the board of directors. The elder Oke resigned in 2012 as his son was moving up the ranks from director of player personnel, to avoid the appearance of a conflict of interest. The Petes fired coach Mike Pelino that year and replaced him with Jody Hull, the assistant coach who had spent three seasons as a forward in Peterborough. Andrew Verner had also spent three seasons with the Petes during his junior hockey playing career. Pat Casey, who had been on the board of directors for more than 30 years, had been a winger on the original Petes team.

The Petes were innovators once, developing an adherence to education that was eventually adopted throughout the league, with advisors helping keep the school-aged players engaged in their studies. As the game and the city and the players changed, though, the Petes remained in many ways frozen in time.

"When I look at the Petes, in general, there always seems to be something from the past that's underlying," said Cosentino. "Sometimes, the past gets in the way."

As players skated on their first day back from the Christmas break, Oke sat in the Memorial Centre stands, chatting with one of the most familiar faces in the arena. Even though Dick Todd spent most of the winter at his residence in Florida, his face stared out from the arena rafters at every game, practice, and concert that passed through town. Todd grew up as an aspiring baseball player in Toronto, coached by another man who had a banner in the Memorial Centre: Roger Neilson.

It was Neilson who invited Todd to join the Petes, initially as a trainer in 1973, and Todd would become an understudy for some of the greatest moments in franchise history. The team flourished when he finally got a chance to coach, and he became the face of the franchise through the 1980s and into the '90s before jumping to the NHL to join the New York Rangers as an assistant. He won a Stanley Cup.

The Petes lured him back in 2004, after firing another coach. He led the Petes to an OHL title the next year, and then he stepped aside. He returned as a consultant in 2013, and he appeared to be consulting Oke now as the Petes skated down below, their season potentially 10 days from the abyss.

"Anything short of a Memorial Cup," said Cosentino, "and people are going to talk about Mike Oke as being part of the nepotism of the history of the great Peterborough Petes."

●●●

There was an example of what could happen when a team fell too far behind the pack, dropping out of the peloton before disappearing from the race altogether. The Belleville Bulls were the second-closest OHL market to Peterborough, after Oshawa. In many respects, though, the Bulls were closer.

They had played at Yardmen Arena, a 3,200-seat relic from another era. The ceiling was so low to the ice that netting was installed over the scoreboard so errant passes wouldn't damage the screen. There had been no modern concession stands—entire fields of barley could be harvested and milled in the time it took to get through the beer line at intermission.

The concourses were narrow. The press box barely had enough space for a full forward line. Even the ice surface was out of place: Yardmen Arena was the only OHL building with the wider Olympic-size rink. The Bulls were literally playing a different game than other teams in the league.

They had a proud history. Belleville was granted a franchise in 1981, and it had made two trips to the Memorial Cup, including the tournament in 1999 after the Bulls won their first—and only —OHL title. It was the franchise of P.K. Subban, arguably the most dynamic and marketable NHL star of the modern era; more than 40 NHL players passed through Yardmen. It was a place where families would gather in familiar seats through the cold winter months. Parents kept their seats after their children grew up and moved away. If one spouse died, the other kept their seat, because the Yardmen was where they fit into a circle of friends. For a segment of the populace, sitting in those stands was part of what it meant to be from Belleville.

Dr. Robert Vaughan had founded the team and carried it for more than two decades before deciding to sell majority control to an out-of-town businessman in 2004. Gord Simmonds was not from far away, with his home in Uxbridge and his family's whole-sale electronics distribution company in Pickering, a 90-minute drive west of Yardmen. Simmonds bought the remaining shares three years later.

Simmonds did not own the arena—it belonged to the city, and he spent years trying to nudge and prod it to upgrade the facility. His fans were getting older, he said, and they were starting to demand the arena install railings to help them reach their seats. The city delayed and demurred and deflected. There was always talk about arena improvements at council, but never any meaning-ful action. In markets such as London and Windsor and Kingston, teams were starting to play in modern hockey palaces designed to attract prospects and generate revenue. Yardmen Arena was a place of worship, but not capitalism.

In 2015, Belleville lost its team. Simmonds sold it to Michael Andlauer, who owned an AHL franchise in Hamilton. The plan was to move the Bulls to Hamilton and rename them the Bulldogs. They would be playing inside FirstOntario Centre—a theatre of broken dreams, having been built for an NHL team that never arrived—and in a market with more than 550,000 residents. About 50,000 people lived in Belleville, or only about 30,000 fewer than lived in Peterborough.

The Bulls would finish out the 2014-15 season at Yardmen, then move away forever. Belleville qualified for the playoffs, but they were not expected to go very far and lived up to those expecta-tions, losing the first three games of their first-round playoff series against the Barrie Colts. The fourth and final game was held inside Yardmen Arena. The Bulls lost 4–2 to complete the sweep, but the stands were full at the final whistle. Fans stayed in their seats, and many wept openly. Bulls captain Adam Bignell, whose father had been a Belleville captain, skated out to centre ice with his jersey in his hands. He laid it down and skated away, his shoulders slumped.

Brandon Prophet was a defenceman with the Colts. They had just booked passage to the next round of the playoffs, but the mood was sombre. "You're ending a tradition, a heritage, a family, that has lasted way longer than you've been alive," he said. "Some of the people have been going there since they were kids. It's ending a monumental event that has been going on in the community for years."

Prophet would be traded to Peterborough the following season, eventually becoming captain of a team that played in another aging arena. While the Petes did not play on an Olympic-sized ice surface, neither did their rink conform to modern OHL standards. When that Petes team missed the playoffs—which was starting to occur with unprecedented frequency—there was no supportive millionaire owner around to cover the revenue shortfall.

But Dave Lorentz, the high school principal who joined the Petes board in 2013, would insist there was no danger of the Petes going the way of the Bulls. "It's going to take a lot for this thing to sell," he said.

●●●

Peterborough travelled to Guelph for the first game after the holiday break, on a night so cold the walk from the parking lot to the arena felt like an Arctic trek. The Petes had fallen to seventh in the Eastern Conference—only eight teams would make the playoffs—and despite their brave talk, they were just as brittle as the snow that crackled like glass underfoot.

There was hope the 10 days away had helped players forget. The holidays were going to clear their mind, wipe clean the sticky sense of dread that seemed to clog their throats after the first missed pass of a game. What had been happening since Michigan was still difficult to explain, and without the vocabulary, players and coaches grasped at the familiar: they would have to get pucks to the net, go to the dirty areas and, above all, work hard.

Nick Isaacson returned to the lineup after having missed two months with a shoulder injury. The 18-year-old was not going to score goals, but he was responsible in the defensive zone, which would help ease the burden placed on Wells every night. The Petes set goals before the game: they wanted to get 40 shots on net, harnessing the vast offensive weaponry that had made them a top 10 team in October.

Hull, just months away from the end of his contract, had spent the break stewing about the team. His wife's family came over for Christmas dinner. That night, with the two dozen guests filling his home with holiday cheer, was the only night he was not haunted by the chorus of echoes from the Memorial Centre.

He took the losing personally. He had played in Peterborough —it was where he grew up in the game, and it was where he returned as a man. The NHL had taken him across North America, to Hartford and South Florida, Philadelphia and Ottawa, but he had come back to Central Ontario. Hull wanted to coach in the NHL one day, but Peterborough was home.

When the season began, the Petes had set out to play a style of game that suited their roster. As the losses mounted, those systems shifted and evolved. Over the holidays, Hull and his staff made a decision: they would return to their October plan. They held video sessions for players on their first day back, showing them exactly how they wanted them to break out of the defensive zone, how to play through the neutral zone, and how to defend. Forwards were no longer allowed to live outside that system. No more selfish play. No more lugging the puck into the offensive zone at the end of a long shift, only to turn it over and be too tired to skate back and defend.

It was two days after Boxing Day, and the crowd inside Guelph's handy downtown arena was small and silent. It felt quiet enough to hear what the players were thinking. Nick Robertson, the rookie, started at centre between DeNoble and Chris Paquette, the Tampa Bay Lightning draft pick. Jonathan Ang was on the second line. Nikita Korostelev, the Russian who could shoot like an NHL player but skated three or four leagues lower, was on the third line. The Guelph Storm held seventh place in the Western Conference. The Petes were a seventh-place team as well, but they still had first-place dreams. The Petes were also easier to read than the Storm —they made a mistake on the third shift of the game, and in the fourth, you could almost hear the fracture.

Peterborough won a defensive draw to the left of Wells, with the puck going right back to defenceman Adrien Beraldo in the corner. There was no obvious outlet pass, so the rookie tried to fire the puck off the glass and out of the zone. He missed, and it sailed high into the stands. Beraldo was sent off with a two-minute minor penalty for delay of game. Moments later, Alex Black, the veteran defenceman, lost a battle for the puck behind the net, allowing Guelph to maintain possession, and the Storm moved it ruthlessly around the zone. Forty-five seconds after Beraldo went to the box, the home team scored. It was only the fourth shot Wells had faced.

Korostelev tied the game two minutes later, but every mistake the Petes made seemed to vibrate along the bench. They allowed two more short-handed breakaways on Wells—one in the first period, one in the second—and could never get that fearsome offence in rhythm.

Oke had made the trip to Guelph, watching from the press box high above the ice. He had been unflappable during the playoffs the previous spring, watching with a cool detachment as the Petes advanced deeper than they had in a decade. The general manager did not make every road game, but he was in Guelph after scouting at a holiday tournament in Toronto. It was becoming clear something was at stake.

"Fuck," he muttered under his breath after a fanned shot.

He clicked his pen, chewed his gum, and fiddled with his phone. He checked the OHL standings. The Petes never got their 40 shots on net, and they never scored another goal. Peterborough lost 3–1, their sixth straight.

Ang ended the second period doubled over on his stick, exhausted and defeated as the horn sounded. A pass missed DeNoble by a dozen feet, and the captain fought to contain his exasperation. After another turnover, Oke shook his head and groaned an "aw, fuck." DeNoble slammed the bench door so hard it echoed off the ceiling.

They had been angry when they left the ice in Oshawa before the break, but in Guelph they were subdued. Nobody snapped his stick in a rage. Nobody yelled. Nobody swore out loud. Players showered and changed quickly, with the rookies loading the bus.

The OHL's trade deadline was looming. In a little more than a week, the Petes would have to decide if they would be buyers or sellers. Would they acquire talent to make a run into the playoffs, as all of the pre-season hope had foretold, or would they sell whatever assets they could? Would they be fighters or quitters? Winners or losers?

●●●

Dave Pogue was not an obvious agent of change. He was raised on a farm outside Peterborough and had never wanted to live anywhere else. He even avoided vacationing abroad, happiest with the pace of life at home in Bridgenorth, a tiny community with a Beer Store, a liquor store, and unimpeded access to the lake. He had a daily routine, and it was forged in iron.

Every day began at 5:30 a.m., with or without an alarm clock. He poured a glass of juice, ate a banana, and hit his home gym for a workout. That was when he caught up on the previous night's highlights on TSN and arranged his thoughts for the day. By 7 a.m., his focus was on work.

Pogue was addicted to work. It seemed like he had held every kind of job that had ever existed in town. He used to run a trucking company, and he also used to spin records and hang out with CanCon legends in his job with a local FM rock station. ("I've got some great stories of, you know, being on the bus, eating chicken wings with Jeff Healey.") These days he described himself as a property owner—commercial and residential—and as a farmer. ("My son's the farmer. I'm the hired help.")

His roots stretched deep into the Central Ontario soil. His late father spent 30 years working at General Electric. The family owned a farm that had been passed down for more than a century. Pogue said they had documents linking the property to around the time Peter Robinson was leading his clan of starving Irish immigrants into town. Pogue had attended Fleming College. The local twice-weekly paper named him the sixth-most influential person in Peterborough.

"I'd be afraid to go anywhere else," Pogue said. "I'm not sure I could function anywhere outside of Peterborough. I love that town. I walk into the street, I walk one block, I'll see four or five people I know. I love that."

He spent his days in perpetual motion, but they ended almost as predictably as they began. His whirring gears slowed after dinner and, by 9:30 p.m., the engine would fall silent for eight solid hours. At 52, his body clock was perhaps the most accurate timepiece in Peterborough County.

"A coma every night," he said. "I'm a great sleeper."

There was one exception, and it was seasonal. Pogue had grown up listening to the Petes on a transistor radio hidden in his bedroom. When the Petes are at home, they usually play on Thursday night. That could push his bedtime back until about 10:00 p.m.

Pogue had been a season ticket holder who was named to the board of directors in 2013, becoming president three years later. He knew the team was struggling on the ice, but he also knew how badly it was starting to stumble off the ice, as well. Seventeen men had preceded Pogue into the president's role, and none did what he did eight months into office: convene a town hall, inviting fans to grill management and get a peek behind the veil.

"For years and years, everybody thought there was this secret society up in this room: 'I don't know what goes on up there, but they must go up there and drink beer and drink wine and spend all the money and not care about hockey,'" said Pogue. "Nobody knew."

The landscape of junior hockey was changing, and the Petes could not afford the status quo. It was getting more expensive to keep pace with teams in the big markets, especially the teams with the fancy arenas like the one in London. The education packages that junior hockey teams funded for graduating players could run six figures a year. Even the annual stick budget was creeping north of $80,000. Something had to change.

The Petes reported a loss of more than $370,000 in 2013. They lost another $220,000 the year Pogue was named president. At the town hall meeting just before the season, with the shadow of the Belleville Bulls still looming over small-market teams, he revealed the financial challenge in public for the first time. He wanted a new arena, but he said the team needed to modify its arena lease with the city first.

He was looking to keep approximately 15 per cent of the revenue the team would otherwise have sent to the city. That would work out to about $350,000 a year. Without help, the Petes would be in trouble.

"There's a lot of ifs," Pogue said. "People took it as: 'The Petes are going broke, they're going to have to sell, they're going to be bankrupt. Destitute.'"

It was not an immediate concern. The Petes had investments. They had a rainy day fund to help cover the shortfalls. But every spring without playoff games at home depleted those funds, which made it harder to remain competitive, which made it harder to make the team an attractive home for top prospects. It was the kind of spiral that could destabilize a proud old franchise.

More than 150 fans ventured downtown for the meeting at Market Hall Performing Arts Centre, a 20-minute walk north of the Memorial Centre. They were frustrated with the years of losing. They asked about the management model, and wondered whether the team might not be more successful with the deeper pockets of a wealthy private owner. Management suggested the current structure was the best way to keep the team in town, because a wealthy owner might not have the stomach for the long-term challenge of sailing such a small vessel in the roiling sea of junior hockey business.

Some of the questions were pointed. Someone suggested the board fire the coach. It had been almost four decades since the Petes had won the Canadian championship, and they appeared to be slipping further from contention every year. Tension mounted inside the room. And it made Pogue smile.

"This is what I love about Peterborough," he said. "Who goes out, takes two hours out of their Thursday night when they could be at home with their family, and comes and gets this riled up about something that really doesn't mean anything in your life? This is fans. This is what sports does, and this is what I love about hockey, and this is what I love about Peterborough. Get riled up. Call me whatever you want to call me. I love it, because I know you're engaged, and that's what I want."

The veil had been dropped. Eleven months after that meeting, Peterborough mayor Daryl Bennett wore a Petes jersey for a meeting with Pogue at the Memorial Centre. The two men were photographed with pens in hand, signing an amended lease agreement. The deal would run through 2023, letting the team keep an additional $340,000 in revenue every year.

It was not a panacea. The Petes were still stuck inside the Memorial Centre, with its square boards and narrow concourses, but it bought them more time to wait for a new arena. Or so they hoped.

●●●

Jody Hull carefully removed his cufflinks and placed them back in the box on his desk. It was getting late, and most of the cars that had been parked outside his office window had long since left. They said it was the coldest seven-day stretch in this part of the world since the 1970s, but the fans in those cars would have gone home happy.

The Peterborough Petes had finally won a game. Two days after their loss in Guelph, the team showed a glimmer of the form they hoped to regain. They trailed the Ottawa 67's 4–2 in the third period at home, but they never broke. Alex Black helped complete the comeback, scoring the winner with 88 seconds to play in the third period, with a crowd of more than 3,500 huddled in the Memorial Centre.

Players celebrated loudly inside the dressing room, with the bass splashing from the speakers and into the hallway where parents and girlfriends were waiting. It was only December 30, but it was also their first win in 23 days.

The arena had grown quiet as Hull finally settled into his office chair. His dress shirt was still white and crisp, but the rims of his eyes were red from a cocktail of adrenaline and fatigue. He had been up front with his players during intermission, after they let Ottawa score three unanswered goals in the second: "There's no one who's going to help us get out of this other than ourselves."

For one night, finally, it worked.

He knew the Petes had talented players on the roster—those who were exceptional and those who could fill the less glamorous roles. The challenge was making sure the effort was provided to fuel those talents. They couldn't afford to have a Jonathan Ang or a Logan DeNoble take a night off. These Petes weren't that kind of team.

Oke popped his head into the office. His son was not feeling well that week, and he told Hull he would be out until later the following day. That was New Year's Eve, but it was also a week until the OHL's trade deadline. There were decisions to be made, and they would shape the rest of the season.

Hull was bad at taking time off during the season, anyway. "I'll be at home, sitting with my family at night, and I'll be watching a hockey game on TV, and it's still going through my mind," he said. "I'll be watching hockey and going, 'Hey, that's not a bad play, can we try that?'" His Christmas vacation had ended on Christmas Day; he was back in his office on Boxing Day, laying out plans for the days to come.

There were only a handful of islands in his life that offered an escape from the drumbeat of hockey thoughts. "One is when I'm plowing snow on my ATV," he said. "I'm so frustrated, I end up plowing our entire fucking road. My wife laughs at me. She goes, 'Why are you plowing the road?' I'm like, 'I just need to . . . it's OK.'" He chuckled. "I go one way real fast, then back the other way real fast, then back the other way fast, then back the other way fast," he said. "It's clean. I did that on Christmas Day because the plow didn't do it."

His wife, Kelly, would warn him he cared too much. "I think probably half the people in town here who follow hockey probably think that I come to the rink at noon and I'm here for three or four hours, and then I go home," he said. "They don't realize I'm here at seven in the morning, every day, and I probably leave at five or five thirty every day."

A lifetime in hockey had taught him to believe in the concept of momentum—that events in a game, good or bad, can carry over to influence subsequent games. Some coaches disagreed, believing every game had its own context and its own variables, and that a mistake or a success from last week had no bearing on today. But Hull believed it. This season was only more proof.

The Petes had played well enough to win in Guelph but had let it slip away. They'd made their own luck at home that night against Ottawa, playing with the same wide-open and fearless style that suited them so well in the playoffs the season before. It was a 12-minute stretch of breathtaking speed. It was a force that Hull believed could be harnessed.

"But at the same time," he said, "I don't think you can get too far ahead of yourself."

He reached for a little spiral notebook on his desk and thumbed through the pages.

"I've got shit written all over my book here," he said. "Sorry. Excuse my language."

The pages were filled with handwritten notes.

"Here's a quote for you: 'History is important, because if you forget its lessons, you are doomed to repeat the failures.'"

Was that from Winston Churchill?

"I'm not sure," he said.

Where did he find it?

"I read a lot," he said.

Was it included in his address to players during the second intermission?

"No," he said. "That might be something I tell the kids tomorrow. Because I don't want them to get caught up in the fact that, because we played a good 12 minutes of hockey, that this is the end-all and be-all, and that we're out of the funk.

"That last 10 minutes of the third tonight will only be relevant if we come out and play the same way on Monday. That's how I look at it. And that's where the lesson is: don't get caught up because we were good one game and think, 'Oh, we're good now. We don't have to listen to the coaches anymore.'"

●●●

Cathy Weiss was a spry, white-haired octogenarian who carried two notable items in her purse on game night. She had candy, which she would kindly offer to people she met inside the Memorial Centre. And she had a gargantuan red brassiere. It was so large that each cup could have doubled as its own floral-print toque, in case of emergency.

She had been going to Petes games for 25 years, her seats right on the concourse behind the home team's net. And every time the home team scored, she leapt out of her seat and twirled the giant bra over her head, in full view of the Queen staring down from her portrait at the other end of the ice.

"I'm not here for notoriety," Weiss said. "I'm having fun. And I sit here with my present husband because the camera can't get at me."

Her late husband developed mobility issues after suffering a massive stroke. They both enjoyed hockey, and watching the Petes play became a welcome night out on the town. Her current husband, who was 91, had never been much of a hockey fan. "But," she said, "he's here now.

"He goes to lacrosse," she continued. "Loves it. He's never shuffleboarded before, and he's doing that. He's never bowled before, and he's doing that."

Peterborough has become a haven for retirees—the 2011 census showed it had the highest percentage of retirement-aged residents of any metropolitan area in Canada. One in five people walking the street was now 65 or older. That trend—and the attendant complaints about things like handrails and music volume—was reflected inside the Memorial Centre. They liked things the way they were.

One player and his billet family giggled about an older fan who had seats just behind the bench, where children would rush to high-five the players as they approached the ice from their dressing room. More often than not, the fan would scold the children for crowding her space. A section away, it was possible to occasionally find another older fan knitting quietly in her seat during the pre-game warm-up.

Weiss was not like that.

The bra-waving began as "just a fun thing" after she had already entered her golden years. "This chap behind me said, 'If you take your bra off, I'll take my shirt off.' And I said, 'Well, I'm still in a training bra.' So the next week, he brought me this."

She motioned down to the bra in her purse. Rex, the man who sat behind her, died a few years earlier. She spoke at his funeral.

"I got this note from his sister," she said. "It said, 'My brother would be proud of you.'"

Weiss had fun at the games, and she had fun with the people she met. The bra was a talking point, and a good way to torment the security guards at the front door. One night early in the season, one of the men asked to check her bag.

"And I said, 'Go ahead, have a big feel.' There were two of them. And one said to the other guy, 'Oh, this one's yours.' The other guy says, 'Can I check your purse? Is there any underwear in it?' I said, 'No, I'm wearing it. Do you want to check that out, too?'"

The bra was also a fixture at Peterborough Lakers games. They were the local Senior A lacrosse team that had just won the Mann Cup, the 15th Canadian championship in franchise history.

"They have a good following, they have good players, and they've done well," said Weiss. "I like lacrosse better. Sorry."

Really?

"It's faster," she said.

TEN

THE SEASON SHIFTS

arly in the first Friday afternoon of January, hours after the Petes had lost for the 9th time in 10 games, the Memorial Centre was silent save for the rhythmic scratching of Brian Miller's broom. The team's long-time trainer was sweeping a path from the dressing room to the ice, clearing away the road salt that the players and passersby had tracked inside.

It was cold beyond definition, minus-22 degrees Celsius, with a savage wind whipping across the parking lot as players arrived for practice. Two of the Russian players parked and hurried inside the arena, past a row of spaces reserved for team employees. General manager Mike Oke had parked in his spot, but another spot was empty. There was no sign of Jody Hull's familiar black sport-utility vehicle.

Peterborough had lost 2–1 to Windsor the night before. It was a home game, and home was the only place the Petes seemed even capable of winning anymore. They were terrible on the road, and had been since the mid-October trip to Michigan. The offence was running dry. They were ragged on defence, and part of Dylan Wells still seemed a bit lost, perhaps wandering the ashes of his dream to represent Canada at the world junior championship. It was not that he was playing terribly. He was just playing like a regular human being, when what the Petes really needed was a deity.

Just before 2 p.m., the team issued its news release: Jody Hull had been fired as head coach.

Oke looked tired as he made the rounds with the two local television stations, choosing his words as carefully as he could. Injuries were a factor in the slump, he said, but even as those players returned, the wins did not follow. Hull was a consummate professional and a valued colleague, he said, and he still had respect for him as a coach. Andrew Verner, the senior assistant on staff, was being promoted into the lead role on an interim basis.

"We have the talent," Oke told one of the assembled stations. "We have the ability within the dressing room."

Back in his office, the burden became clearer. The board of directors held the ultimate say in personnel matters, and it had granted Oke the power to fire Hull after a meeting in December. That meant he had been carrying the decision around for days, if not weeks. He would have had the power with him that frozen night in Guelph, when his cool veneer cracked and he clicked his pen and swore under his breath every time a player erred on the ice. Being a general manager was not like being an owner in fantasy sports, he said after the Christmas break. Players and coaches were not commodities to be moved back and forth on a whim. They were real people, and every move held real consequences.

This was the first time Oke had fired a head coach.

He paused for six seconds before answering when a reporter asked how difficult it had been. The two men had spent their winters in connected offices, they'd travelled together, and they'd both endured the indignity of tumbling down the standings.

Oke tried to speak, but his voice caught. His eyes welled.

"It's hard," he said, finally.

His office door was closed. He lived 45 minutes from the arena, but he had not gone home after the game against Windsor. He stayed in Peterborough, wrestling with what was to come. The two men met in the morning, and it took Hull only 10 minutes to clear out what he wanted from his office.

"I just felt that we needed to do something," said Oke. "I just felt that we needed to go in a different direction. I just felt that it was time."

It was getting close to the end of a long day, at the end of an especially long week.

"I haven't even seen my . . ." Oke said, his voice catching again. "I want to go home."

●●●

Home was in Sunderland, a town of about 1,200. It was a convenient, if isolated, location. His wife taught in the Durham District School Board, which was just one regional road to the south. Oke's route to the arena took him east, a drive he made so often he developed his own unit of measurement.

"I can tell you exactly how long it takes," he said before the season started. "It's a large regular."

Oke wore his dark hair short and brushed back, the line atop his forehead looking like hundreds of tiny spikes along a castle wall. He had two manners of speaking, and he kept them in separate compartments at all times. There was the way he spoke in public—to the television media or to a crowd—which was careful and stilted and dusted with jargon. It was how he sounded on the riser during a sports business conference in Chicago, and it was how he sounded on the local news. He sounded like a police officer.

Part of that might have been earned through practice. Oke had spent more than a decade working in the Ministry of Community Safety and Correctional Services, based in the intelligence department. He refused all entreaties to elaborate on what he did for the ministry, other than to say it was a place where he could use his analytical mind. Oke was someone who tried to figure out the angles within any situation.

Examples of that thinking would sometimes tumble out through his other manner of speaking. Sitting in his element, in his corner of the scouts' box at the Memorial Centre or in an arena where he was on the hunt for the next teenaged hope, he could be profane and funny. During intermission one night, he volunteered a story from his time in school, when computer science courses had become a part of the evolving educational landscape. They were not his strength, so when he handed an assignment in to the instructor, he scratched the inside of the floppy disk with his car keys. His instructor was sympathetic when he returned the disk afterward, assuming there had been a manufacturing error. The instructor offered to pass Oke anyway.

Being general manager in Peterborough required working knowledge of the angles. Some players might have been on the path to professional hockey, but there was still plenty of distance that lay between the Petes and the marquee. Most players would never set foot in an NHL rink without a ticket. Some would play on the fringes, moving to teams in tiny towns in tiny leagues. Some would leave for an adventure playing in Europe. Some would join a university team.

But before then, players broke curfew. Players struggled in school, or struggled to fit in at school. Players were finding ways to get into trouble that never even existed when Oke was a teenager in the early '90s. In November 2014, weeks into his second season as general manager, a 19-year-old forward became an international story: Greg Betzold was a third-year veteran who had been communicating with an unknown woman on the dating app Tinder. Their conversation went public.

"Trust me I know what kind of girl you are," Betzold purportedly wrote.

"Oh yeah and what's that," the woman responded. "Cause I'm pretty sure ya dont."

"A pure bread dumb stupid cunt," the player responded.

"Yeah I'm pretty dumb and stupid with my 93 avg that'll get me into any uni I want without some OHL contract to help my stupid ass get into uni," the woman wrote back.

"Lol 93 average . . . Wow your mommy and daddy must be so proud and yeah let me know how much money your making after your uni . . . And taking dick for a living," was his alleged response.

Another OHL player had also been caught saying terrible things online. Betzold eventually apologized for making "unacceptable private comments," saying in a prepared release that they did not "reflect my true values or views."

The league suspended both players for 15 games. Oke was interviewed by national media, saying what happened was still "a new phenomenon" the team would learn to address. Betzold scored a career-high 43 goals the following season in Peterborough, then graduated into the ECHL, a third-tier professional league.

Parents were also an evolving concern. Children were increasingly focused on a single sport, spending their summers in the arena instead of on a baseball field or a soccer pitch. They enrolled in specialized camps to work on their skating, their stickhandling, their strength, and their speed. For parents, it was not just a financial investment but also a massive commitment of time. They drove to practices and to games and to tournaments. The other parents on the team became part of their social circle. By the time they entered the lobby of the Memorial Centre as parents of players, mingling and gossiping, their total investment could have bought a luxury car or two. It takes a village to raise an elite hockey player—a gated village, with a cover charge and demands for all your vacation time.

Oke was also involved with his son's minor hockey team, and he saw how parents could behave around the rink. For example, it was rare, but not unheard of, for a parent to intervene with concerns about playing time—at least one parent had reached out within the last season, concerned about how their child was being used on the ice. He suggested these dynamics were not unique to hockey. His wife was a teacher, and he had noticed a shift in parenting, and how parents held their children accountable.

"In the past, if little Johnny was misbehaving, little Johnny would come home and dad would say, 'Did I get a phone call from your teacher today saying you were misbehaving?'" Oke said. "And Johnny would shit himself.

"Now it's like: 'Oh no, it wasn't Johnny who was misbehaving—it was your fault, you didn't teach him properly.' That's part of it. It's definitely changed, but society's changed."

For weeks, there had been a sense some of the teenagers in the Peterborough dressing room were not accepting the responsibility they had been given. DeNoble, the captain, suggested as much after that back-breaking loss in Oshawa. The coaches had been using coded words all season; now, as the wind whipped outside, some of the adults inside the Memorial Centre were grumbling about the kids who cost an adult a job he adored.

●●●

At precisely 2:02 p.m., with Miller having swept away the road salt, Verner broke the silence on the Memorial Centre rink. He was first onto the clean sheet of ice, turning a lap in his goalie skates as word was still filtering out into the city. It had only been 10 minutes since the Petes issued their official news release under the title "Jody Hull Relieved as Head Coach of Petes."

Verner had a few moments for himself before he stopped to sip from a water bottle on the boards at the home team's bench. Derrick Walser and Mike Duco, the assistant coaches still in their first season with the team, were on the ice a moment later. The coaches skated quietly, the hum from the ventilation system louder than any sound they made on the ice.

Nick Robertson was the first player on the ice, followed by Cole Fraser and John Parker-Jones, the 17-year-old rookie who'd had the misfortune of scoring his first two OHL goals during blowout losses. His first was against Oshawa, the only goal Peterborough scored that night in a 4–1 rout. During the enforced silence of the post-game walk to the team bus, Parker-Jones had allowed himself a brief smile and a quick handshake from a visitor.

Players continued to file onto the ice. Some tried to look stoic, others opted for sombre as they turned a few warm-up laps. Semyon Der-Arguchintsev, the small Russian forward, was the first to show signs of life. He playfully bumped into DeNoble, and the captain smiled for a moment before he resumed showing whatever kind of emotion the players were supposed to be feigning.

None of the three surviving coaches were guaranteed to survive for much longer. Verner, Walser, and Duco were all heading into the final months of their existing deals. Verner had the deepest roots in the region, having played for the Petes and made his home in the area. Walser was married with young children and had moved his family to Peterborough after a decade spent playing in Europe. Duco was three days from his 31st birthday, and the youngest of the three by a decade.

After practice, one of the coaches voiced concern about the growing crevasse between expectation and ability. The season-long questions about the defence had never really been answered. Timms was agile but not fast, and one of the coaches said a shoulder he had injured the previous spring was still bothering him. The Petes had lost two veteran defencemen to graduation before the season, and while neither of them made the jump into the professional ranks, their absence was felt in all situations.

The Petes did not have great foot speed on defence. One of their best skaters was a rookie taken behind Robertson in the OHL draft. Cameron Supryka's father was working as an assistant coach in Kingston, and his mother was an accomplished personal trainer in Belleville. From the moment he stepped onto the ice at rookie camp, it was clear their son could fly. Supryka's was the kind of stride that scouts love and poets celebrate. He was only 16, though, which meant his gifts were going to benefit whoever was coaching him in another two or three years.

After practice, Walser wondered whether the team's early success was a quirk rather than a feature of its composition. The Petes won when their forwards were screeching around the offensive zone like a squadron of jet fighters. They had put up five goals against Oshawa in the second game of the season, and they scorched Niagara for eight goals a couple of games later. They rolled over Windsor 5–1 in October, and that was a game they should have lost. They were fun and exciting and exhilarating. Then, at the very next game, it was like the taps had been turned off. They rusted quickly and were never reopened.

In hindsight, Walser wondered whether the flow had stopped because other teams needed the extra weeks to implement their respective systems. Once those teams settled into their schemes, the ice suddenly grew tighter. There was less runway for Peterborough's jets. Opponents started to learn that the Petes were not going to be a physical team. They could see the players in maroon were skilled, that they could be dangerous, but that they also took risks. Peterborough could be pressured into turnovers. Forwards did not always commit to helping out on defence.

Hull knew the issues. He'd tried to fix them. And now he was gone, dispatched into the cold without the job he loved.

●●●

In the old days, the Petes only replaced their coach when there was another generational talent waiting nearby. They spent the better part of three decades with coaches who would wind up with their names hanging from the Memorial Centre rafters, or inscribed on the Stanley Cup, or both.

Scotty Bowman became the Petes' third coach after the team's arrival in Peterborough, and they played for the Memorial Cup in 1959. Bowman graduated to become the most successful coach in NHL history. The succession plan after he left was not dictated entirely by luck, but neither was it entirely by design.

"They kind of stumbled into it a little bit," said Mike Davies, the sage hockey reporter at the *Peterborough Examiner*. "Roger was never intended to be the coach."

Roger was Roger Neilson, who became coach after his predecessor resigned in the middle of the 1966–67 season. After he guided the Petes to a win over the Niagara Falls Flyers in December, a dispatch in the *Globe and Mail* described Neilson as the "temporary coach." He would become one of the most celebrated coaches in hockey history, first in Peterborough and then across North America. Neilson was a university-educated hockey mind from Toronto, and he became a national news story for his inventive interpretations of the rule book.

Several of those headlines rolled off the presses after the Petes lost a pre-season game before his second full season in charge. The story was not the loss but how they reacted when the other team was awarded a penalty shot. Neilson had wanted to make a substitution—not to change goaltenders but rather to take his goaltender right off the ice and have a defenceman stand in the crease. The referee was baffled by the request, reportedly taking 10 minutes to consult the rule book before permitting Neilson to make his change. According to the *Globe*, the Peterborough defenceman waited until the opposing forward crossed the blue line, and then he charged. The forward was upset, and fired a quick shot that glanced off the defenceman's leg before the two players crashed into each other.

The league dug into its texts again after the game. "There's nothing in the rule book against it," Scotty Morrison, the league's head referee, told the *Globe*.

A few weeks later, a lower-level junior coach tried the same thing, copying Neilson. His team lost, but a possible trend was being set, and its roots were in Peterborough. (That Petes goalie left the team the following year, reportedly unhappy with his ice time.)

Neilson was also a scout, reportedly driving more than 20,000 kilometres in a single spring. In 1972, with the Petes approaching the second Ontario championship in team history, the *Globe* described the annual midget over-age draft as the "Roger Neilson Benefit Draw."

As the Petes marched through the playoffs that spring, another innovation came to light. Neilson, who taught at Crestwood Secondary School, borrowed a relatively new piece of equipment from campus to use in the arena: a video recorder.

He had an associate from school record the hockey games. Neilson used the video to show players how they could improve, and where they should be skating on the ice in certain situations. He told a reporter he only showed select clips to players, rather than making them re-watch entire games. The London Knights had also reportedly dabbled in video, but Neilson was the first to embrace its use, as he told the *Globe*: "Next year, I'm going to ask permission to use the equipment on the road as well."

Neilson also set himself apart in the belief that players needed to do more than just play hockey. Teenagers of a certain age were expected to attend high school, and those who were older were expected to enroll in post-secondary courses or keep part-time jobs. Neilson—who was also a devout Christian—fined players if they were late to school. He demanded monthly report cards. Some veterans grumbled about how the coach seemed to control their lives, but the system worked. They won, and they won often.

Neilson led the Petes for a decade. When he left for the professional ranks, the team hired Garry Young, who had been general manager of the California Golden Seals, an NHL expansion franchise, and coach of the St. Louis Blues. He was not a fit in Peterborough, and left after one season.

They did not have to look far for his replacement. Gary Green made the University of Guelph's varsity team but quickly realized he would not be able to make a living as a professional player and became a coach instead. He was running a hockey school in Toronto when he approached Roger Neilson to work with the Petes as a volunteer. Neilson retained him as an unpaid assistant. When Young left, the Petes gave Green the role of coach and general manager.

He was 25 years old and billed as the youngest person to coach in major junior hockey. The Petes won the provincial title in his first season. At the end of his second, in 1979, they won the Memorial Cup—the first in franchise history. By then, Green was being viewed as a prospect around the NHL, with teams calling him before the Petes hoisted their trophy. It was reported he sold his home before Peterborough won its final game in Verdun, Quebec. He left, working briefly in the American Hockey League before joining the Washington Capitals, where he became the youngest head coach in NHL history.

Peterborough was a national champion for the first time, coming off back-to-back Ontario title wins, and the team needed a new coach. It went looking in Toronto again, and emerged with a 29-year-old who had been teaching physical education at Forest Hill Collegiate Institute. Mike Keenan was given the role of both coach and general manager. He was stern and serious, reportedly making players roll over on the ice if their team allowed a goal in scrimmage. After consecutive appearances in the Memorial Cup, the expectation was not that the team remain merely competitive; Peterborough was supposed to contend for another title, and anything less would be a failure. Keenan was ambitious enough to recognize the signs.

He did not fail. With Larry Murphy, the future member of the Hockey Hall of Fame, on defence, they won the Ontario title for the third straight year. They did not win the Memorial Cup, but they got close enough to see it, losing the national championship in overtime.

Keenan left after the season, signing on to coach with the Rochester Americans in the AHL, but he did not stay there for long, quickly graduating into a long NHL career in which he won both the Jack Adams Award as the league's top coach and the Stanley Cup. No NHL coach has won as many regular-season games as Bowman (1,244), but Keenan (672) made it into the top 10 all-time—giving the Petes two of the most successful coaches in NHL history.

After Keenan, the Petes hired Dave Dryden, a former NHL goaltender and the older brother of Canadiens legend Ken Dryden. He did not last long, and when the Petes sought a replacement, they did not look very far afield. They hired Dick Todd, the team trainer, who had also served as their business manager and assistant coach. News of his promotion did not ripple far outside Central Ontario, but it would end up becoming one of the most important moves in franchise history.

Todd looked like the film version of a high school principal, sometimes wearing a thin moustache beneath wire-framed glasses and bearing a dour countenance. He would never win the Memorial Cup, but he would still guide the franchise to new heights. Peterborough won two OHL titles, was a finalist for another two, and always seemed to be in the mix. For the 14 seasons Todd was behind the bench, the Petes never had a losing record, and they registered three of their five most successful regular seasons— including a 1993 campaign with a 17-year-old Chris Pronger on defence and an 18-year-old Cory Stillman at forward, in which they won 46 out of 66 games en route to the OHL title. (They made it to the Memorial Cup final, but lost to Sault Ste. Marie.)

Todd was coach when Hull was a player on the roster. He was the coach when Verner, now an assistant, was still a young goaltender with professional dreams. Both Hull and Verner knew what it was like to be in Peterborough when the team was winning. And while the Petes never won a title with Hull, they had also never missed the playoffs in any of his four years behind the bench.

Verner was a star prospect once. He was the first goaltender taken in the 1991 NHL entry draft, ahead of future NHL regulars such as Chris Osgood and Steve Shields, but he never appeared in a game and moved overseas to build his career. He played in Austria and Finland, Sweden and Germany. His career ended in the United Kingdom.

His dark eyes had a mischievous twinkle, whether he was stealing a bite of Duco's green apple after the young assistant had fallen asleep or snapping photos of him as he dozed, mouth agape and head propped up by a neck pillow. He had smiled as he studied the latter photo on his phone, checking for both composition and the potential for embarrassment at an unspecified later date.

Verner was also a star attraction at the team's annual Christmas party, for his cunning as well as his dancing. The cunning was tied to his historic dominance of the post-dinner trivia contest, with players and coaches and executives divided into tables and pitted against each other. Verner seemed to possess an unnatural grasp on the minutiae of Christmas-related trivia—which included questions such as naming the precise tonnage of cranberries produced in Canada each year.

When he submitted his team's answer sheet for grading, he named it: "Team Verner (Google)."

The party ended with everyone in the room singing "The Twelve Days of Christmas," and with each table required to act out the movement of their assigned day. Verner's table got day 10. And so when the 10th day of Christmas rolled around, the senior assistant coach of the Peterborough Petes climbed atop his chair and lunged back down to the floor as he yelled "10 lords a-leaping."

Hockey took Verner further afield than he originally planned. As quickly as he joked, he could also tell a story about growing up as a professional overseas, learning a foreign language, encountering local customs, and acquiring the kind of broader perspective that sometimes feels suppressed in North American hockey circles.

As is the case with many hockey players, Verner was superstitious once. Until he had to forage in the wilds of Austria, his pre-game meal had typically consisted of chicken Parmesan, a cold glass of milk, and a drink with ice in it. He had to learn to be flexible. "If you go down to the south, and in Italy, you can probably find it," he said. "But when you're stopping at a gas station on the way to a game, it's tough sledding."

The sledding ahead in the present day was not going to be much smoother. Peterborough had 29 games left on its regular-season schedule—plenty of time to mount a charge back up the standings. They had fallen behind, but it would only take a spark. A few big goals. A dramatic comeback win. Just a flicker of hope.

Verner had a mandate that extended beyond winning as many games as possible: he was going to give more ice time to the younger players on the roster. Robertson, the American rookie, had been used sparingly before the coaching change. In many respects, Hull was a progressive coach, but he had been closer to the old school of thinking when it came to using his talented draft pick. Robertson would now be free to be more expressive on the ice, knowing that a single mistake would not be the end of his night.

From the outside, the mandate seemed to place Verner in a difficult spot. He was being asked to spend more time developing young players for the future, but he was also in the last year of his contract, and the Petes, confident as they might have been, were not in much of a playoff position.

Still, it was not something that worried him. Despite his roots in town, he was not concerned about facing unemployment. He had signed a one-year deal by design—his design.

"That's the way I do it," he said with a shrug. "I know I could go somewhere, if I need to."

Verner said he had turned down offers to move up to the AHL, one step below the big show. He had a young family in Peterborough, which was a factor in his decision. If the Petes decided not to offer him another contract, though, he figured he would not be out of work for very long.

"I know I can get something, so that takes a bit of the pressure off," he said. "I'm not chained by that."

●●●

By firing his head coach, Oke played one of the biggest cards a general manager holds in his hand. If the team was truly struggling because players had stopped listening to the adult in charge, there was now an opportunity to find an adult who could command the room. If that adult failed, the focus would start to fall squarely on the man in management.

Oke was facing a series of decisions. The OHL trade deadline was only three days away, and the Petes had to decide if they had a team capable of winning. If the answer was no, there was an immediate follow-up: Who could they trade, and what could they get in return?

He still had high expectations for the team—maybe not as high as after those first few weeks, when the team was first in the standings and positioned for more, but he genuinely felt the injuries had undone the momentum on the ice. Injuries happen to every team in hockey, but they just seemed to be piling up in Peterborough this season, and every absence added more weight to those left in uniform. In Oke's mind, that weight was what ultimately caused the whole thing to collapse.

There was a knock at the door. It was Verner. Oke invited him inside, and he settled into a chair as the general manager spoke.

"We haven't met the expectations individually, and we haven't met the expectations, collectively, as a team," he said. "And the players know that. They've admitted that. They have said that publicly in interviews."

The players were running out of time to support their brave talk with action. Peterborough had a game in Ottawa the following night. It was the last game before the trade deadline. If they rallied behind the new coach, they might be able to convince management the season was worth saving. If they did not, one or more of the veteran players could be moved.

Would firing Hull get their attention?

"I'm sure it does," Oke said. "I'm sure it does have an impact."

"None of them have gone through this," Verner said with a little shrug. "Maybe two guys have seen a coach get fired in their life. They're junior hockey players."

ELEVEN

SELLING A CHALLENGE

urrender came not with a white flag but with a press release. Three days after firing his head coach, Oke traded Jonathan Ang for a younger player and two draft picks—a second-round selection in 2020 and a third-round pick in 2022. Players eligible for the 2022 draft were 11 and 12 years old the day the Petes announced the trade, meaning none of them were quite ready to replace the team's alternate captain for the stretch drive of the regular season. The Petes were ninth in the OHL's Eastern Conference, having fallen out of playoff position after another weekend loss.

During his time with the team, Ang could frustrate coaches and bewilder management. He was the fastest skater in the city, but he had a habit of taking bad penalties. He could dominate a game just as easily as he could disappear from view. He ran hot and cold, sometimes on the same shift, but he had NHL potential and was one of the veterans in the room—only 28 players had ever spent more time in the maroon jersey than Ang had over the last four seasons. With the distribution of a single press release, he was gone.

On social media, frustrated fans howled for Oke to capitulate with more of a flourish. They wanted the Petes to ship away as many of the veterans as possible and stockpile assets for another fight on another day. Nikita Korostelev was leading the team in scoring, but what did all his goals matter if they were being scored in a season nobody would remember? Was Oke doing his best to trade his veterans for draft picks? Spread them out across the province, they said—mail them away and wait for a fresh batch of hope to arrive in exchange.

Hope was useful, but it was not everything. The Petes were important to city life, but even at the height of their powers, they never animated the region as a year-round obsession. They were not the Permian Panthers, the high school football team in Odessa, Texas, made internationally famous by *Friday Night Lights*. There, the football stadium was the centre of all existence, and author Buzz Bissinger traced the spokes outward, chronicling how the team shaped not only the local political scene, but how residents viewed themselves in the world.

Peterborough was too pragmatic for any of that. Nobody was lining up overnight for tickets to see the Petes. The city's social life did not ebb and flow with the tides of the regular-season schedule. The Petes were not oxygen, certainly not like the Panthers were to Odessa. They were more like the weather: people would talk about them most often when they were exceptional, when they were terrible, or when they had done something strange.

Everyone knew about the Petes, and many had opinions on them, but that awareness did not always compel people to drive to Lansdowne Street, hand over a pair of toonies for parking, and watch the team from inside the Memorial Centre. Even Roger Neilson would sometimes coach home games in front of hundreds of empty seats.

"You can't measure how much people live the Petes by how many times they sit in the stands," said Burton Lee, the team's executive director, business operations. "How I look at it is, I have yet to meet someone in this city who doesn't have a connection on some level."

Peterborough had developed the reputation of attracting an older, quieter crowd to home games. But as the bigger markets started building bigger arenas, the Petes were starting to draw some of the smallest crowds in the league. In London, Kitchener, Oshawa, St. Catharines, and Windsor, teams averaged more fans than the Memorial Centre had seats.

This was where the team's fate off the ice veered sharply from the unfolding drama on the ice.

As the Petes tumbled down the standings, their attendance did not follow. Not only were they still drawing crowds, they were drawing more than they had the previous season. Attendance jumped by a fifth—a single-season spike larger than any the OHL had seen in four years. The last? In 2012, when the Erie Otters welcomed a rookie from Newmarket named Connor McDavid.

Peterborough did not have a Connor McDavid on the roster. They were a struggling team without any names on the marquee. And still, many of their biggest crowds of the season were yet to come, with more than 3,700 fans in the stands some nights. Their attendance was increasing by 20 per cent when the rest of the league's was growing at around 0.3 per cent.

The Petes had been changing the way they were doing business. Lee seemed to be at the root of that success, and a large reason for that might have been the fact he was an outsider who brought in new ideas without being constrained by notions of the way things had always been.

For the first time, the team was starting to track data: who was attending its home games and which of those fans might be willing to attend another (even if only after getting a gentle nudge from a sales rep). They also launched a mobile app: with one press of a button, the team could make devices across the city buzz with news of a trade, a game result, or a deal on merchandise. It had been in those ties to the past that the Petes had fallen victim to the same complacency that started eating away at the grassroots of the game itself —the inertia of conventional wisdom that said hockey never had to be marketed, at least not beyond publicizing when fans should expect to buy their tickets and fill their regular seats. The Petes were taking steps to become a modern sports entertainment company.

"You talk about receipts in shoeboxes? We *were* receipts in shoeboxes until three years ago," Lee said.

Lee arrived five years earlier, and within two years he was put in charge of business operations in the front office. Growing up in Delhi, in Ontario's tobacco-farming region, he was sports-minded without being hockey-obsessed. He floated through university before moving to Thailand with his future wife, who had accepted a teaching position. Lee coached basketball and worked a little as an English tutor. He started picking away at an MBA through correspondence.

When he returned to Canada, the Toronto Argonauts gave him a job, where he had to wear a suit while making minimum wage in the sales department. Though it would not have mattered to him at the time, the CFL franchise shared challenges with the Petes: the Argos were a proud old brand that did not resonate as easily across the city as they once had. Their fanbase skewed older and whiter. They were losing ground.

Lee left the Argos to take a job with the Sarnia Sting, but the plan was always to find a way back to Peterborough. His wife, Heather, was from there, and that was where they planned to raise a family. When Lee told his manager in Sarnia he was interviewing for the job in Peterborough, he was gently pulled aside with a warning: "You don't want to work for the Peterborough Petes." The team had its way of doing things, he was told, and it had done things that way for a half century.

Oke, the general manager, interviewed Lee. Pogue and Lorentz had just recently joined the board. While he picked up on some possible reticence—"Some 'who is this guy, coming from out of town, and why is he trying to do this?'"—he got the sense that, at least on the business side of things, the Petes were willing to change.

The team had a small front office staff when he arrived. One employee tried to balance the portfolio of three people, selling group tickets while answering the phone for media relations and working on marketing; the team parted ways with that employee and chopped the salary into smaller pieces to give to younger replacements. Lee started holding weekly meetings, with regular evaluations. Targets were set. Incentives were offered. The front office would approach the city like skaters attacking the net.

One of the biggest challenges turned out to be the arena itself. The Memorial Centre was not built with a robust operations structive in mind. There was space for three offices: one for Oke, one for the coach, another for the assistants, and none for the business staff. Office administrator Cathie Webster, the team's longest-serving employee, had her desk by the door, and the rest were arranged in tight quarters like carefully placed puzzle pieces.

Lee walked around the arena, looking for space to expand. Was there a forgotten nook under a stairwell, or an empty room by the beer kiosk? They crammed two of the new hires into the back of the office, in what was once solely the copy room. Interns were moved into the alumni lounge upstairs. In the office, there was no such thing as a private conversation. For Lee, that was a benefit: if there was ever a problem, it wouldn't remain secret for long. "That's the luxury of our open-concept sardine can," he said.

Matt D'Agostini was the brother of former Petes goaltender Andrew D'Agostini, and he was initially hired as a kind of gopher. Lee put him in charge of group sales: he would be the one to call the minor sports organizations, the local employers, and anyone else capable of marshalling a field trip down to the rink. Those tiny, adorable youth hockey players who entertain the crowd by playing at intermission? They can be a gold mine for group sales —what parent, grandparent, aunt, uncle, or close family friend would not buy a ticket for the chance to watch them skate on the Memorial Centre ice?

On game night, D'Agostini was a casino greeter. He had an uncanny ability to remember names and small personal details, and he used that gift to make small talk anywhere from the front door to the beer line. When a group bought tickets, he would make sure to wander through with a clipboard, asking for names and email addresses to enter the fans in a contest. That was how the Petes collected data.

Steve Nicholls was a part-time elementary school teacher hired to sell season tickets. He made 50 calls every day, and he would keep calling a number until he got a firm rejection. Nicholls called every city councillor, but only two got back to him, and they teamed up to buy a partial season package. He tried the mayor but was referred to His Worship's brother. The brother had also been dodging his calls.

Greg Sinclair was in charge of sales and marketing, which meant he got to make use of the brand-new video board the city installed above centre ice. He was in constant motion on game night, making sure sponsors received the attention for which they had paid.

Tamara Burns returned to Peterborough after working with the Belleville Bulls, and she helped run the social media accounts, among other media-related duties. She asked questions of players and coaches in the media sessions after home games. She also wrote the ever-positive post-game news releases, which, with the way the Petes were playing, turned out to be one of the most difficult jobs in the city.

Shelbi Kilcollins was a 23-year-old intern fresh from St. Francis Xavier University in Nova Scotia, and she wrote for the game-day program. To support herself in Peterborough, she was also a server at a local restaurant and worked in two local clothing shops.

Someone working in a sales role might earn a salary of $30,000 a year, plus commission. Everyone in the office seemed to work all day, every day. Lee had positioned his desk in a back corner, just outside the door to Oke's office, and he oversaw the operation more as a mentor than as a dictator. He had just turned 30, and was tall, with a disarmingly sharp sense of humour. Lee lived in perpetual motion. He interviewed players for content on the website, MC'd at the team's Christmas party, and helped out on game night, from pitching in on social media to requesting the DJ play a more upbeat country song after the Petes scored.

"You have to trade off the fact that we're a junior hockey team in Peterborough," he said. "We pay people very low salaries. I can't expect someone to work 80 hours a week. Many of them do work 80 hours a week, but that has to be, to me, of their own choosing."

On a Monday night in September, just before the season began, Burns, Sinclair, D'Agostini, and Lee had all gathered inside a local restaurant on a night when players were scheduled to serve as celebrity waiters. The local television station was there to film players bringing food to the customers, but there was a problem: the television camera operator had to leave early to attend a city council meeting, which had an important issue on the docket—a proposed $35 fine for residents who parked cars on their lawn.

It was only 6:15 p.m., and there were no customers in the restaurant for the players to serve. In order to make sure the television station got the shot it needed—and the shot the team wanted—they had the players deliver water to a table of Petes employees.

Everyone at the table was, on average, 20 or 30 years too young to have been a season ticket holder at the Memorial Centre. Peterborough had plenty of young hockey families, but the challenge for the Petes was that those families were usually busy with their own hockey games during all of those long winter weekends. And if they turned out to have a free Sunday afternoon, there was little reason to expect they would gleefully run right back into another arena to watch another game. Even if it was the Petes.

The typical Petes season ticket holder had already celebrated their 50th birthday. They likely grew up in the city, or returned to retire after spending their working years elsewhere. Those were the people most likely to have $1,000 to spend on a season ticket for hockey. There were some young professionals on the register, but they were far from the majority. Lee figured that was just the result of simple demographic mathematics: older residents tended to be the ones who were more established and more financially secure. If they were 50, their children were likely a bit older. In turn, that would give the parents more free time for pursuits like OHL hockey on a Thursday night in the winter.

What the team had to focus on now were the locals who had not yet passed the half-century mark. They had to make sure that those people knew about the Petes—and that, when those people turned 50, they would want to buy season tickets, too.

There were signs Peterborough was on the verge of significant change. The pragmatic city, the city that avoided the boom-and-bust cycles of places like Oshawa, would soon be drawn just a little bit closer to the noise of the urban core. After years of waiting, Highway 407 was finally scheduled to be connected to the 115 by spring 2020, allowing for easier access to the Greater Toronto Area. Officials were planning for more traffic and the potential for more people moving to the area. Those residents might not have the same natural, ingrained connection to the local junior hockey team. It seemed like an opportunity.

●●●

Richard Peddie was a mediocre high school student from Windsor, Ontario, who became the first president and chief executive of Maple Leaf Sports & Entertainment. In 1998, he joined a company that owned a hockey team (the Maple Leafs), a basketball team (the Raptors), and a new arena (the Air Canada Centre). By the time he retired, almost 14 years later, he had turned it into something Canada had never seen.

He led the company into real estate, buying into a development next to the arena. He developed digital cable channels, which laid a foundation for high-level internet content. The company branched into the restaurant business, launching Real Sports Bar & Grill, which ESPN Mobile promptly anointed "North America's Best Sports Bar."

For $10-million, Peddie bought a Major League Soccer franchise (Toronto FC) that, a decade later, was being valued at more than $240-million. He officially retired on December 31, 2011, and eight months later, 79.53 per cent of MLSE was sold for $1.32-billion.

None of his teams ever won a championship while he was in office. The Leafs and Raptors both endured some of the harshest stretches in their respective histories. It got so bad with the Leafs that one frustrated fan showered them with waffles during a home game. ("Who brings waffles to a hockey game?" forward Colby Armstrong asked, correctly.) Peddie accepted the blame for those failures as he left the building for the last time. His expertise had been on the business side, where he could read the landscape and move before it shifted.

"That Leafs brand is incredibly resilient," Peddie said. "When you figure how Harold Ballard screwed it up, in an old arena— one of the oldest arenas . . . if you did that in any company, you'd be out of business. And we were still there."

The season ticket packages that did make it to the open market were snapped up quickly. Peddie said 70 per cent of all season ticket holders had held them since before 1970, and by and large, "they were white." During his time at MLSE, he said, the Leafs had a season ticket renewal rate of 99 per cent.

"No one gets 99 per cent," said Peddie. "Maybe the Cubs and the Boston Red Sox. But year after year, no one gets 99 per cent."

It was rare for a season ticket holder to go to every game—given the high cost, it was not uncommon for a person to sell the majority of their tickets into a group of friends.

"So the only way diversity is happening is if you're part of a team —a syndicate," said Peddie. "It's still a pretty white crowd."

The landscape was shifting. The face of Toronto was changing, with new Canadians settling both in the city and in its suburbs. Peddie led MLSE to explore what impact those changes might have on the products the company sold. They found new Canadians typically became fans of the Leafs within about five years of arriving in Southern Ontario.

"It was, 'Listen, I'm working at this place and my buddies on the line are talking about the Leafs—I better know what's going on,'" said Peddie. "Or it's, 'My son or daughter is going to school, and all their friends are wearing Leafs garb. I'd better do it.'"

Toronto was not a hockey town, he said; it was a Leafs town. The city's graveyards were filled with the remains of junior and low-level professional teams that could never find a foothold. It was the same out in the suburbs: Brampton lost its OHL franchise in 2013, and all these years later, it was still not clear if anyone had noticed. When the Mississauga Steelheads swept the Petes out of the playoffs, they did it in front of mostly friends, family members, and scouts in their suburban Toronto arena.

The Leafs were resilient, but no empire lasts forever. In order to get new Canadians onto the corporate hockey treadmill, MLSE began using its lower-level hockey team, the Marlies. Working with help from immigration lawyers, the company distributed tickets for some of its American Hockey League games at Ricoh Coliseum. Peddie called it a "market trial device."

Resiliency is not the same as immunity. Peddie suggested *Hockey Night in Canada* was not appointment viewing like it was when he was a child in Southwestern Ontario—his was not even a hockey family, but they still watched the CBC every Saturday night. Now, with hockey available every night on any platform you can name, Saturday night does not have the same pull.

The other warning signs: flatlining participation rates at the grassroots levels of the game, the cost to play, the competition from other sports and activities. The question about whether the Leafs are assured to maintain their local primacy 20 years from now is not quite as easy to answer as it might seem. Evolving tastes and patterns mean that even the Leafs—the biggest brand in the biggest sports company in Canada—might not be able to keep opening the doors and assuming the fans will stream through for eternity.

"So far," Peddie said, "the Leafs are OK. Does that last forever? No. And the belief that it lasts forever is hugely dangerous."

What was his solution?

"Above my pay grade," he said with a smile.

●●●

Two weeks after the Petes traded Ang to Sarnia, Mark Milliere sat down in his north Toronto office to discuss how television helped nudge the evolution of hockey in Canada. He was senior vice-president and general manager at TSN, the first all-sports station on Canadian television.

"What changed is, we started to cover hockey on steroids," he said. "I look back and I go, 'My gosh, the NHL actually owes us a lot of gratitude for us helping grow their game.'"

In 1984, decades before Canadians could watch hockey highlights on their phones while riding the subway, they tuned into a new cable television station. The Sports Network launched with promises of "round-the-clock coverage of professional and amateur sports, 24 hours a day, seven days a week," covering everything from "tennis to tag-team wrestling."

They were the first to treat sports like news, with the dinner-hour highlight show *SportsDesk*. As they grew, they added more hockey programming. In 1998, a rival network was born in Sportsnet. Shortly after that, events such as the NHL trade deadline became all-day theatre, featuring players and pundits and, eventually, a T-shirt cannon to fill the void between trades.

Information was fed into a churning loop. Reporters would break news of a trade, then pundits would debate the merits of the move before the players were interviewed on camera. The growth of internet platforms such as Twitter and Instagram added horse-power to the engine.

Milliere said the volume of conversation the network created around the game, about trades and scores and storylines, helped drive broader interest in the sport. "It spawned another sports net-work, and then another sports network. And now we have five feeds, and they have five feeds. There's sports radio stations that never existed."

In 2013, the NHL thanked TSN for its efforts by awarding full national broadcast rights to its blood rival, Sportsnet, in a deal that obliterated the existing landscape. Sportsnet's parent company, Rogers Communications Inc., agreed to pay the league $5.2-billion over 12 years. It was the largest rights deal in NHL history.

TSN was reduced to regional games, meaning it no longer had the right to carry its games into homes nationwide. The CBC was hollowed out even further, loaning out its iconic *Hockey Night in Canada* brand in exchange for carrying games on its airwaves. The network did not earn any advertising revenue as part of its sublicensing deal with Rogers.

Suddenly, a Canadian sports network was left without any coast-to-coast NHL games. TSN adjusted its programming schedule. It focused on the remaining staples—curling, the Canadian Foot-ball League, and the world junior hockey championship—and it expanded into other areas. There was more NBA; the network carried Major League Soccer games and served as home to the World Cup.

There was still plenty of hockey talk. There were still the panels and the trade deadline shows. But the network continued on, minus a national hockey package, without collapsing in on itself like an aged star.

"I think it's evolving tastes," said Milliere. "If you went back 25 years ago and said, 'OK, you didn't have national hockey' . . . there was no Raptors."

It helped that Canadians were starting to excel in sports other than hockey. Andrew Wiggins and Kia Nurse became part of a wave of young stars in basketball. Milos Raonic and Eugenie Bouchard were household names in tennis. Brooke Henderson was an emerging marquee name in women's golf. Between TSN's other rights deals, Milliere felt like the network was well positioned for the future.

Hockey is still hockey, though. It remains at the top of the media consumption mountain in Canada. And Milliere does not see reason to be concerned with eroding registration rates at the youth level—even if they do not play the game, he said, people will still watch.

"It's not in my line of sight to see that drop in participation, or that stagnant growth, and declining interest in hockey," he said. "Ratings are a funny thing. If Canadian teams are bad, yeah, viewership is bad. If a Canadian team goes on a massive Cup run, or is having a great season, ratings are good."

He recognized some of the pressures, though. TSN helped build the world junior hockey championship into an annual holiday tradition: Canadians celebrate the holidays, then settle in to watch the best teens in the land compete for gold on the international stage. And more often than not, gold was the colour of medal the kids brought home. Canada won five straight titles from 1993 through 1997, and it won five more from 2005 through 2009.

And then Canada hit a dry spell, winning only 2 of the next 10 tournaments and failing to secure even a single medal in 4 of them. Canada was still churning out many of the best players in the world, from Sidney Crosby to Connor McDavid, but other countries were catching up. And some had not just caught up but had potentially passed the Canadians—their nearest neighbours among them.

The United States was producing top-end talent. Auston Matthews, who learned to play on a small sheet of ice in Scottsdale, Arizona, was selected first overall in the 2016 NHL draft. Jack Eichel, another American, went second overall a year earlier. The U.S. was starting to win more often internationally. It was true on the women's side, as well, where the Americans finally broke through with a gold medal win over Canada at the 2018 Winter Olympics in PyeongChang. It was not an aberration—the U.S. had beaten Canada for the gold medal in 8 of the previous 10 world championships.

TSN has long been home to Hockey Canada events. The network signed a 10-year deal to retain that exclusivity through 2024.

"It's not inconceivable that as we continue to go this way, and they kind of go the other way, that they just might start dominating the game of hockey," said Milliere of the U.S. "And once that happens, I really think the bloom comes off the rose for the love of the game. Because it's not our game anymore—we don't win at it anymore. That could be really problematic."

For the time being, those audiences seem safely enormous. In 2017, the network announced that more than 17 million Canadians had tuned in to watch at least part of the world junior gold medal game between Canada and the United States. The following year, 14 million tuned in as Canada beat Sweden for the title.

In 2016, when Russia played Finland for the title, only 2.7 million Canadians tuned in to watch.

●●●

A highway was going to help drive change into Peterborough. They were still finishing the bridge from the 407, which rose above the 115 against a backdrop of open field and possibility. It was not going to magically place the city on the way to anywhere important, but what it could do—and what some business leaders discussed in local media—was turn Peterborough itself into a destination. Families looking to escape soaring real estate costs closer to Toronto could move north. They could flip their city dwelling for a larger home in Peterborough, and with the arrival of the 407, they could commute.

While projections varied, it seemed that within a decade the city could add at least another 10,000 residents.

"Growth in Peterborough has been very slow and steady," said Ken Hetherington, the veteran inside the Peterborough planning department. "Now, I think, everybody is bracing for this to happen. And all of a sudden, we start doubling our unit counts. I don't know if I have staff to be able to take care of a lot of that. It's exciting for the community."

There were already signs of change downtown. An old YMCA building across the street from city hall was being converted into lofts. The developer advertised its "historical charm" and "urban chic," and a report suggested 30 of the 130 units had been reserved more than a year before completion. There was another loft development down the street, closer to the heart of downtown.

More people wanted to live downtown, Hetherington said. And that was important, because "we've been harping on that since I got here."

The Ministry of Natural Resources placed its giant offices downtown. The movie theatre was across the street. An old stretch of aging appliance stores—Hetherington called it "appliance alley" —now had a row of trendy coffee shops. There was talk that, if the

Petes were to get a new arena, they would try to build it on another reclaimed patch of downtown property.

"Your money goes further up here," he said. "You're still in an urban municipality, if you feel like living in an urban municipality. The hospital is brand new. You've got the service-based industry that supports a retirement community. There's a lot of options."

The federal government was also studying a project submitted by VIA Rail, raising the possibility of a renewed rail connection in the Windsor–Quebec City corridor. Within that project was the possibility of commuter rail service between Toronto and Peterborough. Promises of critical public transit were not unique to Peterborough, and nor was the heartbreak when those promises were abandoned.

Stuart Harrison, the president and chief executive of the Peterborough Chamber of Commerce, said the new service "was closer than you think" to finally becoming a reality.

"It's inevitable, with the 407 extension—and if the train thing actually comes about—that we're going to see new people starting to live here," said Mike Watt, who owns three clothing retail stores in the downtown core. "Because we will become one of those commuter cities."

Watt was born in Sarnia but moved to town to study English at Trent University. He was 22 years old when he graduated, and he used the $3,000 he saved working as a DJ to open his first store in 1999. It was not like the other downtown clothing stores, the ones your grandfather might have shopped at to get his shirts, suits, jackets, and underwear all under one roof. This was aimed at teenagers, and it was just across the street from an arts-minded high school.

Nobody in town was selling fashion for them. It was loud and brash and counterculture. And it turned into a hit. Watt, now 43, owned three stores on George Street: Flavour, Plush and Save Our Soles.

"There used to be a stigma, in my industry, to liking sports and liking hockey," he said. "It was, 'Well, if you're a skateboarder, you don't like hockey. And if you're into punk rock, you're not into sports.'"

Watt loved hockey. He played intramural hockey when he was a student at Trent, and he still got out to play on Friday nights in town. The Petes had their own line of merchandise, and they had their own store inside the Memorial Centre. It was mostly the standard fare, with the familiar logo pasted on toques and shirts and expensive replica jerseys. Watt had an idea.

He approached the team about designing a new line of merchandise. It would not necessarily have the team logo blasting across the chest. Shirts would look less like hockey jerseys and more like what he had on display in his store. The Petes were not selling that kind of merchandise—younger fans were not generally going to wear the team's replica jersey to a pub night downtown, or to a music festival, or to class on Monday morning. It became apparent that a deal with Watt might help extend their brand beyond its accepted demographic.

It was agreed that Watt would create and sell the new Petes-themed clothing inside his store. It was displayed prominently at the front, and even that was by design. Grandparents walking past the store could see it and step inside to buy it, and they would never have to walk through the rest of the store, which targeted a specific, younger audience. The young customers, meanwhile, would still see the new merchandise as they walked toward the clothing they had in mind when they dropped by for a visit.

"We wanted to talk to a younger clientele [for the Petes]," said Watt. "Because their voice was not resonating with a younger generation. Ours does."

It was a welcome change in direction for the franchise.

"They haven't had guys at the helm like that in the past," said Watt. "These guys want to see the Petes, the brand, the arena . . . they want to see evolution."

TWELVE

LOST AUDIENCE

Hajni Hos fell in love with a Canadian. She was a lawyer in Budapest, and he was farm-built and handsome, with dark hair and sharp green eyes. Steve Ross was in Hungary as a volunteer working with the Presbyterian Church in Canada, assigned to help impoverished Roma children. She was serving as a local volunteer. She had a reasonable grasp of six languages, but English was not among them.

How did they communicate?

"It was just body language," she said with a laugh.

"It was quite understandable," he said. "Let's say that."

"We knew what everyone wanted," she said, still laughing. "Quite clearly. Quite early."

Ross returned home, but went back overseas for a humanitarian aid project in Ukraine, not far from the border with Hungary. They reconnected, got married, and, in 2006, settled in Canada. They lived at the Ross family's dairy farm in Norwood, a short drive east of Peterborough. Hos went from living in Budapest, a city of more than 1.7 million, to living in rural Central Ontario, sharing a property with 70 sheep. The farm was where she worked on her English—for a while the running joke was how she struggled to pronounce it "horse barn" and not "whores barn."

"When I started to work here and attend board meetings," she said, "my language was very dirty."

Hos was sitting behind her desk in a brightly refurbished space inside St. James United Church, a short walk from the downtown core, on a weekday in September. She was executive director of the New Canadians Centre, a non-profit that had been helping newcomers settle in the region for almost 40 years. The centre helped guide immigrants around hurdles and roadblocks that were often invisible to the locals. Ross was a front-line worker with the centre. He was sitting in a chair by the far wall.

A year earlier, the centre had helped resettle 250 Syrian immigrants in the region. In a typical year, it would work with 800 clients, half of whom were first-time visitors. Clients came from every imaginable background—they were refugees and they were people who had lived in Peterborough for 60 years, realizing as they began edging toward retirement that they only had British citizenship. They were migrant workers and they were engineers who had married a local, trying to figure out what certification they needed to work in Canada.

Hos and Ross worked in an office only 700 metres from the Memorial Centre. And as far as they knew, all of their clients through all of their years shared one notable thread: none of them seemed to develop much of an interest in hockey.

"I don't think you would find too many clients—if you even find one—who plays hockey," said Hos.

"Not in Peterborough," Ross agreed.

"It takes attention away from academics," said Hos.

Academics is the first priority for most refugee families, she said. Even in their own home, she and Ross would have arguments—"or discussions," she said a moment later—over the different expectations they had of the public education system. Parents new to Canada might often wonder if the children had it too easy: "What do you mean, they don't have to memorize the times tables?'"

The distraction from academics was only one barrier to entry.

"You can't afford it," she said. "Especially if you're a newcomer and just trying to start your life here—although we can't generalize, because some newcomers are wealthy—it's not really an affordable thing. It's not like swimming lessons at the Y."

It was a different story from the one Nelson Riis told of growing up as the son of immigrants outside Calgary decades earlier, when there was never a question of whether he would play hockey. That was how he connected with his friends and with his community —it was just what he did, because it was what everyone did.

According to the 2016 census, more than 7,100 of the 79,725 people living in Peterborough were immigrants, and more than half of those were under the age of 24, which would have placed them in prime hockey-playing years. Whatever meaning or connection the game might have had generations earlier, it did not seem to be reaching the new Canadians who walked into the bright, helpful offices in St. James United Church.

"I cannot think of one kid who has entered hockey," said Ross. "Not one."

"For many Canadians, hockey's what you do," said Hos. "But the demands of signing up for hockey, and the trouble that goes with it, it's not worth it."

Sometimes, the Petes approached the centre with large blocks of tickets, 50 to 100 on offer at a time for a free night—a no-strings-attached chance to watch a game and see what it looked like in person. It was an opportunity to see the famous Petes, the team synonymous with the city for hockey fans from Central Ontario to Central America. The rink was a nine-minute walk from the New Canadians Centre. Who could say no?

"To be honest with you—and it's not the Petes' fault—sometimes it's difficult," Ross said with a shrug. "We've had times when we haven't been able to give all those tickets away."

"Free hockey tickets," said Hos.

"Free hockey tickets to a Petes game on a Thursday night," said Ross. "There's a lack of interest, even amongst the young people."

Hos still remembered how Canada looked through the eyes of a new arrival—it was beautiful, she had thought, with its wide-open spaces and crystalline lakes. She also remembered what it felt like, as a trained lawyer from a big city, moving into the heart of all that natural beauty. "I would be home alone, and it would be June, and there would be these eyes in the grass everywhere, and I thought a pack of wolves had come to attack me, to eat me up," she said. "They were fireflies."

Despite her legal training and command of several languages, Hos knew when she decided to move to Canada that she would almost certainly never be able to practise law here, not unless she went through the entire process of law school a second time.

She applied to work at McDonald's. She did not get an interview. A typical immigrant problem, said Hos. "No one is brave enough to take the risk and hire you for your first job in Canada." Finding that first job, she said, is one way a new Canadian can put their own roots down. Having children will plant you deeper; making friends and developing a fluency in the culture will make you feel just that much more at home. They are all important, she said, because there are a thousand examples of signs—invisible to just about anyone born here—to remind someone they are from somewhere else.

Even more than a decade after landing in Peterborough, with a supportive family and a husband with a strong connection to the region, Hos said she still did not feel fully integrated, though the differences seemed subtler now. The fireflies and the language were not as daunting, but she had not conquered everything.

She had never, for one thing, faced anything like Valentine's Day —at least, not as the parent of a young child. One day in the middle of winter, the children came home from daycare with a list of all their tiny classmates' names. "And I was thinking, 'Oh, great —finally, it's mid-year, and they tell us who their classmates are,'" Hos said. "Steve didn't tell me. I had no idea you are supposed to send cards, right? You feel awful."

There were more examples as the children got a bit older. Lunch bags were not part of the daily routine when Hos was growing up in Hungary, because the schools fed the children. When they started going to elementary school outside Peterborough, she was shocked: "What do you mean I have to send them with food? Are you kidding me?

"The first thing you see, as an immigrant in Peterborough, is how beautiful it is—how beautiful the nature is, the river," she said. "Canada is a very developed country. So I think, first, you see very positive things. And then the culture adjustment is a little bit of a shock. If you could choose wherever you could go in the world, Canada is a great place—no matter how white or old people are, they are still quite friendly. There is discrimination and racism— I'm lucky because I'm white, right? I never was living in an African American person's shoes. No one knows I'm an immigrant until I open my mouth."

A couple of months earlier, word filtered back to the centre about an incident on a city bus involving a man and one of the Syrian mothers they had helped to settle. Her children were being loud, as children across the galaxy are known to be, but it was not the volume that made these children different, it was the language: they were speaking loudly in Arabic. And a man stood up and started to yell at them. Someone on the bus called the police, and uniformed officers were waiting at the next stop to remove the belligerent passenger.

"The bus driver came back and said to the mother, 'We are so happy that you are in Peterborough, you are so welcome here, and we are so sorry that this has happened to you,'" said Hos. "It was, again, one person doing something bad. But many others—plus the system—reacting in the positive way."

She had heard another story, from a client who arrived from Somalia. They were waiting for a bus in the middle of winter. It was freezing outside, and as snow began to fall, an older white woman from town walked over to the client to apologize for the Canadian winter. It could get bad, the local said, but you get used to it after a while.

"Our client looked at her," said Hos, "and with her broken English she said: 'Snow is bad, but better than bullets.'"

On November 14, 2015, another incident made national head-lines. The only mosque in Peterborough was set on fire an hour after community members had gathered inside to celebrate a couple who had just had a baby. Police said a substance was placed inside through a broken window and set ablaze. No one was injured, but the damage was estimated to be about $80,000. Prime Minister Justin Trudeau issued a statement saying he was "deeply disturbed" by the targeted arson, and that "Canadian authorities will not abide innocent and peaceful citizens being targeted by acts of vandalism and intolerance."

"You will always have those people in every community," said Hos. "But what was amazing about this mosque fire was that, within 24 hours, there was an online fundraiser. And within 24 hours, they raised $110,000."

"They had to stop it, actually," said Ross, "because it was too much money."

"There will always be the ones who you can't convince," said Hos. "But then there is the reaction, and how the community reacts together."

Peterborough still has a small-town feel, she said. It is not like Toronto, where it takes 100 calls to get anything accomplished, and where local agencies can fight and bicker over tiny details. In Peterborough, especially in times of crisis, people come together to get things done. You can bump into a city councillor at the grocery store, or end up at a table next to the mayor at the Keg outside the Lansdowne Place mall.

Resettling the Syrian refugees was illustrative of that hands-on willingness to help, she said. When the New Canadians Centre announced it would hold a workshop describing how private sponsorship of the refugees would work, they expected about a dozen people to attend. Instead, 100 people did. They advertised another workshop a few months later, this time on how locals could help out with the government-assisted refugees. "And 400 people showed up," said Hos. "We broke every single fire code in the building."

They matched every Syrian family with a group of 10 volunteers. These groups were assembled strategically: each one had a volunteer who had a van they could drive. Each group had someone with kids. Each had a retiree and a doctor. Someone was in charge of being a lead with school and school-related issues. None of the families were ever placed in hotels, like they were in Toronto. People rallied together, she said. Peterborough did it right.

The centre already had plenty of success stories, one of which began decades earlier, when one woman arrived in Peterborough with three young daughters. Her husband had been murdered in 1988 trying to help a relative at Afghanistan's border with Iran. Soriya Basir was a single mother trying to raise a family in a strange new country.

The New Canadians Centre helped the family. Eventually, one of Basir's daughters would spend a year working as an outreach coordinator with the centre. And a few years after that, she would launch a surprise run for mayor. Maryam Monsef began her campaign without a dollar in the coffers 100 days before the election, but she pushed incumbent Daryl Bennett harder than anyone could have predicted. She was a political rookie, a 29-year-old from Trent University. She lost by only 1,331 votes.

Less than a year later, she became the first woman to represent Peterborough-Kawartha as a Member of Parliament. Monsef beat Conservative rival Michael Skinner by more than 5,300 votes. She was named to Justin Trudeau's cabinet.

Hos chuckled again. "So I can brag about how I was the boss of a minister."

It was spring in 1996 when Monsef arrived in Peterborough with her mother and two sisters. They had escaped the Taliban and travelled through Iran, Pakistan, and Jordan before boarding the flight that would finally ferry them to safety. They touched down in Montreal, and it was reported they took a cab all the way into their new town, with the Swedish pop group Ace of Base supplying the soundtrack on the car radio.

Monsef was struck by how fresh the air seemed. The countryside was verdant and the people inside the city seemed to smile more than expected. She could not speak the language, but years later she would say, "It was really a dream, coming here.

"The beauty of the place . . . there's some juxtaposition with how scary it actually is to not be able to communicate with the people who surround you, to not really fit in," she said. "And worse than that, to not know how to fit in."

They spent time in shelters and in a Casa Maria Refugee Home —a non-profit run by the Sisters of St. Joseph of Peterborough and affiliated with the Catholic Church—where all four of them lived in the same room.

Slowly, she started feeling more at home. She learned how to ride a bicycle.

"Girls didn't ride bikes where I came from," she said. "We certainly couldn't find a space big enough where we could try to learn how."

She got a job delivering one of the local newspapers. She learned about Halloween—"We knock on people's doors and they give us candy? For free?"—and she learned the language. She went camping and drank hot chocolate and was taken on a sleigh ride, all in her first year in the country.

Eventually, the four of them moved into their own apartment. Monsef shared a room with one sister—the middle sister, "the organized one"—and started to feel more at home. Slowly, at least.

"What was it like? Challenging," she said. "The age that I came here at, I think, marks the beginning of a series of turbulent years in most people's lives. And that turbulence, for me, was compounded by the fact that I didn't fit in, and I didn't speak the language. And I had a hard time making friends."

What helped ease part of the transition was the network in place to help new Canadians. "The community ensured that we experienced Thanksgiving and Christmas in somebody's home, from that first year onward."

One element was missing from her story as she continued to learn about Canada. Monsef had seen hockey on television, but that was the extent of her early connection to the sport.

"There were a few valiant efforts where people tried to teach me how to skate," she said. "I have vivid and somewhat disturbing memories of me, on skates, very nervous, with little kids holding my hands and helping me."

Even in the early days, though, it was almost impossible to live in Peterborough and not know about the Petes. "No matter what you know or don't know about hockey, when people talk about something enough, you start to ask questions like: 'What is Petes?'" She laughed. "Fortunately," she said, "it's a question that many people were more than happy to answer, with a lot of detail, and with a lot of pride."

●●●

Hajni Hos said her brother had dabbled in hockey as a child growing up in Budapest, but whatever highlights existed of his career had faded into the sands of her memory. Her first real recollections of the game began when she and Steve Ross were still dating: they visited his relatives for Christmas, and they rented one of the local rinks for a family skate. She could barely move. They tried to make her feel welcome, but it quickly became obvious there were limits to their hosting abilities. She missed after they fed her a pass in front of an open net.

She tried to watch hockey on television, but could never quite get a handle on the rules, or even find the puck as it zipped across the surface.

Back in Hungary, a Canadian team visited, and she and Ross went to the game with a group of friends. "Steve told everybody that one reason why Canada is great is because they are really nice people, and if they are better than the other team, they are not destroying them," Hos said. "So after it was 9–0, all the friends were looking at Steve."

Even now, after more than a decade living in the heartland of hockey country, there were parts of the game she did not understand. She would yell during games, but she knew the terms she was yelling were not always the right ones.

"It shocks me how much Canadian ladies, especially rural ladies, doll themselves up for a hockey game," she said. "It's a whole experience. I [would] be so happy, finally, not to wear high heels and makeup, and go in my worst sweater. It's almost like a fashion show."

"These are minor hockey moms," Ross said. "And you can't just go in your sweatpants. You're going to the rink."

Hajni and Steve have two young children, a nine-year-old daughter and a four-year-old son. Their daughter had already given swimming and figure skating a try. A year earlier, they had the option of registering her in an all-girls hockey program, but they hesitated. Friends who had children in hockey seemed to live in the arena all winter. They always seemed exhausted, yelling at each other under the strain of carpools and practices and out-of-town tournaments.

They signed her up anyway. This year was going to be tricky, though: the start time of the weekly practice had been moved to when they usually went to the United Church in town.

"The price is one thing," said Ross. "The fact that you have to tell a parent that hockey is three days a week and oh, by the way, the parents got together at the first meeting and there was a vote: we want to do six tournaments this season. Who can do that?"

"It's like, $10,000," said Hos.

"They have substituted church on Sunday: 'Well, now we go to hockey practice,'" Ross said. "How many families do that? Lots. Sunday morning, that's where they are. And then all through the week. This is their social network. This is their outlet. You have to enter into a culture."

Ross was not unfamiliar with the culture. He started playing hockey when he was six, back when the season started after the annual Norwood Fall Fair, on Thanksgiving weekend. (The fair began in 1868, one year after Confederation but about 36 years after Steve's family first set foot in the area from their home in Scotland.)

They began after the leaves turned, and they were finished by the middle of March. That was just how it was done. Now, Ross said he had heard about local children starting as young as three, and training that began in the last week of August. With the fundraising and the costs and the time needed, the game was feeling increasingly inaccessible.

It was certainly true for the children he worked with through the New Canadians Centre. They would know hockey exists, he said. They would know some of the branding, and some of the more popular symbols and logos. They could identify a stick, but their curiosity did not usually extend much further. "They have literally no interest in it," he said. "Absolutely zero interest in it."

There were plenty of reasons why they were not connecting. If they liked soccer, they could still follow their favourite teams online, and they could easily find their way into a local game. If they were from China and followed badminton, or from India and adored cricket, the distance between their new home and their old home no longer required them to sever those connections.

"You can watch those things on TV," Ross said. "It's not like moving from Denmark in the '50s and not being able to watch your favourite sport from back home. They can watch those things, they can follow it online." At home, Hos manages to stream Hungarian programming.

"If you're coming from Syria, you might know that hockey is a big sport in Canada, but there are lots of sports in Canada," said Ross. "And they might not realize that Ron MacLean is on TV every Saturday night saying, 'Isn't it great to be Canadian? We're worshipping again as Canadians, our religion, our sport.'"

"I often told Steve, if he would have used all his brain cells that he's used for hockey in his life, he could have been a brain surgeon," Hos said. "No, really: it is amazing how much Canadian 40-year-olds know about hockey. It's really part of Canada. Part of your life, right?"

Like many Canadian parents, they were busy people with busy lives. It could be stressful. They had missed three daycare pickups for their son, Hos said. Hockey, with all its demands, did not fit easily into the jigsaw puzzle of their weekly schedule.

"That's the problem right now," she said. "Either it takes over your life, and you have to be able to afford it, or . . . There's no middle."

THIRTEEN

TRYING SOMETHING NEW

Shelbi Kilcollins woke up for work at 7 a.m., only two hours after she'd gone to bed, and she drove down to the Memorial Centre for the most stressful day of her rookie season. She had joined the Petes as an intern that fall, but the game operations manager left for another job, and now Kilcollins was in charge of how a Petes game looked and sounded to fans inside the arena. She'd had more shots of espresso than hours of sleep to prepare for this particular game in March.

"I interviewed for this job a couple of days ago," she said, rushing through the office an hour before the game to cross another item off her to-do list. "I said I was like a Jack Russell. Very eager."

The Petes were not the story, not after a recent 10-game losing streak. This would be the rare night when all attention would be on the front office. The team was scrambling to engineer a pre-game event that no major junior hockey team had attempted in Canada: they were going to host a citizenship ceremony for 40 new Canadians at centre ice just minutes before the puck dropped on a Thursday night game at home against the London Knights.

It was an audacious logistical project for a small staff, but it was important to Burton Lee, the team's business manager. It was something he'd dreamed of trying since he arrived in town five years earlier. Making the game more inclusive, he said, was "probably the most important thing we think about every single day."

Kilcollins was not immediately concerned with the broader symbolic implications of the gesture—she was worried about the famously crusty London coach, Dale Hunter, whose team had finally just pulled up to the arena. Even if everything went according to plan, the ceremony was still going to delay the start of the game by 19 minutes. The Petes were hoping the Knights would watch from their bench rather than wait inside the dressing room. It would be a nice gesture.

Kilcollins dropped off a card and a small bag of chocolates for the surly Hunter and raced away. There were so many moving parts involved, not least of them the clock, which was ticking away. They were expecting 40 new Canadians, but they would not know exactly who would be taking the oath until they signed in that night. Everything had to be accounted for, right down to the colour of the tablecloths—they could not be red, lest it be interpreted as supporting the governing Liberal party, so the tables were covered in black. The Petes staff had rehearsed as much as they could earlier in the day, laying the carpets and tables out on the ice, then snapping photos and creating maps to make the process as smooth as possible when people were in the stands that night.

There was a problem. An official told Lee one of the new citizens was an elderly woman who needed a walker. The plan required her to walk over carpet placed on the ice until she reached her folding seat somewhere by the blue line. If her walker were to catch a seam in the carpet, there was a fear she could end up slipping and hurting herself. The official suggested the woman might need more time than was in the schedule to reach her seat.

"Nobody's going to give us an issue about how long it takes her," Lee said.

Nobody was exactly sure how the crowd would react to the entire event. Peterborough was an exceedingly white town, but it had opened its doors wide to Syrian refugees, and its voters had sent Maryam Monsef to work on their behalf in Ottawa. That did not mean Peterborough was immune to the harshly anti-immigrant undertones amplified when Donald Trump claimed the White House. An alt-right march had been scheduled in September but scrapped in the face of a massive backlash. That did not stop one man from wearing a Nazi-themed shirt through the crowd of anti-racist protesters assembled in a downtown park. One protester was arrested after the Nazi was punched in the head.

It would only take one protester to ruin the ceremony. More than 3,000 fans were expected to be in the stands, and a single person yelling or booing could shift the tenor entirely, turning the team's well-intentioned idea into a video clip racing across social media and into the national news cycle.

Lee was moving around nearly as much as Kilcollins, and sweat beaded on his forehead. He was not nervous—his only real fear was that someone might fall or track dirt onto the ice, which would require a second flood and delay the game another 15 or 20 minutes. He did not think anyone would heckle new Canadians. At least, he hoped nobody would.

"If someone yells," he said with a shrug, "someone yells."

Many of the scouts and other visiting hockey people were positioned three storeys above the ice, eating the complimentary pregame meal in their assigned suite. Kyle Dubas, the rising front office star with the Toronto Maple Leafs, was sitting on his own in the stands. Mark Hunter, his colleague in Toronto, was also in the building. Hunter owned the Knights with his brother, the head coach.

As the Petes put on the finishing touches for the ceremony below, the mood in the suite seemed verging on sour. One scout said they had just driven in from Gatineau, and that the delayed start would increase their risk of getting stuck in the snowstorm bearing down on the area. An older man who lived in the area grumbled about all the time and energy the hockey team was expending on the newcomers. "They don't give a rat's ass about hockey," he said.

A social media account listed under the name of another scout complained to the whole internet: "7:05 start pushed back for 'citizenship' night in Peterborough. One of the most unnecessary pre game ceremonies I've seen. Have to get that good PR though."

A London-based reporter also weighed in on Twitter: "How do you fire up a losing franchise? Well, I can tell you, it's not by having a full on citizenship ceremony like the Peterborough Petes are currently doing."

The Petes, meanwhile, were in the hallway down below, getting ready to head onto the ice. Despite all the losing, there was still a flicker of hope for the playoffs. Peterborough had won two of their last three games. Nick Robertson engaged in one of his pre-game rituals with a teammate—a high-five followed by the motion of tickling fingers and capped with a headbutt.

Just as they were about to head out, a squeaky voice emerged from the sea of young faces gathered by the door.

"Logan," the child called out.

"Yeah?" the captain answered.

"Can you score a goal for me?"

"Sure," he said, a little surprised.

All three coaches, Andrew Verner, Derrick Walser, and Mike Duco, were chatting idly about the longest pre-game ceremonies they had ever seen. Someone mentioned Taylor Hall had a long one in Windsor when the Spitfires retired his number earlier that winter. All three men nodded. Someone else mentioned the Oshawa Generals staging a marathon to honour John Tavares. They all nodded again.

"They'll have a long one for me," Verner said with a wink.

The new Canadians were lining up along the wall farther down the hallway. There were only 39, not the 40 the Petes had been expecting. That just meant one of the grey folding chairs that had been carefully placed on the red carpet would remain empty. A thousand plates were still in the air, and if one of them crashed now, it would make the kind of noise people around town would remember.

"Everybody keeps 'good lucking' me, and it's making me nervous," Kilcollins said, running to attend to her next demand. "I feel like it's the Super Bowl."

Petes staff rolled out the carpet, carefully placed all the chairs, and made sure the black cloth was on the table at the front, right under the scoreboard. There was a flag, and there was a chair for Monsef, the Member of Parliament who had taken the oath of citizenship with her family two decades earlier. It is a beautifully powerful ritual, and one that can evoke matching emotions. Monsef was well aware of that risk as she walked past with a smile: "I'm wearing a lot of mascara."

Kilcollins's bag of chocolates for the visiting coach did not work as hoped—the Knights bench remained empty. Across the ice, where the home team sat, Petes forward Pavel Gogolev looked a little shorter than usual. He was standing on a clearing next to the bench, but he had removed his skates. The 18-year-old was standing in his socks as the ceremony began.

Brian Miller, the veteran trainer, stopped dead in his tracks as he reached the bench from his workshop. "Why's he got no skates on?" he asked, to nobody in particular.

"Russians, eh?" someone answered from the stands.

"We're not going to be on the ice for a half hour," Gogolev said. Miller shook his head.

For the most part, everything was still going according to plan, until the ceremony started. The wireless microphone sounded a bit scratchy, and it was too faint to be heard in sections of the 62-year-old arena. In the concourse above the Petes bench, fans continued to chat and mingle in the beer line. Some watched a television mounted against a wall. A few looked down to the ice as the officials began to speak. The woman in the walker made it to her seat.

Nobody yelled. Nobody heckled. Fans applauded as their newest fellow citizens accepted their certificates and returned to their seats. They waved their tiny Canadian flags. Technology had failed the Petes, but the fans in the stands did not. Monsef addressed everyone seated in chairs on the ice: "Welcome home."

DeNoble skated to centre to complete the ceremony. Austin Osmanski, the defenceman from Western New York, welcomed him back to the bench: "Welcome to Canada, Nobber."

After singing "O Canada," the new Canadians walked off the ice, and arena crews rolled up the carpets and folded the chairs behind them. Lee glanced at his phone to see how badly things had fallen behind schedule. They were only seven minutes off what they had promised.

Up in the box, the scout with the Twitter account remained unimpressed: "Nearly a half hour of moral grandstanding. We're the nicest. We're the most inclusive."

Near the Petes bench, an usher shook his head: "If they wanted to do this, they should have started it at 6:30."

Back in the hallway underneath the stands, John Anderson was smiling, fresh paperwork in his hands and children tugging at his shirt. Born in Ghana, he had moved to Canada 10 years ago after earning a scholarship to study the economics of agriculture at the University of Guelph. He fell in love with a Canadian girl. They got married and settled in Orillia, where they were raising their young son and daughter. This was his first trip to Peterborough but not his first time inside a hockey arena: he'd gone to games at Guelph as a student and had been to see the Maple Leafs at the Air Canada Centre. "Oh," he said with a broad smile, "I love hockey." And he was passing it on: "He's a skater," he said, gesturing to his young son.

Keno Wilson was standing inside an arena for the first time. He had moved to Canada 13 years earlier from Jamaica and had lived in Brampton before relocating to Peterborough. He was a long-haul truck driver who did not get much time off, but he lived on Charlotte Street, a dozen blocks north of the Memorial Centre. "Who knows?" he said. "Maybe I'll come to a hockey game after this." A dozen people walked right out the front door of the arena after the ceremony, but he was planning to stay.

As Wilson left for his seat, a young family of four was trying to build consensus over what to do. The carpets were rolled and stacked, and the chairs stowed. The Petes and the Knights were getting ready for the opening faceoff. The father asked the young boy if he wanted to watch the game.

"I don't want to watch," the young boy said, shaking his head. "I want to play."

Steve Nicholls, the team's season ticket coordinator, arrived before the final verdict was delivered. He told them he had four really good seats, close to the action. "Better than what everyone else has."

Nicholls darted back into the Petes office and reappeared a moment later. He led the family down to a section of seats in the lower bowl, below the portrait of the Queen and below where a handful of long-time hockey people were grumbling about all the fuss over inviting new Canadians into the arena.

Mike Oke was staying to watch the game, though not for the same reason most of the team's fans were still watching. Only eight teams from the OHL's Eastern Conference would make the playoffs, and the Petes were in ninth place. They had nine games left to play, and they were nine points out of a post-season berth. It was possible they could sneak in, but the math was not on their side.

"We basically have to win out," Oke said. "It's not going to happen."

It was still hard to digest. Six months earlier, making the playoffs hadn't even been a question. How had the season turned so dramatically? Back in September and October, everything was falling into place as if by cosmic design. All the players they expected to return from the previous season had done just that, and an unexpected gift arrived two weeks into the season, when Nikita Korostelev came back after failing to land a professional contract in the American Hockey League.

Nobody expected that Oke would have to fire his head coach. Oke respected Hull and valued him as a long-time colleague, and the firing wore on him. He had to admit defeat on the season three days later, when he traded Ang. It was getting hard to ignore what they were saying about him on social media. He tried to do as much as he could, but there were limits. Players had no-trade clauses. He could not move anyone he wanted, anytime he wanted. Most of these players were still only teenagers.

The Petes scored first after the ceremony, but as had too often been the case, they ceded the ground they had gained. The Knights scored second. DeNoble made good on his impromptu pre-game promise and scored in the second period. The Knights scored again to tie. DeNoble scored again in the third, but the Petes could not hold on. They held the lead three times, and all three times, they let it slip away.

It was tied 3–3 late in the third period when Knights forward Alex Formenton collected a pass inside his own blue line. He peeled away from Robertson and coasted past a half-hearted poke-check from winger Adam Timleck. Formenton was approaching top speed as he crossed the neutral zone along the right boards. He blasted past Declan Chisholm and sliced in toward the net. Chisholm was the team's quickest defenceman, but he was suddenly skating with sand on his blades. Alex Black assumed Chisholm would make the play and did not get over to help until it was too late. Formenton swooped in front of Wells and plopped the puck into the net like a piece of mail.

He beat all five players on the ice, and he broke the Petes. Sitting in the suite high above the south end of the ice, Oke watched the last three minutes melt off the clock. He leaned his chin on his left hand as he idly pawed the screen of his mobile phone with his right. There was nothing more he could do this season. It was the first time London had led all night, and everyone in the arena seemed to know it would last. They were right. The Petes lost 4–3.

There was no yelling as players left the ice after the game. Nobody had it left in him to break a stick or slam a door. They filed past the fans quickly, and with their heads down. A little girl with a flower fixed into her dark hair did her best to cheer them up.

"Good try."

"Good try, Dylan."

"You can't win every game."

Nobody broke stride, and nobody smiled.

"That was depression," Verner said, a few minutes later. "They felt like they had that game."

There was a ready-made excuse, if he wanted to use it. The Petes spent a half hour moored to the bench before the game, while the Knights relaxed in the relative comfort of their dressing room. It would have been easy for a coach of a losing team, now into the final weeks of his contract, to blame something out of his control. Other coaches have blamed lesser events with less on the line.

Verner, the goaltender who had seen the world through a life in hockey, was not one of those coaches. "It's a long ceremony, undoubtedly, and we knew that going in," he said. "But I was ready. If anyone had complained, I was certainly ready to ask where their grandparents came from. Because there's a good chance they came from Scotland or Ireland or England or Italy."

A win would have been helpful, to say the least, but the ceremony was important, too.

"I have been all over the world, and I'm proud to call Canada home," the coach said. "Most of those people on the ice tonight probably know quite a bit more about Canada than a lot of the guys around here."

FOURTEEN

INTO THE ABYSS

On the night of the last gasp, only a half dozen scouts bothered to show up to the big suite three storeys above the ice. There was only one playoff spot left in the Eastern Conference, and the Petes were 11 points out with six games to play. If they lost, they were out. If they tied, they were out. If the team they were trying to catch won any of their six remaining games, the Petes were out.

They were chasing the Mississauga Steelheads, the same team that had swept them clean out of the playoffs the previous spring. The Steelheads happened to be visiting the Memorial Centre that night, but if there was a grudge, not many hockey people seemed interested in watching it unfold. Up on the bulletin board above the coffeemakers, where newspaper clippings were pinned and removed with regularity early in the fall, the most recent notice was from late October. A page had also been torn out of game program from November, celebrating a new design on the team's bus. The last time anyone had posted the standings on the board, the Petes were still in fourth place. They now sat 9th out of 10 teams.

"Only five games left," one of the front office workers said wearily, already looking past tonight's elimination game. "Only five games to go."

Mike Oke was in the box. The burden on his shoulders had not eased. The team had not named a permanent replacement for interim head coach Andrew Verner. On the surface, there was no rush to stencil a new name over Jody Hull's old office door. If the Petes lost to the Steelheads, it would be another six months before they had to play a meaningful game. There was a risk in waiting, though, especially if the job sat vacant through the OHL draft. Agents and parents would want to know who was in charge before they sent their teenagers up to Peterborough. If a draft pick did not like the direction a team was taking, he could refuse to report. It was possible the Petes could lose him to the NCAA.

There was also frustration in the fanbase. It had been simmering, and some had finally bubbled out of social media and into real life. Steve Nicholls fielded a call from a season ticket holder upset with how the team was performing. Nicholls, the part-time teacher, suggested the man go straight to the source.

He said he should call Oke.

So the man called, and Oke picked up.

"I was expecting to leave you a message," the man said, flustered. "I'm not really prepared to talk."

The two men started discussing the season. The caller was unhappy about some of the moves Oke had made earlier on; he wanted to know why the Petes had traded a useful veteran like forward Tyler Rollo to London to make room for Nikita Korostelev, another over-age player.

Oke pointed out that Korostelev was leading the team in scoring, and by quite a large margin.

The man was also upset Oke had not made more moves at the trade deadline, once it became clear this was not the team to mount a charge deep into the OHL playoffs. Oke told the man that junior hockey players can have no-trade clauses in their contracts—Jonathan Ang, the one player they managed to ship out, had to be talked into accepting the move.

"You're saying we can't get guys into Peterborough," Oke said. "And I mean, geez, we can't get them to leave."

Eventually, the man pledged to renew his tickets.

Around the arena, the suffering took many forms. Barb Wells often seemed to be approaching a form of physical agony when her son, Dylan, was in net down below. Every time an opposing player wound up to shoot, an invisible switch sent a pulse of electricity to her seat. Where Dylan's father chewed gum or sipped coffee, his mother jolted forward, sideways or backward, depending on the play. She had been a goalie parent for more than a decade, and it looked excruciating. She'd heard about what had happened in Oshawa a few months earlier, how her beautiful, blue-eyed little boy got angry after that game and smashed his stick into the concrete wall outside the dressing room. She did not say how she knew.

"I heard," she said with a smile. "I hear things."

And?

"He got an earful after that one," Barb said. "Because I just don't approve of that."

If you need to vent, make sure you do it out of view. Find a quiet spot and scream and yell and punch a wall. Especially now, in the OHL, you never explode in front of the fans. Even with an older crowd like the one in Peterborough, there are always children around. She still believed in those values, even after a season like her son was being put through this year.

Dylan Wells arrived at training camp with one of the busiest winter itineraries in town. He was a 20-year-old with an NHL contract and a real shot at making Canada's world junior team. Of all the players on the roster, he seemed like the surest bet to ascend. One day, his name was going to move from local cable access broadcasts to national television.

Instead, the Peterborough defence left him on stage by himself. Only one other goaltender in the league would end up facing as many shots as Wells, and only one other was going to let in more goals. The league does not publicly disclose more detailed statistics, but if it did, the goaltender from Peterborough might have won the title for most short-handed breakaways saved in a single season.

Barb and Rob Wells saw many of those in person, having made the three-hour drive around the elbow of Lake Ontario and up into Central Ontario. They drove through the blowing snow, the ice, the sleet, and the rain.

"It's this season," Barb said with a shrug. "It's been an awful, horrible season. You've just got to let it go. You know what? It's over, it's done."

There were still no easy answers about the cause of those struggles.

"When they were winning, they sucked," she said. "It was just, they sucked less than everybody else."

It wasn't just the biological parents who suffered. More than any other sport, junior hockey relies on a network of adults to open their homes to the children of strangers during the season. They are known as billets, or billet families. Sometimes, they are known by another term: landparents.

In Peterborough, prospective landparents are required to undergo a criminal background check. General manager Mike Oke also visits the home. Once they are approved to host a player, they are asked to treat their unfamiliar teenager "like any other member" of the family. Landparents are required to provide a smoke-free home with a bed and a "good mattress," as well as a private desk for homework. They are also enlisted to help enforce curfew and make sure the players meet expectations in school.

For all that, they get two season tickets and a weekly stipend of $85 for each player they house.

"You don't do it for the money," said Tracy Adamo, who was billet mom to forward Adam Timleck and rookie goaltender Hunter Jones.

As a 17-year-old, Jones was listed at 6-foot-3 and 195 pounds. It stood to reason that $85 a week might not cover the cost of groceries. It might not have covered the cost of his breakfast for a week, let alone three full meals and snacks every day.

"My kitchen is never closed," Adamo said. "It's just non-stop. They're cooking in there all the time. And I always say to them: 'The kitchen is open, all hours of the night. You want to eat? You go right ahead. It doesn't bother me—but just clean up after yourself.'

"If you don't clean up after yourself, then we're going to have a problem. Oh my gosh."

Adamo grew up in Sault Ste. Marie, where her father was an assistant coach with the Greyhounds. Her sons were toddlers when the family settled in Peterborough. They were 22 and 21 now, and neither had a living memory of a winter spent without a Petes player living in their home.

"You're their mother," she said. "You're their away mother."

"They become a part of you," said Julia Tanner, who had been landmother to defenceman Matthew Timms for the past four winters.

Tanner was a registered nurse who lived just outside of town, and she had been a billet for more than a decade. She had a different Petes jersey for every night of the week. She had accumulated so many, in fact, she could have worn a different one to more than half of the team's home games. Her father started taking her to the Memorial Centre when she was seven or eight years old. She went to the same high school as Brent Tully, the Petes defenceman—they had homeroom together. He was taken by Vancouver in the fourth round of the NHL draft but never played a game with the team, and, after a career in Europe, he returned to Peterborough.

Tanner and her husband had season tickets before they were married. They became billets after a night shift in the delivery room. Dr. Bob Neville, the long-time Petes board member, was working that night, and he knew she loved hockey. He said the team was looking for billets. She said she was intrigued. She got a call from the team at 10 a.m. the next morning, and her first billet walked in the door a few days later.

"I love hockey," she said. "So I love the fact that these kids are playing because they want to make it to the next level. And I love the fact they're not here to get paid millions of dollars—they're here trying to make it. And it's so hard to make it."

Tanner loved having the boys hang out at the house. She loved watching them walk into town as baby-faced teens and leave as young men—as family.

She drove down to watch the Petes in Michigan. Timms lived with her longer than any of the other billets she had housed over the years. At a concession stand in Flint, she found herself in line with Timms's father, who told her she was the best billet in the history of all billets. She smiled at that one.

"Because I spoil them," she said. "I spoil them rotten." If a player likes chocolate chip cookies, she'll make them cookies. If they like muffins, she'll make a fresh batch. If they like a snack, or a certain brand of soda pop, she'll keep it in store.

Still, she said, they don't change up their routines all that much. "They eat what we eat. Right now, just as an example, Matt Timms loves this cheese sauce I make to put on broccoli. And he freaks out every time I make it." The broccoli might be the exception. "I wouldn't do it if it was just for my husband and I."

It had been a difficult season for everyone, but Timms seemed to have some of the worst luck. He hurt his shoulder in game three of Peterborough's first-round sweep of the IceDogs the previous year, and it turned out to be a stubborn injury, following him through most of the summer. His foot injury at the team barbecue happened in September, as the team was gearing up for its run at first place. He came back just as the season started to fall apart.

In some respects, the landparents had a better view than the other adults around the team of what was going wrong this season. When the kids got together to play cards, it was in their homes. When they hung out or played video games, it was often under the landparents' rooves.

"It started off great," Adamo said. "Everybody was on the same page, and gung-ho."

The injuries did not help, she said, but you can only use that excuse for so long. From her vantage point, the issue was team unity.

"The guys, they tell you: there's no closeness," she said. "There's no closeness."

She said that feeling had been building for the last three or four years. A decade ago, the boys all had a sense of common purpose. One night, when a teammate was shipped to a team in the other conference, they did more than just send a text: they all came over to the house.

"You looked outside," Adamo said, "and there they were, all in a group, hugging, saying goodbye to each other. It was the most surreal thing."

That was seven or eight years ago, and that team had all remained friends. It was not the same today. Nobody gathered on a front lawn when Ang was traded to Sarnia. The last few teams had seemed divided into cliques. A few of the billet moms had raised the concern with management before the playoff run, but the team was winning, which helped to mask the issue. It was laid bare this year, when the team folded immediately at the first signs of adversity.

It even affected the team's famous Tuesday movie night, which was seen as a means of bonding, of preventing cliques from forming. The tradition had withered, Adamo said.

She shook her head. "This was supposed to be the year."

With hope gone, all that was left now was the blame. Some of it was attached to Jody Hull through his dismissal. The rest would be assigned later, possibly over the summer, through sober reflection. For the time being, the team was no longer searching for a spark. It was just trying to find the energy to limp to the end of the season.

The Petes had two days to recover from their loss to London before heading to Erie for a game against the Otters. DeNoble gave Peterborough a 1–0 lead 45 seconds into the first, which seemed to get them moving. They fell behind by a goal early in the third period, trailing 4–3, but it was close. They still had a shot. Winning a game on the road would be a welcome moral victory.

Peterborough took a penalty and conceded a power-play goal. It was difficult to catch on the television replays, but as the puck crossed the line, the soul of every Peterborough player left their mortal frames and went to wait on the bus. Erie beat backup Hunter Jones three times in 29 seconds. The Petes turned a 4–3 game into a 9–3 blowout loss.

They had to play the very next night, back across the border in St. Catharines. It was the arena where the Petes had capped their first-round playoff sweep 12 months earlier, having brushed the IceDogs right out of their series without breaking a sweat. Peterborough outscored Niagara 21–10 over those four games. Wells was stellar in the only close one, helping the Petes win in overtime.

On one hand, it had only been a year. On the other, that year sometimes felt like the longest decade of their lives. This time, the Petes lost to the IceDogs, extending one of the franchise records no one wanted to set in the first place: it was the team's 18th straight loss on the road. By the time the season was over, that number would be 20.

A light snow dusted empty parking spaces outside the Memorial Centre before the elimination game against the Steelheads. It was the second-last Thursday game on the schedule, and despite the early-March chill, it was starting to feel like the last days before summer vacation. The Petes spent the winter progressing through the five stages of grief, and there was a quiet sense that everyone had followed Oke down the path to acceptance. Players still had incentives to perform—from NHL aspirations down to personal pride—but for the team, dreams melted long before the spring thaw.

Even the basics seemed to be a challenge now. The official was ready to drop the puck after the anthem, until someone spotted the Steelheads goaltender waving his glove over his head. The lights had not come on above his net. It was also dark at the other end of the ice, around Wells.

On-ice officials delayed the faceoff while the arena staff fiddled with the lights. On television, the broadcast crew chuckled and suggested the old barn might be to blame. For a moment, all the lights went dark and the arena was thrust into blackness. Then only some lights came back online. They tried again. It took them another minute before it was bright enough inside to meet OHL standards. The crowd cheered.

Mississauga scored first, but quickly ceded control of the game to Korostelev, the Russian winger who would be looking for work in a matter of days if the Petes missed the playoffs. There were moments it seemed obvious he would become a fixture at the next level. His patience with the puck, and his ability to make it move wherever he wanted, could make him look like a glitch in a video game. Nobody else could do the things he could do in tight spaces. It was understood that, if he ever improved his skating, he would be terrifying, rather than merely frightening.

He scored twice and assisted on another goal from Semyon Der-Arguchintsev, giving the Petes a 3–1 lead. On another team, in another year, that offensive spark would have jump-started the machine. The Petes were at home, after all, playing in front of their fans and friends and parents, with everything at stake. If they lost now, the last nine days of the season—four practices and five games—would be stripped of all meaning, a season-ending streak of exhibition games.

The Petes gave a goal back, but scored another. They led 4–2 after the first period, and 6–5 heading into the third. It was not until Mississauga scored its sixth goal that the Memorial Centre fans finally offered their commentary on the season. The intermission flood was not fully frozen when the Steelheads broke across the blue line. The Petes were scrambling. Defenceman Austin Osmanski froze in front of Wells, dropping down to block a shot instead of covering the Mississauga forward standing by himself by the far post. With Osmanski standing in his way, Wells's view of the pass was obstructed. Ryan McLeod had enough time to send an email before he tapped the pass into the open net to tie the game.

In the stands, fans booed loud enough to be heard.

Nobody needed to read the script after that goal—everyone knew how it was going to end. Mississauga scored again to take a

7–6 lead but gave Peterborough a chance to tie the game with a power-play later in the third. The Petes had their second unit on the ice when Osmanski missed the net with a high wrist shot. Rookie forward Pavel Gogolev was playing at the other point, and he misjudged the bounce off the end boards. He was playing too deep in the zone and got caught as the Steelheads raced away on a two-on-one. Osmanski backpedalled, then dropped down to his stomach to cut off a pass. It did not work: the pass got through, and Wells could not get over in time to stop the shot.

Wells looked toward the bench for a long time after the goal. It was a short-handed goal, the same kind that had beaten the Petes all year. This time, it helped to knock them out of the playoffs. Peterborough fell 8–7 at home. It was over.

It was a fitting microcosm of the season, Verner thought: a good start, a bad middle, and an indifferent end. He addressed reporters inside the same dressing room where Hull used to speak after games, and he made many of the same points his predecessor had made before he was fired. Coaches walked players through what they needed to do. They gave them assignments. And those assignments were either blown or ignored.

In the alternate universe of early October, when the Petes held first place in the conference, the players would have been looking forward to spending the final week of the season getting ready for the playoffs. Instead, they would be in uncomfortable meetings with the coaching staff after practice.

Verner had a list of questions he planned to ask returning players. Where did they expect to be playing next season? What kind of playing time did they have in mind? What level did they want to reach by the end of their careers?

"Do you think you have a spot on this team next year?" Verner would also ask them. "Be careful."

FIFTEEN

SAVING THE GAME

There was a pond back in the woods, behind her aunt and uncle's farm in Cavan, just west of Peterborough, where Cassie Campbell-Pascall learned both how to skate and how to fend for herself on the ice. She was one of the youngest cousins—sometimes the youngest by more than a decade—and she got to test herself when the family gathered for Christmas.

"That's probably where I learned how to be a pretty good player," she said, "because I played with all the older boy-cousins."

That was a benefit. But there were also drawbacks. The youngest was the one the older cousins sent back to the house for food when everyone started getting hungry. Campbell-Pascall's task was to run back through the woods to the house, where her aunt would have a pack waiting for her with fresh supplies. It was an easy job. The older cousins probably suspected as much, so they added a wrinkle: "They used to tell me that this old man, who lived in the chicken coop, hated little girls.

"I used to run by that chicken coop as fast as I could," she said. "Because I thought this old man was going to get me."

She laughed, now.

"Oh my god," she said, "my cousins were so mean."

Campbell-Pascall avoided the imaginary old man long enough to become one of the foremost pioneers of Canadian women's hockey. She was a star on the Canadian roster when the women's game made its Olympic debut in Nagano, in 1998. She was captain for the next two Olympics, ending her career with back-to-back gold medals after wins in Salt Lake City and Turin.

She built on the foundation set by forerunners such as Fran Rider and Angela James and became one of the first household names in Canada's women's game. Campbell-Pascall joined *Hockey Night in Canada*, becoming the first woman to work as a colour analyst. She helped guide the Canadian Women's Hockey League as a governor. They named a community centre after her in her hometown of Brampton, a suburb northwest of Toronto. Hockey had taken her around the world from that frozen pond in Cavan, but it did not prepare her for her next phase in the game.

Campbell-Pascall, acknowledged Canadian hockey legend, was now a Canadian hockey parent.

Her daughter, Brooke, played organized hockey for the first time in 2017. She was seven years old, and she had clearly inherited the hockey genes. Her father, Brad Pascall, was a former Buffalo Sabres draft pick who worked for Hockey Canada before joining the Calgary Flames as assistant general manager. There are hockey families, and there are hockey families that could be on a postcard. Brooke was growing up in the portrait of a Canadian hockey family.

At the end of the season, Brooke was offered a spot on a spring hockey team in Calgary. Her mother's initial reaction was to decline, but first she emailed her husband, who confirmed her gut feeling. They declined the spot.

"Everyone kind of looked at me like, 'What? You're not interested? Like, what are you doing?'" she said. "And I'm like, 'Nope —she's moving on to soccer, and we've got piano.'"

Brooke was going to spend her spring away from the rink.

"It wasn't so much the parents on the team, but I think the association was just, like, 'What?'" she said. "I think we just need more people to step up . . . It's not professional hockey. It's minor hockey. It's minor sports. And I think we're getting the two confused a lot lately."

Campbell-Pascall remembered hockey being fun. She remembered the tournament her team played in Peterborough, but only for what happened in the hotel, when they all played mini-sticks in the hall and spent every other waking moment in the pool. When the hockey season ended, it was time for soccer.

There was no industry built around the kids like there is now. Campbell-Pascall had heard of teams in Ontario—and she was sure it happened in other provinces—where parents paid the coach a six-figure salary and travelled to tournaments every other weekend. It got to the point where one child's minor hockey team ate up most of a parent's entire salary. Pressure replaced fun. With all that money on the table, the goal was not the game: it was getting to the highest possible level in the game.

"Then you've got all these experts outside the associations who are making money off our children," said Campbell-Pascall. "There's so much pressure to do all these things for parents now. I've just scratched the surface, and I'm sure my time will come. But she's really got to tell me that this is what she wants to do, right? It's still about fun for her, and if it's something she loves and something she wants to do.

"It's tough out there for parents."

●●●

On a rainy June afternoon in 2017, Tom Renney, Hockey Canada's highest-ranking executive, was talking about the threats to hockey's supremacy within the country. It was not just the cost, nor the competition from other sports, he had told a news conference: it was the lure of a sedentary lifestyle, and of video games.

"We have to understand that minor hockey associations, through the volunteers across the country, are working very hard at making the rink—whatever it looks like, wherever it might be—a destination," Renney said later. "We are in the experience industry. And the hockey experience, at least for us, has to supersede any other, in terms of activity."

Canada was changing, he said. Minor hockey executives were going to have to find a way to make the game more appealing to new Canadians. They would have to knock holes through the barriers that had been allowed to grow around the game, pushed skyward by the tectonic plates of money and ambition.

Hockey was going to have to find Canadians, rather than the other way around.

"People identify with Canada through the game of hockey," he said. "We can never take that for granted. We can never think that we've arrived."

Hockey Canada was rolling out a program he believed would remove some of the barriers facing young players. The Initiation Program—also known as IP, for short—was designed to change how children were introduced to the game. It had been on the books for decades, and versions of it had already been implemented elsewhere in the hockey-playing world, but it was finally being mandated in Canada.

It revolved around one basic concept: match the size of the ice to the size of the players. Children did not sit in adult-sized chairs at adult-sized desks when they went to school, the thinking went, so why were they being asked to play on an adult-sized sheet of ice?

From now on, children entering the system would play on a smaller sheet. A five-year-old would play from sideboard to sideboard, rather than end to end. Their ice would be chopped into thirds, creating enough space for two games—one at each end—and room for drills and water breaks in the middle, by the team benches. The adult-sized ice would effectively be turned into three miniature rinks.

Studies had shown the compacted games allowed children to touch the puck more often, which made them feel more engaged in the play. The children made more passes and attempted more shots. That meant the goaltenders also benefited, because they would face more shots, rather than standing alone at one end of the ice, waiting for the miniature herd to migrate back toward them. It was not a regular game, but the evidence was overwhelming. It made sense.

Splitting the ice into thirds would also allow coaches to divide their teams into tiers. Players who had advanced quickly would be able to play against other advanced players. On the adult-sized sheet, they would normally be able to pick up the puck and race toward the net in a straight line. With the smaller ice, they would have to work on their lateral mobility and improve their decision-making processes. It would force them to use their head start as a base upon which to build, rather than coasting on it during games.

Children who were slower to develop, or who were still taking their first steps into organized hockey, would be able to play against other beginners. Rather than watching faster children race around them for an hour, they would have the chance to touch the puck, to make plays and become more a part of the game. They would be more engaged, and more likely to stay in the sport.

Development was being prioritized above competition. The scoreboard was being de-emphasized. It was how they were doing it in parts of Europe, especially in Sweden, where children under the age of 13 played in leagues where standings and personal statistics were not kept. Based on population and participation statistics, those countries were already outperforming Canada in some areas of minor hockey development.

As the children progressed through the program, the size of the ice would get bigger. By the time they were seven, for example, they would be playing half-ice, rather than cross-ice. Eventually, they would take the skills they learned on the modified ice to the full sheet. Renney believed more players would reach that point in part because the children who developed at their own pace would be encouraged to remain in the game for longer. They would not leave for another sport, because hockey would be too much fun to leave behind.

Moving children into games on smaller ice surfaces was not a revelatory idea. Some minor hockey associations had already adopted it, while others ignored it altogether. The political structure of minor hockey in Canada meant that it was possible for a four-year-old in Saskatchewan to play cross-ice games while a child across the border in Alberta was still playing full-ice games.

Hockey Canada finally decided to mandate its program across the country in 2017. Effective that fall, every child born in 2011 or later would be required to follow the prescribed progressions up the ladder. They would start by playing cross-ice, graduate to half-ice, and finally move into the full-ice games around their 10th birthday. The rule would be enforced across each of Hockey Canada's 13 member branches.

"Make the experience what it's supposed to be in the first place," said Renney. "If we understand why we do this—if we really ask ourselves that question—we'll understand why we should."

Eventually, Renney wanted to extend the program through novice and atom and into peewee, when the players were approaching their teens. That was the sweet spot, he said. That was the age when a child developed the sporting tastes that would follow them for a lifetime. Encouraging participation was the key, he said: "Not to be an NHLer, but to play hockey."

The question now was: Would Canadians embrace changes to the way their children played hockey?

●●●

Despite widespread (though not yet universal) acceptance, the idea had faced years of resistance from pockets around the country. In August 2017, months after Hockey Canada mandated its cross-ice plans, a group of 30 minor hockey association executives in Toronto wrote a letter to Renney. They asked that the mandate be deferred for a year.

Local associations said they had not received enough guidance to properly prepare for a season of modified ice, and that they could not comply with the mandate. And if they could not comply, they would not be able to offer the select-level programming to the children. Hundreds of five-, six-, and seven-year-old players would see their season cancelled.

These children were registered for teams in the North York Hockey League (NYHL), a decades-old organization that provided players a level of hockey over and above their house league teams. Its executives made their case: they said Hockey Canada's requirements were "rolled out with inadequate communication, transition times, education tools for parents/public/volunteers, financial support for new equipment such as ice barriers, and an overall lack of training/support." They said they needed more time to get their arenas and their staff ready for cross-ice. If they were not granted a deferral, the season would be lost.

The Initiation Program was already up and running in many cities, and some rolled their eyes when the uprising in Toronto crept into the news cycle. It's the city every other Canadian city loves to hate—perhaps the rebellion should have been expected. Of course Toronto would claim special status. Only in Toronto would minor hockey associations think they were any different than anyone else in the country.

It was still a difficult position for Hockey Canada. More children played hockey in Ontario than in any of the other member branches, and the Greater Toronto Area was the largest, richest part of that branch. A deferral for Toronto could raise hackles elsewhere. On the other hand, if Hockey Canada held firm and declined the requested deferral, there were whispers some parents would take legal action. This was all for children who were only a year or two into elementary school. They were still learning to read.

Renney pledged to convene a meeting, but nothing more.

The minor hockey executives were called to a lecture hall at the University of Guelph-Humber campus in the second week of September. It was still warm outside, and the room filled quickly, making the air heavy and stale. Officials from the top three levels of hockey government were down at the front, with Hockey Canada, the Ontario Hockey Federation, and the Greater Toronto Hockey League all represented.

Many of the executives wore clothing from their respective minor hockey associations, lending a burst of colour to the room. The mood did not match the palette, though. They were expecting to discuss the specifics of a one-year deferral on cross-ice hockey at the select level. Hockey Canada had other ideas.

Renney, it turned out, had not made the trip to Toronto. Instead, he was piped into the lecture hall via speakerphone.

"The concern I have is that you, as the leading MHAs, have not recognized the virtues of IP and cross-ice hockey to the point where we could have maybe avoided tonight had we been better informed, possibly?" Renney said, his voice rising on the final syllable. "Or recognized the value of it, maybe?

Maybe, maybe not. In their letter to him, the other executives had in fact pledged to implement the cross-ice program after the one-year deferral, though it was clear that not everyone in the room embraced the concept. Two executives from an association in the west end of the city shook their heads and overtly passed notes as Renney spoke.

Change was not easy, he said, especially against the strong tide of the game's history in Canada. But it was crucial that changes be made to the way children were introduced to the game. Hockey was losing ground in Canada.

"This is not about getting as many kids to the National Hockey League," Renney said. "This is not about getting kids to NCAA schools or the CHL. We are in the experience industry. The bottom line is that the experience is controlled, the environment is controlled—and the environment is enhanced—by adults."

He was speaking without stopping. The focus of minor hockey had to be on the children, he said, and not their parents. There was empirical evidence to show cross-ice hockey was better for young children. On the anecdotal side, it was simply more fun.

"If we're not careful, we're going to coach five- and six-year-olds out of the game, because it's been hot-housed and they've had to drink the game from a firehose as opposed to identifying with the skills—cognitive, physiological, and emotional skills—to play the game," Renney said. "I would suggest to you that the game is not an endurance test."

As he continued, it became clear in the room the meeting was not going to be a discussion about the merits of the plan—it was a lecture.

"We have to understand: Are we actually improving the situation? Or are we an impediment because we're satisfied with where things are, we're afraid of change, or we think that we've got the answer as it is," Renney said. "This has been mandated across the country for a reason. I support it completely."

He thanked everyone again, then disconnected without taking questions.

But there were still plenty of questions. When Hockey Canada announced its mandate in January 2017, it had pledged to get the details of rule changes and other guidelines into the hands of volunteers on the ground. That ended up not being the case. Word about the modified ice program was issued through a news release posted on the Hockey Canada website, along with stories placed in mainstream media outlets. From there, it went to the 13 branches —including the Ontario Hockey Federation—and was supposed to be disseminated down to the regional bodies.

It was the same leaky delivery system that sought to give Maple Leafs tickets to children who wrote a 100-word essay outlining their love for hockey and received only three entries, because the announcement had reached only a fraction of the hockey-playing population. Now it felt as if regional administrators were risking sanctions for refusing to adopt a system whose contours had never been properly explained.

Phillip McKee, the executive director of the Ontario Hockey Federation, was the meeting's emcee. After Renney disconnected,

McKee introduced another speaker at the front of the room. Stephen Norris had intense eyes, a shaved head, and an English accent. He was a sports scientist who worked as a consultant with Hockey Canada, and he had flown into Toronto from Calgary on short notice for the meeting.

It turned out that he, like Renney, was not here to discuss the specifics of implementing the Initiation Program.

Norris wanted to make sure every executive in that room fully understood the importance of changing how Canadians coached the game to their children. He lectured on the physiology of young players, and how they develop at different speeds on and off the ice. He offered tips on how coaches could maximize their ice time, and he bemoaned the focus on games and results over practice and development.

"Even with just two lines, they're sitting on the bench 50 per cent of the time," he said. "You turn up for an hour, and how long are you sitting on the bench?"

Occasionally, he would throw out a statistic designed to shock the audience. Canadians used to comprise about 98 per cent of the players on NHL rosters, he said, but in the span of 25 years that number had dropped below 51 per cent. He gave the number a moment to breathe before he continued.

"This is disgraceful," he told the room, animated but not angry. "If we were the board of directors of PepsiCo, we would all be fired. The entire community."

The two men from the west-end minor hockey association who'd been passing notes during Renney's call grumbled.

"And I remind all of us in this room: you don't really want to be a child's last age-group coach, do you?" he said. "What a sad indictment that is."

Norris asked the audience to imagine the Canadian hockey system as a pyramid. The children formed the base, with hundreds of thousands of young hockey players serving as the bedrock for every level above. The NHL players were at the top. With fewer children playing hockey, the base was beginning to shrink, which lowered the pyramid's peak.

Inertia was partly to blame, he said. Coaches were not upgrading their skills and techniques. They were not using the information he said Hockey Canada had placed "at their fingertips."

"And all around us, the rest of the world is marching on," he said. "The Americans, handing us our ass over the last decade."

Norris emphasized the word *ass*.

"And what are we doing here?" he asked. "We get wrapped up in the emotion all the time."

For the moment, Norris had everyone's attention.

"We've narrowed our pyramid, because we've watched our participation rates drop, so that now, at 17 years of age, our pool of so-called talent—so-called talent—is as narrow as Sweden and Finland," he said, twisting his voice into incredulity at the names of the two Nordic countries. "And yet we start out with tens upon tens of thousands of orders of magnitude more players than them."

Canada, he said, was at risk of falling down the same hole England had with soccer 50 years prior—of taking the country's love of its supposed national game for granted, failing to develop home-grown talent in an organic way, and watching its supremacy in the sport shrivel up.

"The number one reason for leaving sport?" he said. "Not having fun."

Arguably, a cancelled season would be least fun of all. The tension in Toronto was breaking out of the hockey bubble and into

the mainstream news. A report aired on Citytv showed one young
player who was left in tears after being pulled off the ice during
a pre-season tournament. He was born in 2011, but he was on a
team of players who were a year older. The older children were
allowed to play on the full ice, but under the letter of the new
law, their 2011-born teammate was not. He had to watch from the
other side of the glass.

This was the issue many of the assembled executives had been
hoping to discuss: that there were children who were already playing on a full sheet of ice, and that it was unfair that they be moved
backward, forced to play on a smaller surface—or, if their associations failed to accede to the new mandate, not at all. When it
became clear that Hockey Canada was not going to budge—that
the institution was not, in fact, particularly interested in having
that conversation at all—the room got punchy.

One west-end executive challenged the notion that coaches had
all the information they needed at their fingertips. The man said
he had spent three months seeking and failing to receive any guidance while trying to build a variation of the Initiation Program for
his own association. He was actually willing to spend the $50 for
Hockey Canada's manual, but he could not find a copy anywhere.

There were other complexities the executives wanted to discuss.
Some were still not sure how cross-ice was supposed to look inside
the local rinks. What was the best way to divide the ice into sections? Some associations ordered foam dividers, but without assur-
ances that they were fire retardant, some cities wouldn't allow them
to be stored on city property. Someone suggested a firefighter's
hose would suffice as a cheaper alternative, but others worried the
hoses were themselves a safety hazard. Another executive said the
rink where their association was based would not allow volunteers

to move barriers at all, only city workers, meaning it would have to hire another worker just for the hours the cross-ice games were held. And what about the gameplay itself? How many five-year-old players were supposed to be on the ice at the same time? Were teams even allowed to use goaltenders? One fundamental question wound its way through the proceedings: Would the associations be given the opportunity to make better-informed decisions before being strong-armed into rule changes?

Corey McNabb was the next speaker. He was Hockey Canada's manager of player development, and he carried himself with the air of a man who had seen some things; he too had flown in from Calgary for the meeting. His assignment was to continue the hard sell on the benefits of modified ice for children.

The notes were familiar: that even NHL teams were using smaller ice surfaces at practice to improve decision-making and turns and puckhandling in close quarters; that full-ice hockey doesn't help kids develop the most important skills; that the cross-ice format would ultimately mean more playing time for kids, and that even if it looked unusual to a hockey purist in the stands, the kids might actually be enjoying themselves.

Short tempers got shorter. A coach in the audience started arguing with a representative from the GTHL about whether the regional body had bothered to make information on the Initiation Program widely available. The GTHL spokesman said it had. The coach disagreed. They went back and forth with diminishing civility.

McKee, the emcee, finally broke in: "Corey's giving a presentation, so give him the opportunity to go through it."

"There are logistics here that we have to get through," the coach shot back.

"And we'll get to those logistics," McKee said. "We'll have that opportunity at the end of Corey's presentation to do it. Show him respect, because he's showing us respect to be here—to fly across the country."

McNabb resumed his presentation with murmurs floating through the seats above him. He reiterated the availability of the material. Decorum was hanging on by a thread.

By the third hour, someone in the audience tried to steer the conversation back to the issue that many assumed they had been summoned to discuss. Nobody aside from the panel of speakers had been expecting a lecture. They wanted to talk about the immediate concern: What was going to happen with the 2011-born players this year?

The question from the seats was about the fate of 2011-born players who had already signed up to play with children in an older age group. Those children made their teams after trying out in the spring. Their parents had already paid their fees. The jerseys had been purchased, and children had already begun practising together and making friends on the team—what would happen to those children? His voice rising in anger, he said phone calls with Hockey Canada, the GTHL, and the NYHL yielded nothing concrete. Did anyone have an answer?

From a national level, McNabb said, there were bylaws in place to govern such matters. He said he was not aware of the specifics in Toronto, with the NYHL. He was unable to complete his final thought aloud.

"See? You don't know," the man said, exasperated. "You can't even tell us."

"I can tell you what the national one is," McNabb answered, calmly, "but I don't know what every single—"

"Everybody says, 'Hockey Canada has got to tell us,' and then you call the NYHL and it's, 'The GTHL has to tell us,' and you call the GTHL, and they said they don't know," the man said, incredulous. "So we're into a season now—"

McKee tried to interject.

"I'm not finished," the man said. "We're into a season now where everything's picked, and you're telling us kids can't play up, even if they played up a year before. Is that fair to a six-year-old, who has to go, 'See you guys—I'm no longer on your team,' two days before a season starts?"

Murmurs filled the room. McKee stepped in again. In the Ontario Hockey Federation, he explained, they never stopped players from moving up an age bracket, but when they implemented mandatory cross-ice, it meant five- and six-year-olds would play cross-ice no matter what. You want to move your six-year-old up onto a seven-year-old team? It's cross-ice hockey.

The room erupted.

"Think about what you just said," the man in the audience said. "You're going to get all the minor novices—the 2010s—to play cross-ice so those two kids who are on the team can play cross-ice, because they have to follow your rule?"

"It's not beneficial to those kids," McKee said.

"So grandfather it in," the man said. "But don't tell us two days before a season starts."

The crowd dissolved into clusters of arguments. McNabb stood silently at the front of the room, while Norris watched from a seat nearby. Hockey Canada did not offer to grandfather the 2011-born players out of plans for the Initiation Program. Minor hockey executives did not get their deferral, and they did not get detailed instructions on how to implement the new changes. After four hours, it seemed likely that no one who sat inside that room left happy.

●●●

Two weeks after that meeting, Hockey Canada and the OHF issued a news release: they would grant the minor hockey executives a one-year deferral, and the 2011-born players would be allowed to play traditional full-ice games with their select-level teams. Renney conceded the governing bodies had work to do on their communication skills: "To see even one player's season called into question because of an implementation issue of our mandate is one player too many."

There was one catch. As part of the agreement, the NYHL was required to stage two so-called cross-ice festivals for the 2011-born children. They would show parents how the game would look with modified ice. The games would also give organizers a trial run for all subsequent seasons, when games would all be held on the smaller ice.

Afterwards, Paul Maich, the chief operating officer of the NYHL, was unmoved. Maich had white hair and photos of his grandchildren on his desk. He also had a binder filled with the results of a survey of league parents done after the second festival. He read one of the survey questions aloud: "How would you rate the overall experience from the select cross-ice game your child participated in?"

Forty-seven per cent said they were "very dissatisfied," while only 1 per cent felt "very satisfied."

"So you can see," Maich said, "that it is a huge majority that don't want any part of it." The national hockey executives needed to realize they were dealing with a business, he said, and that the parents and their children were the consumers.

"Hockey Canada thought, 'Well, they don't have any options —this is like school, we set the curriculum, you do what we tell you,'" Maich said. "Sorry, folks, but these guys are actually paying the freight, and they're going to decide where their kids are going to play.

"And now, we've got a number of private enterprise organizations that are putting together full-ice programs in those age groups."

Those private groups operated outside Hockey Canada's umbrella. The children who played with those groups were not included in the national registration totals. McKee estimated there were as many as 20,000 children playing in unsanctioned leagues across Ontario, outside the national body's purview and not beholden to any institutional rule changes.

It fractured the system. The more children that played outside the system, the more difficult it would be to implement changes. On a local level, it could hurt registration numbers at minor hockey associations, some of which had already seen membership bleed away. On a national level, a broad-based movement into the private sector had the potential to weaken Hockey Canada's authority.

Maich wondered if the new mandate was going to drive more families outside the umbrella. He had heard that a handful of organizations in neighbouring Mississauga were looking into forming a league where children could continue to play full-ice games. Some resistant coaches in Vaughan were also supposedly putting together their own programs.

"We're talking about five- and six-year-old children," Renney said later. He believed cross-ice hockey would help retention rates —that it would make sure all children had a chance to feel part of the game. "This is not an endurance contest. This is about five- and six-year-olds in a space that allows them to be successful and have fun, and touch pucks and bump into each other and fall down and get up and laugh and giggle."

The children, who were provided with pizza and drinks and movies between their games at the cross-ice festival, were not surveyed about their experience—just the parents.

Parents often helped reinforce the existing structure of minor hockey. There was peer pressure to enroll children in extracurricular activities such as skating camps and spring hockey, but the parents still had to enter their credit card numbers. Parents had more choices. There was more opportunity to become a consumer in minor hockey than ever before.

McKee would later smile sheepishly and admit that for all his talk about saving the game, he too was part of the problem. Namely, that he gladly accepted hand-me-down clothing from relatives for his five-year-old, but when his son started to play hockey, they went right out to the store to buy new Bauer equipment.

"We're our own worst nightmare in this," he said. "It doesn't have to be expensive."

He'd had an idea.

"If I'm a minor hockey association, how am I making sure that every kid in the game can get into the game for $50?" he said. "Skates, helmet, everything."

When students decide they want to try football in high school, they are not expected to go to a store and spend $300 on a brand-new helmet—the school will often have a bank of equipment, filled with helmets and shoulder pads, and fit the children before the season. McKee suggested minor hockey associations could follow a similar path. Children in the youngest divisions have a helpful tendency to grow quickly while not logging too many miles on their equipment, usually growing out of it before it reaches the end of its lifespan. McKee suggested the local associations could build incentives for parents to donate the equipment: "Don't give it to Play It Again Sports."

Many associations already have a bank for goaltending equipment. By expanding their collection, they could address two barriers to entry: cost and unfamiliarity. Parents who had no previous experience in hockey could take their children to the local rink and have them outfitted by volunteers for little to no cost.

There were programs to help, too. Scott Carlow and Ryan Hurley were driving around Ontario in their big black pickup pulling a trailer filled with equipment for their Try Hockey program. The private sector had also developed plans to address the issue: Canadian Tire launched the First Shift program, which provided Bauer equipment "head-to-toe," along with six weeks of on-ice instruction, for $199.

One issue with the former was scale: Try Hockey was still just two men driving around the province in a truck. An issue with the latter was awareness: something still had to spark enough interest in a family to register for the program.

"The best chance we have? It's 13 branches across the country identifying with the same process, identifying with the same programming, identifying with the same reason why we do this," said Renney. "And then you've got a chance."

Scott Oakman, the executive director of the GTHL, wondered if the hockey season could be broken up to accommodate parents uncomfortable with dedicating a full winter to one sport. Maybe the local associations could follow another school-based model and start offering seasons like semesters: there would be a fall season and a winter season, and parents would have the option of signing up for one or both, depending on their appetite.

There were sparks of innovation elsewhere. When an association north of Toronto noticed its retention rates among young girls was falling sharply, they developed a plan: they invited women who had grown up in the system to come back for an hour or two on the ice and mentor the girls. Then they ordered pizza for everyone. Their retention rates went back up.

"I still think hockey is Canada's game," said Fran Rider, the hockey pioneer who helped establish the Ontario Women's Hockey Association. "We've had situations where posters go up in a rink for an adult team, and we get a call back: 'I've got 60 women, what do I do?' The passion is still there for hockey, as players. But we are struggling against technology, finances, and a changing society."

The easiest solution? Hockey has to be fun.

SIXTEEN

TEARS AND RENEWAL

By the time the Petes finished their final practice of the season, the biggest story in town had nothing to do with hockey. The team held its final workout at the Evinrude Centre because a travelling game show had taken over not only the Memorial Centre but also most of its parking lot.

Players had trouble finding places to park as they carpooled back from their workout on a Wednesday afternoon. Inside the main bowl of the arena, workers were running through the final soundcheck for *The Price Is Right*, the long-running daytime television staple adapted for the road. Sixty prizes would be won that night, not including all the giveaways.

Burton Lee and his wife had tickets, even though he knew he could never accept a prize. "Can you imagine if I got called down?" he said. "'Rigged! Rigged!'"

Two players wandered toward the stands as the crew continued show preparations.

"What is this?" Nikita Korostelev asked Tamara Burns, the team's communications coordinator.

"*The Price Is Right*," she said, a little surprised.

Korostelev and Pavel Gogolev furrowed their brows. Both had been in Canada for years. Korostelev had arrived eight years earlier to attend the Hill Academy, a sports-focused school north of Toronto. Gogolev had five years under his belt, following a similar route. Despite the time spent in Canada, neither player had stumbled across the show.

"It's a game show," Burns said, finally breaking the silence. "You can win money."

Korostelev shrugged and walked back into the dressing room. Gogolev was intrigued.

"Can I go?" he asked.

"You need a ticket," Burns answered.

"Can I get in for free?" he asked.

"No," she said.

Gogolev slumped his shoulders and walked back across the hall to the dressing room. Almost a month had passed since the Petes won a game, a seven-game losing streak in which they were knocked out of playoff contention and rendered obsolete for another spring. They lost two more games after Mississauga officially ended their post-season chances. There were only three games left, all stacked over the next three days—at home to North Bay on Thursday, in Oshawa on Friday, and home against Hamilton in the finale on Saturday.

All of the adults had somewhere else they had to be that afternoon. Oke was in Toronto on a scouting trip. Duco would soon be on his way back to the Evinrude Centre to run practice for a minor hockey team. Walser had the most important job of them all that day: it was his turn to make dinner for his children, then take them to gymnastics.

He was also preparing for his son's upcoming hockey tryouts, even though he was still waiting to hear about his own immediate future in the game. None of the remaining coaches knew for sure what lay ahead, because none of them had contracts past the end of this season. One way or another, life was going to go on, with or without the Petes.

Without a place to park because of the game show ruckus, Walser pulled his silver Mercedes into the space normally reserved for Oke. He was older than Duco, but he was not as established as Verner. He had no idea where he might be in the fall. The Petes were still looking for a head coach to replace Jody Hull, fired two months earlier. If they were going to clean house, Walser thought, they were going to clean house—but he didn't think you could pin the year on four coaches.

By 5:30 p.m., all the coaches had left the building. The doors were going to open for the game show, but one player was still inside. Dylan Wells had just finished what was almost certainly his final OHL practice, but that did not mean he was going to deviate from his routine. There were still weights to lift, an ice bath to take, and muscles to stretch.

He was waiting on direction from the Oilers, who had signed him to a three-year entry-level contract. He got a signing bonus of $92,500, and he treated himself to a silver Audi. He bought it used, but it was still the nicest car any player was leaving in the Memorial Centre parking lot on a regular basis.

Like the Petes, the Oilers were also going to miss the playoffs. They could call him up to the big team, but it was more likely they would send him to one of their minor-league affiliates. That meant he could be leaving Peterborough to join the Bakersfield Condors, the AHL team in California. There was also a chance the team could send him to Wichita, Kansas, in the ECHL. Wells was still young enough to return to the Petes for one more season, but all signs pointed to the launch of his professional career.

Everyone around the team was already looking ahead to what was next.

"It feels like yesterday," Wells said. "Guys are always saying, 'Aw, it flies by.' Sometimes, the first couple years are tough. It almost feels like forever if you're struggling or if you're missing home. Now, looking back at it, it does really fly by."

It was 6 p.m. before he was finally ready to leave the arena. It was quiet, with *The Price Is Right* about to start in the main bowl. Wells had no real interest in the show, though. He had somewhere else to be, too: his billets had just gotten a new pet, and they were all going to puppy school.

●●●

Technically speaking, all of the Petes players listed on the lineup card were on the bench for their final Thursday game of the season, but only a few of them really seemed to show up. Peterborough gave up three goals in the first period and two more in the second —five goals on 20 shots—to ensure no one would remember anything about the time they played the North Bay Battalion.

What happened after the game, though, was an entirely different story.

Alex Black, the tall red-headed defenceman, had returned from a weeklong suspension handed out for being out past curfew. The team said he had broken an undisclosed rule for the second time in as many weeks. Black was in his final year of eligibility in the

OHL, and there was a thought that he might end his career serving that suspension.

He was not a star, but he was a veteran. When injuries shortened the roster, the Petes needed Black to log difficult minutes against players who were far more skilled. He was still game, even when he was clearly overmatched.

The Petes allowed him to return to the team after two games. This was his first home game back in uniform, and it was his first chance to address the local media since the suspension.

Mike Davies, the respected local newspaper reporter, asked Black about "the elephant in the room." The post-game media scrum was underway in the usual space, the dressing room across from the Petes office. But it was unusually quiet. Nobody could be overheard washing their hands or flushing a toilet in the adjoining restroom. Nobody made a sound as Black started to speak.

"At the end of the day, I think it was a major miscommunication from all parties," he said. "I did break a rule. I was out past curfew. I can admit that. But I don't think they did their due diligence to figure out what I did."

Hockey players are not generally known for speaking their minds in public. They almost never question authority figures. It is a collective personality quirk handed down through the generations, passed from one smelly hockey glove to the next. Wayne Gretzky and Sidney Crosby have become Canadian hockey avatars not just for their ferocious skill on the ice but also for their determined avoidance of conflict off it.

Black was nearly finished with the game, and he wanted to protect his name. He told his version of the story. He said he received a call late on the Wednesday night in question. It was around 1 a.m., long after curfew, even for the over-agers on the roster. A close friend was on the other end of the call, and she was in distress. The

OHL had been talking to players about the importance of mental health awareness, he said. He felt compelled to act.

He said his friend only felt comfortable speaking with him, so he headed out to help. He did not tell his billets, and he did not tell the team. In hindsight, he said, he knew he should have let someone know where he was going, but the clock was ticking and he raced out without a second thought.

"I went and got her, brought her back to the house, calmed her down, talked about what was going on," he said. "I think I helped her. I dropped her off."

General manager Mike Oke did not get the entire story before he sent him home, Black said. "At the end of the day, I can look myself in the mirror and know I did a good thing. I know I helped a person, and I'm still helping that person."

His parents were proud of him. Curfew or no curfew, Black said, he knew he'd done the right thing.

There was brief silence in the room.

"I didn't know there was so much to the story, Alex," said Davies. "I appreciate you being that forthcoming."

"I wanted to, because Mike didn't really have the choice," Black said of his general manager. "It was the night it happened, so he didn't really know as much. I don't want to say anything bad about him, but I looked like kind of an idiot, and I wanted to clear the air. I don't know how he's going to think about it, and I don't know how the organization is going to think about it. But I'm a big boy—I'm 20 years old. I wanted to clear the air."

It had taken Black about three minutes to clarify the situation to Davies and the other two reporters in the room. Out in the hallway a few minutes later, he looked relieved. It was easier to explain it all now than it had been in front of his coach and general manager. Black said he was exhausted and frayed, having gotten home at 5 a.m., when he was called into the office three hours later to meet with management.

The first time he missed curfew, earlier in the season, Black admitted he had been out drinking with friends the night before a game. It was nothing dramatic. He had not crawled through the front door at 4 a.m. missing a shoe. He got back at 1:15 a.m., but he still got caught.

That was the context Oke was working with when Black's billets called to tell him the veteran had missed curfew again. He summoned Black into the office and told him he was being sent home. Black said he was too tired and still too shaken to explain himself. They asked him what he'd been doing the previous night, and he told them he picked someone up and took them home. And that was it.

"I was completely devastated," he said. "I got home and I went downstairs and cried. If it would have been for going out, boozing, trying to get laid, I would have had no one to blame but myself. But the reason it hurt so bad is because I was trying to do the right thing and help someone who is close to me."

He conceded he put the team in a bad spot, and he also knew how bad it looked in the media. Coaches from the universities he was considering would wonder about his character. It would be one of the top Google hits under his name.

"I don't know how they're going to react to that," he said. "But they made me look like a dick in the paper, because they said I did the same thing twice. And my parents said I should say something. I thought I should say something. And I'm glad I said something.

"At the end of the day, it's my life. And I don't want to look like a dick twice."

●●●

The request came over the public address system with five minutes to go in the second period against North Bay. Peterborough
was trailing 5–0, so there was no noise to disrupt the announcement: "Would the team dentist please report to the Petes bench."

A few seconds later: "Would the team dentist please report to
the Petes bench."

Nobody had been hit in the face with a puck. There was no
blood, no evidence. Neither trainer was sent scurrying across the
ice on a tooth-retrieval mission. The call remained a mystery until
a few minutes after the game, when Cole Fraser emerged from the
home team's dressing room. The most intimidating player in a
Petes uniform smiled his baby-faced smile for just a moment, and
it featured fewer teeth than usual. He'd cracked a tooth the previous season, and he'd chipped it again during this game. But it had
nothing to do with the Battalion: he was trying to open a bottle
of Gatorade with his mouth when the cap popped off his tooth.

It appeared that a sports drink bottle had become a metaphor
for a hockey season. It was down to the final weekend now. Fraser
was one of the players guaranteed to return next season, but he
still had not established a firm hold on what had happened to the
team this time around.

"I don't even know if I'll ever know," he said with a little shrug.
"It's just been a weird season. As a team, we came in and we
thought we were going to be really good. Obviously, we had the
talent, and then things started going downhill."

Peterborough finally snapped its road losing streak with an 8–4
rout of Oshawa, in a game that meant nothing for the Generals in
the standings. The Petes were back home the next night to face
Hamilton, which left many of its most recognizable players out of
uniform. The Bulldogs had clinched first place in the Eastern
Conference standings. They already knew when they were going

to open their first-round series. Their only concern was preserving their roster for the playoffs.

There was no such certainty for the Petes. Mike Oke still had to hire a coach, and that coach would likely have input on whether or not the existing assistants would get new contracts. Verner, Duco, and Walser were all waiting. Players were waiting, too. DeNoble was in contact with a team in the ECHL about signing a contract for the stretch drive of the season. Korostelev was aiming to land somewhere in the AHL. Billets wondered if players would be returning to their smoke-free rooms in the fall.

On the final pre-game show of the season, the hosts on 90.5 FM tried to highlight the positives. It had been a disappointing season, sure, but there was still reason to be hopeful. Wells would be eligible to return next season, but even if he moved on, the Petes still had Hunter Jones. "This is a player that they've been talking about the last couple of years," one of the hosts said. "That he is ready to become, kind of, that next starter."

In the Memorial Centre, Dave Lorentz was standing just outside the alumni lounge as fans walked past. He was on the board of directors, the group that had given Oke permission to fire Hull in January. They would also sign off on whoever was going to become the next head coach. Ultimately, those directors shaped the product on the ice. None of the fans were protesting the directors at their day jobs, though. And as he stood beside the door, in the concourse above the ice, Lorentz said he had not heard an angry word.

"I think they're frustrated," he said. "But they understand. They know about the injuries."

It was still too early for bitter reflection. So without any rage to fuel the building, the season finale took on an unexpectedly festive air. Parents and relatives and friends drove into town, not so much to see the game as to observe the milestone. Some of them were going to stay for the post-game afterparty, and at least a few of them seemed to have started early. A group of young men leaned over the stands as captain Logan DeNoble prepared to step onto the ice for the final pre-game warm-up of his OHL career. They were his friends, and when they caught a glimpse of his familiar No. 28, they began to heckle: "Come on two-eight. Your last game in junior, two-eight. Your last game in the show. Let's get those feet moving."

Within a few minutes, the entire team, standing in full equipment in the hall, was giggling. Some of the players tried to hide it. Others did not even bother. It was St. Patrick's Day, and there was no reason to be upset. Not anymore.

Midway through the third period, the Bulldogs were up 5–2, and players from both teams looked interested mostly in getting out of the game without an injury. DeNoble stole the puck inside the blue line and moved closer to the net. There was a shot for him if he wanted, but he passed instead. Both his linemates were there with him, along with two mildly engaged Hamilton defenders. Brady Hinz could have shot, but passed to Adam Timleck, who was trailing the play. Timleck could have shot, too.

Timleck and DeNoble were friends, and even though he only had a split second to make a decision, he fully understood the moment. Instead of shooting, Timleck redirected the puck back to DeNoble, who was suddenly standing beside a half-empty net. The puck was bouncing when it arrived, and it took a second to tame. DeNoble was drafted as an afterthought in the 13th round, 242nd overall, and somehow found a way to play on the same ice as his grandfather. And his final statistical entry for the Petes was the 31st goal of his season, scored in front of friends and family at the Memorial Centre.

That was when the mood started to shift in parts of the stands. Some of the fans were wiping tears, and some were starting to sob. Interim coach Andrew Verner sent DeNoble over the boards as often as he could in those final few minutes, making sure he was on the ice as the buzzer sounded on the season.

DeNoble was fighting tears by then, too. He was the last player to leave the ice, followed by Oke, and then by Verner and Duco. Parents and friends filled the narrow hallway leading down from the craft beer stand to the dressing room. It was the same place they waited before trudging back out to scrape their windshields after frozen Thursday nights in January. It was where they had celebrated the wins in the playoffs the previous spring, and where they'd expected to celebrate more this year. This was the end for some of the parents, too: the predawn practices, the games, the tournaments in faraway cities. It had become part of their lives, part of their social calendar. And now it was over.

Julia Tanner was standing next to Tracy Adamo, her eyes red. Timms had been with her for all four seasons of his Petes career, but it seemed unlikely he would be back for a fifth. He was young enough to play another season, but there was friction. His father was not happy with the coaches and believed the departure of Grimes —one of two assistants allowed to leave over the summer—had a larger impact on the team than many knew. He was prickly over the perception that the defence was the root of the team's struggles, noting the Petes had scored 17 fewer goals this season than last. It was not clear where his son would land next season, but he had reached the point where he needed "a change."

Tanner was not losing a defenceman. She was losing a teenager she enjoyed having in the house, who'd become part of her family. The next time she made her special cheese sauce for the broccoli, it would have to be for a reunion, rather than a dinnertime surprise on a random winter Wednesday.

"Sad," she said, her voice catching.

"It's overwhelming, as a billet," Adamo added.

"It's like the end of an era, you know?" said Tanner. "My player, I don't know what he's doing next year. All these kids you get close to, they're gone."

Her door would always be open. There would be visits. The first player she ever hosted lived in Owen Sound now, and they were still on such close terms that Tanner could walk right into his house whenever she was in town. That was one of the most rewarding parts of being a billet—the bonds could be for life. The hardest part was having to say goodbye.

"You don't get to see them every day," she said. "Some of them, you don't get to see them again ever."

DeNoble waded into the crowd a few minutes later. He hugged his father and made his way toward his mother, who was standing by the customer service kiosk. The Petes never made it to the Memorial Cup like he'd dreamed. Their 5–3 loss in the finale left them with 23 wins through 68 regular season games, a drop of 19 from the previous year. Peterborough finished 9th of 10 teams in the conference, 17 points out of a playoff spot. They'd been first in the conference in October but sat 41 points away from that peak as the players continued to filter into the hallway. DeNoble was going to have his name added to the plaque next to the office. He was going to be linked to the team forever.

Black was a standing a few feet away, immersed in the group of young men who'd been heckling and cheering before the game. He had been talking to university coaches, too. He laughed when someone pointed out that university students generally get to set their own curfews: "Thank fucking god."

Wells was still in his team-issue shorts when he emerged from the room. He got to his mother first, and Barb embraced her son warmly. She rubbed his back, kissed him on the cheek, and held the back of his head gently with her hand as they both started to cry.

Nick Robertson was showered and changed. He had scored Peterborough's second goal of the finale, which gave him 15 for his first season of junior hockey. Despite his injuries and how sparingly he saw the ice in meaningful situations under Hull, Robertson finished eighth in OHL scoring among rookies. He hugged his mother, Mercedes, and gave his girlfriend a quick peck on the cheek; they'd met in town over the winter. Mercedes stepped back and took a picture of the young couple in the hallway. She was proud of her youngest son. He was only 16, living away from home for the first time, and not only had he learned to cope with injury and decreased ice time, he had adapted to a new environment. She said she had not heard about how her son was the first on the ice for practice, and the last to leave.

"I like that," she said. "Absolutely. That means he's in the mindset. He knows it's his job; he's here for a job, he has a purpose. Anything else, other than that, it's a distraction."

Robertson had a goal, after all.

"Get drafted higher than his brother," she said. "That's his motivation. He hasn't forgotten that."

Robertson was not going back to the United States to relax. He wanted to get stronger, faster. He would be back on the ice, maybe to return to Canada as part of the American entry at the Hlinka Gretzky Cup, the annual showcase for the best under-18 players in the world. That was where he could start to boost his name recognition ahead of the 2019 NHL draft. Scouts would begin to follow him like lost puppies, moving from arena to arena.

The NHL was where everyone would know his name. An entry-level contract would make Robertson a millionaire on his own. There would be fans, jersey sales, endorsement deals, charter flights, and hotel beds with thread counts higher than anything that ever existed in Peterborough, Ontario, Canada.

But there was something he had to do first. After they drove back down the 115 toward the 401, past the stubborn pockets of snow lurking in the shady corners of the fields, Robertson would have to ready himself for another task. It was waiting for him in Michigan.

He still had to get his driver's licence.

EPILOGUE

Nick Robertson gently clarified that he did not recall the details of his own premature birth. He was in the room, obviously, but he could not remember the tubes or the medication or the raw terror that held sway over his parents for months after his arrival.

It was his story, of course, but it also belonged to his family, and their unique pathway that had now produced not just one, but two NHL prospects. The Toronto Maple Leafs used their first selection in the 2019 draft to take Robertson, overlooking concerns about his size to focus instead on the vast potential of his skill. He went in the second round—the same round in which his brother was picked two years earlier.

So much of the immediate post-draft news coverage rightly focused on the story of his birth, and the heroism both his mother and father had shown in somehow balancing the schedules of three hockey-obsessed little boys. But none of those early questions really mined the psychological fossil fuel buried just below the surface, which had powered so much of Robertson's already considerable competitive drive. He wanted to be taken in the first round, and he wanted to go earlier than his brother. In the end, he dropped to the 53rd overall pick—14 spots lower than where the Dallas Stars had taken Jason in 2017.

"It was a little frustrating," Robertson told reporters in Toronto three days after the Leafs finally called his name. "Talking to my dad, saying, 'What's going on? I thought I said the right things.'"

He looked relaxed and comfortable in the spotlight, like he had been training for it alongside his on-ice practice. Robertson made eye contact, as he always had, but he also smiled and joked and showed skill in narrating the events that delivered him to the big stage.

"Obviously, I don't remember it, but I've been told," he said of his difficult first few months on the planet. "But I think that kind of shifted me into the kind of player and person that I am, just being versatile, and persevering and strong."

The Leafs had been interested in Robertson long before the draft. General manager Kyle Dubas had taken in a handful of games in person at the Memorial Centre, watched him play and asked questions of his character, his family, his upbringing, and his interactions with the other teenagers on the roster. The team did its research, and it liked what it found.

Nick Robertson, premature son of California, now belonged to the biggest hockey team in the world.

●●●

One of my favourite places in the Memorial Centre is a spot in the hall just outside the Petes dressing room, where Robertson and the rest of his teammates would meet friends and family after the game. Sometimes it was quiet—the appeal of a mid-February game with Owen Sound has its limits even for mom—but it was more often the central transit hub of raw emotion.

It was where players who had been so stoic on the ice melted at the sight of familiar faces. Whether by rule or by design, neither general manager Mike Oke nor the coaches ever seemed to venture into the crowd, leaving room for the dust to settle (or the smoke to rise). Parents gathered and clustered and gossiped, just like they do in every minor hockey rink. Players who relied on familiar bromides in post-game media scrums were finally liberated, permitted to let the first hints of real human emotion be seen outside the dressing room.

More than anything, it was where the Petes revealed themselves for what they really were. They were only kids, some still not old enough to need to shave. Without their granite-edged shoulder pads and practised glowers, they were high school students and recent graduates living away from home for the first time. From that spot in the hallway, you could watch Cole Fraser flip the switch from terrifying hitman to smiling teenager. You could see Susan Schramm, a kindly woman from Michigan who used to tutor Robertson in math, deliver a care package of candy bars, hazelnut spread, and a chocolate with his initial.

It was where it became almost impossible not to root for the Petes, even and especially as the season around them caught fire, deep inside a dumpster, sandwiched in a train wreck.

Dylan Wells sometimes seemed to float above the chaos unfolding in front of his net. He had as much at stake as any of the adults connected to the team. He had been on track to try out for the Canadian world junior team, where he could have played for a television audience of millions. But even as that chance slipped away, one shorthanded breakaway goal at a time, he maintained outward calm, just as his mom demanded. He could have—and maybe should have—lashed out at teammates, but if he ever did, it was behind closed doors.

His season did not end in Peterborough, and neither did his hopes of making it to the NHL. Wells left the Petes for the Bakersfield Condors, the American Hockey League franchise that served as the top-tier professional affiliate of the Oilers. It was his first taste of life in full-time professional hockey and, as widely expected, that is where he stayed. Wells did not return to Peterborough for his final year of eligibility. He stayed in the pro ranks, bouncing between the first- and second-tier ranks of the North American farm system.

By late March of his rookie season, Wells was in net for the Condors in a game against San Diego that might not have made much news outside—or inside—California, but that did not diminish its meaning to a young goaltender on his way up the professional ladder. Wells stopped 40 of the 42 shots he faced that game, helping Bakersfield clinch its first AHL playoff berth. At 21, he had his entire career in front of him.

Logan DeNoble realized a childhood dream when he made the Petes, but he knew his abilities would not be able to carry him much farther than junior hockey. He gave it a shot, though, by signing with a team in the ECHL after the Petes cleaned out their lockers. DeNoble appeared in three games with the Kansas City Mavericks, but did not record a point. By the fall, he was back in school, playing for the Saint Mary's University Huskies.

The Huskies, like the Petes, were once a dynasty. Saint Mary's took seven straight Atlantic University Sport titles in the 1970s, but had gone a decade since its last win. DeNoble had 16 points in 30 games as a freshman, finishing ninth in team scoring. (The Huskies lost in the playoff semifinals.)

Defenceman Alex Black went to university, too, returning home to the Kitchener area to play at Wilfrid Laurier. Fellow defenceman Matthew Timms was traded to the London Knights, but found himself at a crossroads in the middle of the season: The Knights told him just before the OHL's trade deadline that he was being moved again, this time to the Barrie Colts. Rather than report to a team out of contention, Timms enrolled at the University of Guelph.

Another former teammate continued to fan the embers of their NHL dreams. After leading the Petes in scoring, winger Nikita Korostelev joined the Laval Rocket—just one step below the Montreal Canadiens. He appeared in 10 games and scored a goal, but that was not enough to root him in the soil, and he began to drift. He signed a contract in Russia, tried out for the Columbus Blue Jackets, and was moved to Cleveland (AHL), then to Jacksonville (ECHL), and back again.

Jody Hull had also ended up in Russia, but only briefly. Three months after the Petes fired him as their head coach, he was working behind the bench as an assistant coach for the Canadian team at the world under-18 championship. By August, he was back in the OHL, hired as an associate coach with the Niagara IceDogs.

He said he planned to keep his home in the Peterborough area.

●●●

Following the news out of Peterborough can make it feel like something is wrong with the settings on your internet browser. Some news items seem like they come from the future, others from the past, and a handful more remind you of something you have already seen before. (There could be some irony in the fact that the post-secondary school closest to the Memorial Centre is named after Sir Sandford Fleming, the founder of standard time.)

When the team hired a coach to replace Hull, a former Petes player, it opted for a candidate in Rob Wilson who had been a former Petes player himself. When the team's board of directors announced it had retained the help of a senior advisor, the help was revealed to be Bob Gainey, who had worn the jersey 45 years earlier and quickly admitted to local media he had "some catching up to do in the OHL and on junior hockey."

And when Oke made the team's selection for its first-round pick in 2018, it was yet another teenager who did not want to report to Peterborough. Will Cuylle had the hallmarks of a rookie who could make an immediate impact: he was big, fast, and skilled, and still available when the Petes picked third. But his family had been clear on the subject: They would not send their prodigy to skate a single shift at the Memorial Centre. And they were not bluffing.

Cuylle had options at the collegiate level in the United States. In the end, Oke made the best of his situation by trading the young star to the Windsor Spitfires for a hockey bag full of draft picks. He got nine, in all, including a first-round pick and four second-round picks. Cuylle went on to finish seventh in OHL rookie scoring, and the 26 goals he scored would have tied him for third-most on the Petes.

The reasons behind his refusal were never explicitly detailed in public, but Cuylle did eventually tell the Windsor Star that he "didn't really feel like Peterborough was the best place for me to play."

Windsor had a rink built this century. It had won three Memorial Cup titles since the advent of high-definition television. Taylor Hall was a Hart Trophy winner in the NHL, but before that, he was a star in Windsor. Ryan Ellis, Cam Fowler, Zack Kassian, and Adam Henrique were among some of the other former Spitfires who were now filling NHL jerseys.

Peterborough, meanwhile, had an arena that was on the verge of cataclysm. The city moved to spend $3.5-million to rip up the entire floor over the summer of 2019 to replace 40-year-old pipes that were on the verge of failure. The work was not going to make the weight room more attractive, or update the home team's dressing room to make it more modern and comfortable. It was being done to ensure the barest minimum standards could be met—that the Petes could play on a floor that had ice.

Oke did not have an easy job ahead of him. The team had shown some remarkable forward thinking. It had come up with ways of welcoming new Canadians to the game. It had tried to find ways to expand its base and connect with new audiences, from sending players to visit a local cricket association to hosting an eSports tournament. None of those things have a direct impact on what happens on the ice, of course. And that is where games tend to be won.

The Petes have a history that is deeper and richer than almost any team they play. There are banners in the rafters and photos on the walls, all reminders of greatness from generations that came before visors and WiFi and shame about mullets. Many of the boys in those team pictures grew up to become famous men. From their eternal home deep inside the Memorial Centre, they give voice to where the Petes have been, but not always to where the team should be going.

AFTERWORD

There is a new basketball net in our backyard. It materialized by request on the first Saturday in June, two days after the Toronto Raptors started playing the Golden State Warriors in the NBA Finals. Within minutes of its assembly, an eight-year-old boy in a new Kawhi Leonard jersey was lobbing his new, rainbow-coloured Spalding basketball up into the sky.

Thump. Thump. Thump. Clang. Thump. Thump. Thump. Swish.

The net was on sale for $349.99 at Canadian Tire, and the ball was $22.49. Added together—and not including the six hours of parental labour to assemble it—the total came to about half the cost of a week at hockey camp.

The weekend the hoop arrived, Brock University issued a news release under the provocative banner claim that the Raptors "could change Canada's sporting identity" with their success in the play-offs. The school suggested Canadian sports might have been heading for a "transformational" moment. "Hockey is a bit selective and elite," Julie Stevens, associate professor of sport management at Brock, said in the release, "where basketball has a strong social bond across different areas of class and race."

Television networks were filled with images of Jurassic Park, the small concrete clearing between Scotiabank Arena and the condominium development Maple Leaf Sports & Entertainment helped create. Fans had been lining up at dawn for games that started at 9 p.m., huddled in metal holding pens until officials let them into the main square. They became a part of the growing spectacle.

Every game in the NBA Finals set a new Canadian television ratings record for basketball. The final game averaged an audience of 7.7 million, and 82 per cent of all Toronto households were said to have been tuned to basketball. The Raptors were a bigger draw than the Blue Jays, who averaged 5.12 million viewers during their high-water playoff mark four years earlier.

Suddenly, a blasphemous question was being asked out in the open. It was being discussed on air and in polite conversation: Was basketball poised to loosen hockey's grip on the Canadian winter?

Basketball is cheaper to play. It's more accessible and more attractive to new Canadians. By some metrics, the game has already passed hockey in youth participation. The Raptors are known by their first names—Kawhi, Kyle—and by catchy nicknames such as "Spicy P" (Pascal Siakam). Drake will go to hockey games, but he lives for basketball. By the end of June, Toronto was feeling close to the same. The Raptors were fun, and their bandwagon was wide open and welcoming.

Hockey is, by contrast, far more closed off. And at the grassroots level, it can be a pain in the ass.

Minor hockey demands full compliance. From the first organized practice in September to the final day of the playoffs in April, weekends run on a metronomic predictability. There is a practice and a game on Saturday; a game and a practice on Sunday.

There is also a standing midweek practice, held in the teeth of rush-hour traffic. Depending on the time of year, there can be two practices during the week.

There are tournaments and skills development camps. Local arenas are filled with flyers and other advertising: Coaches promise to improve your child's skating, stick-handling, and awareness on the ice. They might not be old enough to read books without pictures, but that is no excuse for not knowing how to properly use the outside edge of a skate blade.

An all-day camp on a PA day can cost $100. A March break camp can cost about as much as a round-trip plane ticket to somewhere warm, if you wanted to think about it in those terms, which you do not, because you want to preserve your sanity. Besides, everyone else living in the bubble seems to be doing the same thing.

In Toronto, there are minor hockey coaches who are paid five-figure salaries. There are skills coaches who make a living off working with high-level youth programs. There are specialized teams that run in the summer, sneaking out from under Hockey Canada's umbrella. There are children who spend more time on the ice than some NHL players.

It is all getting out of hand, we tell each other in the lobby. It has become too much, we say with a slow shake of our heads. We are crazy for doing all of this.

And then we do it all over again the next weekend. Because that is hockey, and everyone else seems to be doing the same thing.

But we also do it because the eight-year-old loves it, from the floor-to-ceiling P.K. Subban picture on his bedroom wall to the No. 9 he wears on his back as the result of reading Roch Carrier's story more times than either of us can remember. He loves tearing around the ice with his teammates in those precious few free moments before coaches blow the whistle to start practice. At a pre-Christmas tournament in Buffalo, every spare moment off the ice was spent thrashing around the hotel pool or in the rented conference room, playing hockey with mini-sticks until they were so covered with sweat it looked like they'd never left the water.

For a while, they traded hockey stickers, and then hockey cards. Some of them got Xboxes, and they moved like a swarm, from basement to basement, playing NHL 19 on the console between more games of mini-sticks and ball hockey outside. The short stories of their youth updated Carrier's work, with Connor McDavid, Sidney Crosby, and Auston Matthews taking the place of Maurice (The Rocket) Richard.

They were forming connections with peers outside of school—few even went to school together. Those bonds were not only shared with those from around the community, but also with their parents and grandparents who had history in the game. My parents used to give me a red two-dollar bill to spend at the arena concession stand, and now, our children get two dollars to spend on the same junk food.

Parents become friends, then drinking buddies. In those arenas, even a big city like Toronto can start to feel like a small town. Everyone, from labourer to lawyer, from chemist to consultant, can still reliably lean over the arena railing and have at least one thing pull them together in conversation: hockey.

Except, everyone along that railing already has plenty in common. They all have the means to be in hockey, and they have the time the game demands as investment. Everyone has their own car. Everyone has made peace with being at an arena all weekend instead of, say, skiing, visiting family out of town, having to work, or being literally anywhere else.

Those demands leave plenty of people outside. The crowds inside Toronto minor hockey arenas tend to look an awful lot like the crowds inside Scotiabank Arena for Leafs games. On the other hand, the fans inside Jurassic Park look more like the city—and the country—in which we all live.

The problems are structural. Even well-meaning minor hockey associations struggle to reach out to and connect with new faces. The system lacks the conditions that might invite radical thought, let alone revolutionary action.

Communication channels are fractured. When Hockey Canada issued its cross-ice mandate, it did not send clear instructions down to the volunteers who had to implement the program. Were the cross-ice games supposed to include goaltenders? With games going on at each end, what were coaches being asked to do with the leftover ice in the neutral zone? Were games supposed to have referees?

Children are being sorted and drummed out of the game too early. Professional coaches and skill trainers are driving up the costs. Demands cycle into more demands, and at higher frequencies.

Individually, hockey people are generally helpful and generous. Parents will happily run through a blizzard to the car to get a spare neck guard for a child who forgot theirs. In our minor hockey association, where our son plays in the east end of Toronto, executives show up at dawn to help unload the temporary boards for cross-ice games. They work countless hours and care deeply about the programs they deliver.

Mike Oke, the Petes general manager, also worked with his son's minor hockey team, and would spend entire intermissions up in the management box in Peterborough sharing practice drills he thought might work for us in Toronto. He developed a manual for the parents of his own son's squad—filled with team goals, a code of conduct, and expectations—and generously passed it along. An adapted version became our handbook. (Probably about half of the text messages we exchanged during the reporting of this book ended up being about minor hockey. He always wanted to ensure his players had fun on the ice.)

Tom Renney, the chief executive at Hockey Canada, and Phil McKee, the lead executive of the member branch in Ontario, acknowledge the challenges. Their intentions are good and their ideas propose a path, but they are up against a structure buttressed by money and ambition. And that makes it resistant to change.

Despite all this, hockey remains, for the moment, the guiding light in this country. For all of the ratings records the Raptors set, they were still only a fraction of the all-time record for Canadian sports. That record was set when 16.7 million Canadians—half the country—tuned in to watch Crosby score the gold medal-winning goal for Canada at the 2010 Vancouver Winter Games.

Hockey still binds Canadians. It can turn big cities into small towns, and small towns into extended families, all huddled in the lobby for warmth near the bad coffee and hot dog rollers nobody has been brave enough to touch since sometime in 1975. Hockey can still feel like Canada.

There is evidence that bond is loosening, and that is not a bad thing. Canada is changing, and it makes sense that its relationship with cultural touchstones would evolve alongside. What would take its place? In a time of increasingly fragmented media consumption, what would connect the country if not a ritual meeting in front of the CBC on Saturday night? Would anything?

There is a basketball net in our backyard, but for now, hockey will be what crams us together in the car for midwinter drives across town. It will be what gets us into the Tim Hortons drive-thru before dawn. The drumbeat of practices and games and camps will send us through the snow with two dozen other parents, into communities of families doing the same thing.

We will follow our eight-year-old on whatever journey he ends up taking into his Canadian childhood, and then we will prepare to do it all over again: His little sister is registered for hockey school in the fall.

ACKNOWLEDGEMENTS

It was a dark and unemployable night, and Jordan Ginsberg wanted to meet for a beer. We picked a spot near his office, which only seemed fair because he was the one who had a job. I was out of work for the first time in my adult life, having been laid off by the *Toronto Star* a month earlier.

The paper called me on a Tuesday, while I was down in the basement watching the Johnny Depp movie *Black Mass* with my mother. That was also, as it turned out, how I was spending my first full day home from the hospital after surgeons rebuilt the elbow I'd broken (like an idiot) playing hockey with friends a few days earlier. I fractured it on Saturday, had surgery on Sunday, got home on Monday, and got whacked from the job I adored on Tuesday.

So a beer sounded pretty good, under any circumstances.

Jordan never fully explained why he wanted to meet. All he offered me in a direct message on Twitter was: "I have some . . . things I want to run by you that I'm hoping you might be interested in."

What he wanted to run past me was the concept that evolved into this book. He had the idea, he had the vision, and he had the plan. I had a freshly broken elbow, two young children at home, and uncertain job prospects, but suddenly, I had this. Over the next three years, I would also learn what I had with Jordan: a gifted editor, a part-time guidance counselor, a full-time therapist, and a deeply valued friend.

Burton Lee was the first person I met from the Petes. We had lunch in downtown Peterborough, not all that far from the Memorial Centre, and I laid out my plans for the book. He listened intently and asked smart questions, as he often does. The team opened its doors, allowing me onto the bus, into meetings, and into its offices without anything more than the promise of telling the story of its season with truth.

Dave Pogue, Mike Oke, and Jody Hull all sat down for long conversations. We talked often, sometimes at a football field, in a drafty arena hallway, or in a silent office as the clock neared midnight. The team never shooed me away, even when the season started to turn. Tamara Burns and Shelbi Kilcollins let me sit in on countless post-game player interviews and helped me develop a fluency with the team, its culture, and its nicknames.

Writing a book always seemed like an undertaking for other, smarter people. Those people were clever and organized—gifted with a clarity of vision for the story and its outcome. I have never counted myself as one of those people. Anthony Wilson-Smith helped guide me through this daunting process while also pointing out when to expect moments of enlightenment and joy. He was the Lonely Planet guide to plotting a book, and he is a respected mentor to whom I owe a great debt.

Robyn Doolittle was an invaluable sounding board. Bruce Arthur helped iron wrinkled exposition and, as one of my dearest friends on earth, also covered the occasional bar tab when necessary. Sunaya Sapurji is a leading expert in junior hockey and grassroots development, and she lent her expertise throughout the reporting, writing, and editing process. Peter Norman hiked through the later drafts and cleared excess foliage from the trail with clean strikes of his red pen, and Gemma Wain gave it an incisive, thorough proofread.

By the time the project was underway in Peterborough, another had begun back home in Toronto. Alex Mather and Adam Hansmann were two San Francisco–based entrepreneurs who launched an audacious online sports journalism venture. They opened operations for The Athletic in Toronto the same month I met with Jordan, and they hired me a few weeks later. They fostered a culture that promoted creativity, an unwavering focus on journalism, and the freedom to try new things. The team they formed in Toronto, led by James Mirtle and Ian Denomme, quickly became an incubator of emerging talent and wonderful journalistic energy. It has been a privilege to work alongside every member of that team.

This project never would have gone ahead without the belief and support of Penguin Random House Canada, led by chief executive Kristin Cochrane. Jared Bland, the publisher at McClelland & Stewart, was active and encouraging from the very first time we met. Managing editor Kimberlee Hesas set out a clear (and humane) schedule for deadlines throughout the process.

Thank you to Joe Lee, assistant editor at McClelland & Stewart, for his thoughtful reading early on, and for coming up with the title. And thank you to designer Lisa Jager for developing such a stellar look. Erin Kelly and Samantha Church were the marketing lead and publicist, respectively, and through their inventive and tireless work helped spread word of this book across the country.

It would have been impossible to try writing this book, though, without the support of one person in particular. For the better part of three years, my wife, Caroline, found a way to balance a demanding full-time job (she is the talented journalist in the family) with two young children at home. If I was in Peterborough or Montreal or Saskatoon, she was in Toronto, shouldering the work of two parents. She allowed our dining room to turn into a dust-bowl of cue cards, notebooks, highlighters, yearbooks, and wrinkled scraps of junior hockey rosters.

She was the first to tell me to hop a plane across the country for an interview. She was the first person who saw every draft of this story, and she was always the first with an encouraging word. There is not enough space and not enough paper in the world for me to possibly express my gratitude. I can only hope to make you proud.